GW01478402

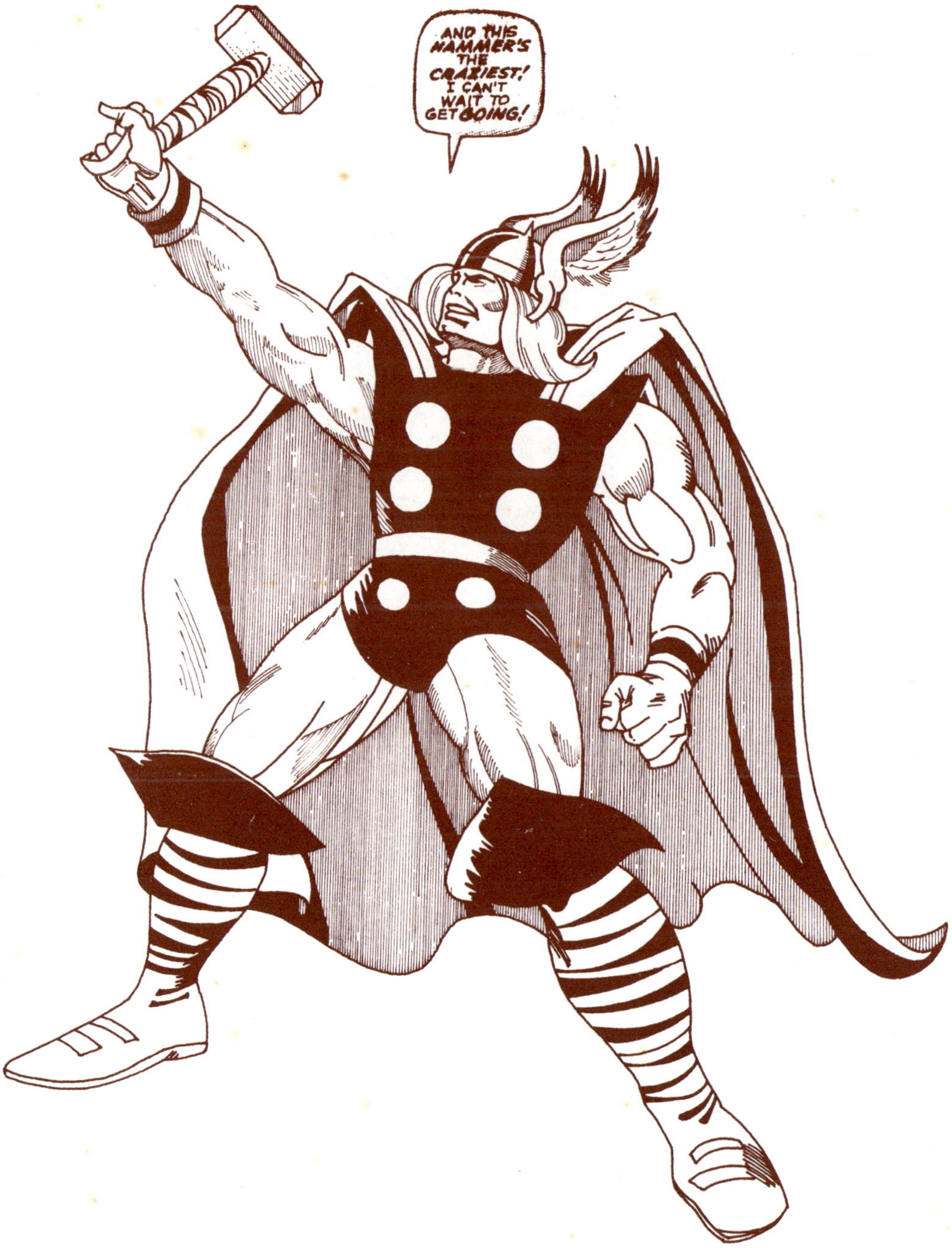

SURVIVAL SCRAPBOOK 3.

© 1973 by Dave Williams & Stephanie Munro

ISBN 0 85659 009 6

	Section
Industry & Craft	A
Shelter & Food	B
Communications	C
Learning	D
Systems	E
Outdoors	F

SELECTIONS

An item is listed if it is deemed :-

1. Useful as a tool.
2. Relevant to independent education.
3. High quality or low cost.
4. Easily available by mail.

These selection criteria, like the format and general approach of this section of Scrapbook are copied directly from the US Whole Earth Catalog. We make no apologies for plagiarism - a good idea is a good idea is a good idea.

Selections have been made by asking people who know, keeping eyes and ears open, judging books by how they got through to us, and using our own experiences. Selections also reflect our biases and interests, and what was available to us - we are strong in some fields, non existent in others, and have quite possibly made weak choices where we were not well informed. This is unavoidable - a Whole Earth Catalogue is an assembly of the experience, skills and knowledge of many people.

FEEDBACK

Feedback is essential. Send in suggestions, critisisms, corrections, ideas in any form you want; scraps of paper, made up pages, letters.
We anticipate that a first supplement, along with a cumulative index will be published in about a years time, in the same A4 ring-binder format.
Rewards, apart from names in print, will initially be in heaven - we are not backed by 0000's of dollars.

BOOKS

Except where stated books are in print at the time of going to press. We have included some out of print books because they were worth putting in, and you can get them from libraries anyway. A number of books are US imports, and are usually stocked by Compendium, Books, Unicorn and similar shops. These are indicated by (US) after publishers name. If a book is available in paperback, that is the edition we quote.

TECHNICALITIES

When all the material for a page had been assembled, a scale diagram of the layout was made on graph paper, and all sizes of reproductions were scaled up or down to fit, using the Boots 85p slide rule and metric measurements (both these saved so many ulcers). Reproductions were then copied, printed and pasted up, along with comments and details. Typing was done on an Adler electric typewrit er using a carbon ribbon (Thanks to Lee Sanders). Nearly all type matter and pictures were copied directly from the books/catalogues, using a Pentax Spotmatic, with f2 55mm standard lens, and printed through an f2.8 El-Nikkor enlarging lens on Agfa Grade 6 photographic paper. Film used was Pan-X or Pan-F, underexposed about 80%, and overdeveloped 30% in Definol to give negatives that suited the enlarging set-up. Getting a spot-on consistent copying system going was one of the most difficult tasks of production.

Thanks to all people listed in the following pages, Bob Gregory for the loan of his bookshop, and everyone else.

Dave Williams Stephanie Munro   (Leeds 1972)

The Intermediate Technology Development Group is based on the theory (or fact?) that the export of complex and expensive capitalist technology to 'underdeveloped' countries does no good to the lives and welfare of the ordinary people in those countries. In fact, they argue, it frequently destroys existing patterns of life and work by undercutting local small scale industries out of existence.

ITDG aims to counter this by the introduction of small scale machinery and hand tools which will complement the existing human and economic structures, and help them develop slowly. They try to encourage the introduction of such low level technology into poorer countries, as well as publicising it in the West. They encourage research by schools and colleges into IT, and organise firms making the right equipment to export it to the right places. Their task is unenviable faced as they are by the operations of big Western companies in these countries, whose ruthless defence of investments and profits needs no further description here.

ITDG direct their activities at the poorer countries. In face of the eco-crisis that is coming (or is it here already?) perhaps intermediate technology is relevant to the West too. The decentralization, small group relationships, and absence of huge financial structures that IT implies are going to be vital conditions for sane survival. Wendell Berry says it in Last Whole Earth Catalogue - 'For most of the history of this country our motto, implied or spoken, has been Think Big. I have come to believe that a better motto, and an essential one now, is Think Little.'

****

The best description of the theory of Intermediate Technology is an article in the excellent magazine 'Resurgence' Vol 1 No 2. by Dr. E.F.Schumacher, founder and Director of ITDG. Photocopies of the article from Resurgence, 24, Abercorn Place, St. Johns Wood, London NW8. Send 25p to cover their costs.

ITDG publish 'Tools for Progress', a catalogue of firms that supply small scale equipment, aimed mainly at overseas buyers. 75p + 15p postage as well as leaflets describing activities of the group from ITDG LTD. 9, King St., Covent Garden, London WC2.

COUNCIL FOR SMALL INDUSTRIES IN RURAL AREAS

The purpose of CoSIRA is, in their own words, 'to help develop the prosperity of small rural firms, and so provide more jobs in the countryside, especially, but not exclusively in areas threatened by serious loss of population.''The countryside' includes towns of less than 10,000 people, and'small firm' means employing less than 20 skilled people. Agriculture, horticulture and retail trades are excluded.

The services they provide include the granting of Treasury loans, advice about technical and legal matters connected with small firms, and credits to help tourist enterprises.

They publish some books and leaflets, such as 'The Thatcher's Craft'-a complete textbook of all aspects of thatching.

CoSIRA is a Government sponsored body, studded with CDCs,ODCs and JPs at top level, but with a wide ranging local structure covering all counties of England and Wales.(Scotland is covered by a seperate,similar body.) They are stringent about loaning money, but their help has been useful to the firms that they describe in their blurbs.

Details of activities and publications from CoSIRA,Information Section, 35, Camp Rd., Wimbledon Common, London SW19.

John Allen & Sons (Oxford) Ltd

Mayfield Tractor

All-purpose attachments. Robustly constructed for long life, yet easily handled.

Choice of engines:
150 cc, 3 hp or 250 cc, 4 hp Villiers, or
170 cc, 3½ hp or 230 cc, 4 hp Briggs & Stratton,
4 stroke engines, 3 speed gearbox.

Attachments:
Scythe unit, reciprocating cutter bar 3ft (91 cm) wide, deals with all rough growth.
Plough, fully adjustable, turns a furrow 6 in. to 7 in. (15. 2 to 17. 7 cm).
Toolframe, 30 in. or 36 in. wide (76 cm or 91 cm) with attachments for ridging, cultivating, potato lifting etc.
Also bulldozer, generator, flexible drive power take off, sprayer unit and rotary cutter attachments available.

Prices ex works:
Mayfield tractor MK 15
Villier 3 hp engine   £101. 0. 0.
scythe unit   £ 35. 10. 0.
plough complete with disc coulter £ 15. 0. 0.

INDUSTRIAL COMMON OWNERSHIP MOVEMENT.

People

Our premises are old and the overheads are kept deliberately low. We pay a great deal of attention to trying to give an efficient, friendly and personal service to our customers. This enables us to survive and hopefully to prosper. Discovering our way towards a radical alternative to the conventional structure of industry, the Trylon community is also concerned with the quality of life at work. It is said that four out of five people in industry are bored and working well below their capacity. Thus one of our concerns is to search for ways in which manual and clerical work may be made a more enriching and fulfilling experience. We think this must be an end in itself and not merely a means of making the company more profitable for the financial benefit of the owners. There is no clocking; everyone is paid monthly by cheque to minimise clerical work and to indicate the high degree of security usually associated only with "staff conditions"; salary differentials are deliberately less than normal and there is considerable job-flexibility. For example, workshop and warehouse members frequently help to run art and craft demonstrations for teachers, those involved with clerical work, both men and women, also carry out development work with resins, the manager sweeps out the passages as well as projecting the cash flow. Members have different motivations for joining the group; for example, it is relevant that several members including the four Directors who have the task of preparing the common-ownership constitution, are practising Christians whose commitment has led them to try to develop a new kind of industrial community. The organisation is a tentative but determined attempt to reflect the view that people at work have material, social and spiritual needs. In order that a pioneering group of this kind may grow, it has become apparent that each member needs freely to accept the wider objectives of the group and to be prepared to make a positive effort to achieve them. The objectives cannot be imposed by "the Board", they must be the common concern of members; industrial democracy has little meaning in other circumstances.

ICOM is a group who seek to spread the gospel of industrial common ownership. The main members are firms which to some degree are owned and controlled by the people who work in them.

Trylon Ltd. (see AE) the plastics firm is an example. Trylon is 15 people , with a regular structure to keep people informed and involved in decision making. They publish a leaflet (T51) which describes the set-up. (Free for the postage from Trylon Ltd., Thrift St., Wollastan, Northants. NN9 7QJ) Extract left.

The address of ICOM is 8, Churton St., London SW1. A useful account of firms in ICOM can be found in Directory of Alternative Work, 3rd. edition. Pages 12-13

DESIGN FOR THE REAL WORLD Victor Papanek
£4.00 Thames and Hudson 1972.
Not how to design but why design , who-for design. If you're
into any design situation - as a professional, or as a student
or teacher, this book asks some very right questions.

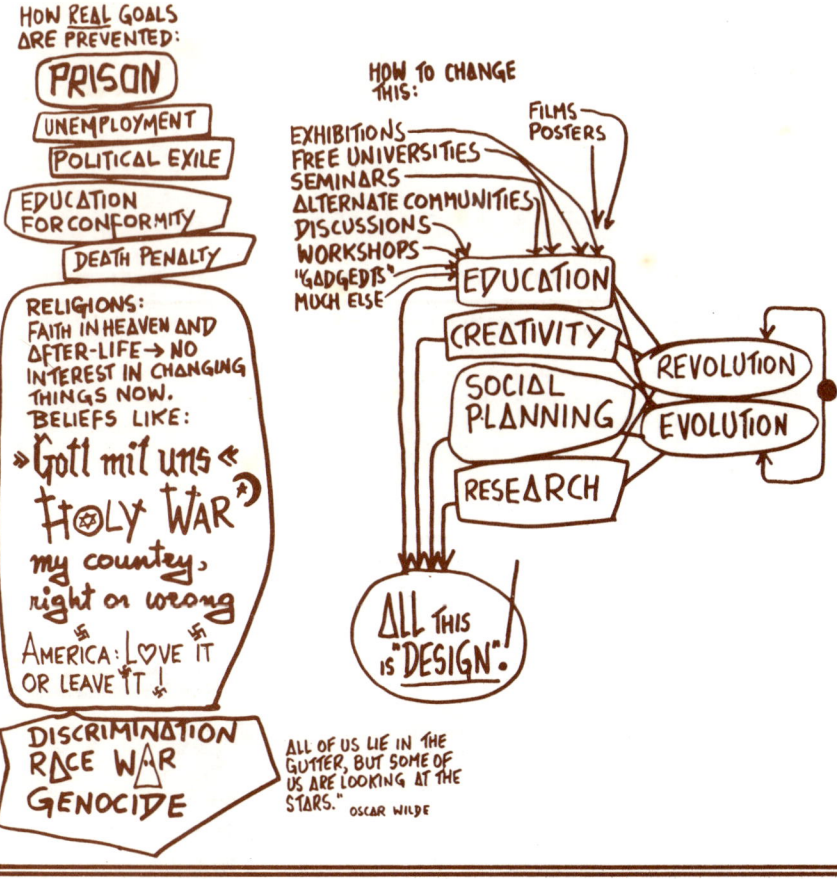

HOW REAL GOALS
ARE PREVENTED:

PRISON
UNEMPLOYMENT
POLITICAL EXILE
EDUCATION FOR CONFORMITY
DEATH PENALTY
RELIGIONS:
FAITH IN HEAVEN AND
AFTER-LIFE → NO
INTEREST IN CHANGING
THINGS NOW.
BELIEFS LIKE:
»Gott mit uns«
HOLY WAR?
my country,
right or wrong
AMERICA: LOVE IT
OR LEAVE IT!
DISCRIMINATION
RACE WAR
GENOCIDE

HOW TO CHANGE
THIS:

EXHIBITIONS
FREE UNIVERSITIES
SEMINARS
ALTERNATE COMMUNITIES
DISCUSSIONS
WORKSHOPS
"GADGETS"
MUCH ELSE
FILMS
POSTERS

EDUCATION
CREATIVITY
SOCIAL PLANNING
RESEARCH
REVOLUTION
EVOLUTION

ALL THIS
IS "DESIGN".

ALL OF US LIE IN THE
GUTTER, BUT SOME OF
US ARE LOOKING AT THE
STARS." OSCAR WILDE

As factories and industrial combines grow in size, complexity, and investment capital, their opposition to innovation grows. Changes in the system, replacements of the system itself or parts of it become more costly to contemplate and more difficult to institute. Directions of change therefore cannot be expected to be initiated by big business or the military-industrial complex (or the tame, captive designers working for them) but will be initiated by the design team.

To do the most effective job possible, a great deal of research will be needed. A great many questions (most of them trans-national in character) need to be asked. All of these are rather big questions indeed:

What is an ideal human social system? (This will mean an in-depth study of such diverse social organizations as American Plains Indians, the Mundugumor of the Lower Sepik River basin; the priest-cultures of the Inca, Maya, Toltec, and Aztec; the Pueblo cultures of the Hopi; the social structuring surrounding the priest-goddess in Crete; the mountain-dwelling Arapesh; child care in Periclean Greece; Samoa of the late nineteenth century, Nazi Germany, and modern-day Sweden; hunting customs among Australian aborigines, Bantu, and Eskimo; the place of authority and decision-making in China, imperial Rome, slums, and ghettos, and the Loyalist Regime in Spain; delegation of authority in armies, the Catholic Church, modern industrial networks; etc., etc.)

What are optimal conditions for human society on earth? (An inquiry into living patterns, sexual mores, world mobility, codes of behavior, primitive and sophisticated religions and philosophies, and much more will be needed here.)

What are the parameters of the global ecological and ethological system? (Here new insights from such diverse disciplines as meteorology, climatology, physics, chemistry, geology, Von Neumann's Game Theory, cybernetics, oceanography, biology, and all the behavioral sciences will be urgently required; as well as ways of establishing links between these disciplines.)

What are the limits of our resources? (Studies comparable to those carried on by the World Resources Inventory Center at Southern Illinois University will have to be brought into continuous contact with changing technologies and new discoveries.)

What are the human limits?

What are the basic housekeeping rules for human life on the planet earth? (Or, in Bucky Fuller's phrase: *An Operating Manual for Spaceship Earth.*)

And, finally, what don't we know?

HOW THINGS WORK
pp 590; £1.25; Paladin 1972.

The Universal Encyclopedia of Machines
or, more correctly, how examples of most
of the common processes and machinery
currently in use in our technology
actually work. Even if you can't use it
to mend the TV, you can still understand
how it works.

WATER CLOSET (TOILET)

When the chain attached to the lever of the flushing cistern is pulled (Fig. 2), the hollow iron bell-shaped unit rises and opens the passage to the flush pipe. As soon as water flows down this pipe, a vacuum is formed in the cavity of the bell and causes more water to flow from the cistern through the bell and down the pipe. The cavity inside the bell thus acts as a siphon (Fig. 1). When a vacuum is formed at C (by initially applied suction), water is drawn through the siphon tube. Once the flow has been started, it will continue. For the siphon to function, its outlet must always be below the level of the water in the tank. When the chain of the water closet has been briefly pulled and released, the bell falls back into position over the inlet of the flush pipe, but the flow of water down the pipe continues— thanks to the siphon effect until the cistern has been drained. As the water level in the cistern goes down, the float descends and opens the water supply valve, so that the cistern fills up again. When the float has risen to a certain level, the inflowing water is cut off by the valve. The capacity of the flushing cistern is usually 2 gallons.

Fig. 3 illustrates another type of cistern. When the rod is briefly pulled up and then released, the water here, too, continues to flow until the cistern is drained. The rod is provided with a freely movable float which is prevented from floating to the surface of the water by two stops on the pull rod. When the rod is raised and the inlet of the flush pipe is opened, the closing pressure which is developed by the water column in the full tank is reduced. The buoyancy of the float predominates and keeps the pipe inlet open. Then the rod descends and the rubber valve disc is thrust against its seat by the inflowing water.

NATURE AND ART OF WORKMANSHIP David Pye
pp96; 90p; Studio Vista 1971.

An extension of many of the ideas touched on in
'Nature of Design'. Good sections on craft,
quality and durability which shake out some
mystique, and hold industry up to criticism.
(Reviews by Bill Challis)

27 Stile.

In a thing as weathered and time-worn as this stile we think open joints and
partial collapse are honourable scars, but if these same timbers when freshly
sawn had been left to stand in the same way, with the joints nearly falling
apart, we should consider it gross bad workmanship. Our judgement is not
simply a matter of sentiment. Age and weather have converted the originally
regulated workmanship of the rails, post and spur into an evidently rough
approximation: a very rough one. So we find the open joints perfectly in key
with the rest of the workmanship—the workmanship of wind and wet.
Because it is consistent we half believe it intentional, or at least regard it as
if it had been.

DESIGN OF DESIGN Gordon L.Glegg
pp93; £1.50; Cambridge UP 1969.

Highly personalised general reading about
recurrent engineering problems. Scarcely
touching upon motivation, the writer light-
heartedly assumes that all design must conform
to the same principles of competative engineering.

Now one of the cheapest ways of designing something is not
to design it at all. Use one that is designed already by someone
else.

I once saw a carpet-manufacturing machine where a very
large number of connecting rods were needed to convert rotat-
ing motions into reciprocating ones. When the machine was
operating they went so fast that all you could see was blur.

When it stopped you could see that they were Ford Zephyr
connecting rods. Readily available, precision made, no designing
time needed, and above all, mass produced and so good value
for money.

A draughtsman was once struggling with a machine-actuating
layout which needed a fairly involved hydraulic set-up. I hap-
pened to spot that the hydraulic principle was identical with
one used on a sophisticated fork-lift truck. Although the
machine being designed had a quite different purpose and appearance, the same hydraulics would do, and they did. Once
again designing was eliminated and proved components and
locally available spares all came in as fringe benefits to a capital
outlay reduced to a fraction. Shop around in other industries
and you may find cut-price bargains.

The author once set about designing a draining rack. It was for the
plates, pot-lids and so forth used by his family while living in a tent.
It had therefore to be very small and very light. Because he started
by thinking 'I must design a draining rack' instead of considering what
kind of result was wanted, his train of thought was conditioned un-
profitably. Racks act by supporting. Any instance of a rack which will
support plates must have dimensions conformable with those of the
plates, and there is a limit below which its size and therefore its weight
cannot be reduced.

After prolonged thought the designer realised his mistake and started
to consider what result he wanted, namely, a row of plastic plates
edge-on in mid air. He then started to search his memory for results
of the same class but not necessarily involving similar objects or, at
any rate, objects which were closely similar. Doing this is not as easy
as it sounds. Because it was not easy his mind ran to a result involving
objects which, if not closely similar, at any rate were suggested by a
very obvious association, namely a row of cups hanging on hooks.
The unconscious association must have been plates – saucers: saucers –
cups. Thus the thought of plates unearthed the memory of cups.

It was then easy to arrive at the required invention, a thin stick carrying a row of thin wire hooks like cup-hooks; for the desired result was
by now well in mind, and the objects in it too, the flexible rather soft
plastic plates, which being rather soft at once suggested that holes
might be cut in their rims.*

Designers and their clients seldom formulate their purposes in terms
of the desired results, but on the contrary habitually do so in terms of
the systems of things which give rise to them. As the example of the
dish rack showed, this may be a bad habit; but it will only be bad if

some new factor in the situation, such as plates made out of easily
drilled plastic, is overlooked. Otherwise the designer's normal habit is
mere common sense. If you want to enable someone to sit, it will be
idiotic to proceed in the way that students of design are sometimes
advised to do, and think out the whole problem from first principles,
as though all the people who for the last four thousand years have been
making and using chairs were half-wits. Where the problem is old, the
old solutions will nearly always be best (unless a new technique has
been introduced) because it is inconceivable that all the designers of ten
or twenty generations will have been fools.

NATURE OF DESIGN
David Pye.
pp96; 90p;
Studio Vista 1964.

Not a technical
manual, but thought-
ful preliminary
reading for some-
one about to solve
a problem by making
something. Marginal
design pedantry, but
not too academic
for general reading.

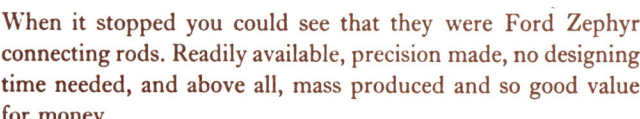

A3

```
THE NEW SCIENCE OF STRONG MATERIALS.
(Or why you don't fall through the floor)
J.E.Gordon.
pp269; 40p; Penguin 1970.

A great book. An idiot's guide to the basic theories
of structures plus a really well written and
entertaining run through the science of materials
from treacle to carbon fibre. An absolute must,
five stars, ten out of ten, 100%  ...(carried off
raving).

(Suggested by Robin Harvey)
```

St Sophia, Constantinople.

From the economic point of view it is in the saving in processing, manufacturing and finishing that new materials can make a really big contribution. We have become accustomed to considering the processes of manufacture as lying at the heart of the economy and we use the word 'factory' pretty well as a synonym for the whole industrial process. Traditionally, advanced countries import 'raw materials' and 'manufacture' them into products for sale. We accept the idea that technological advance requires that industrial plant should need ever greater concentrations of capital and employed labour, closing our eyes to the fact that these dinosaurs are vulnerable and 'socially divisive'. Moreover, looked at objectively, the life which is led within them may be a miserable one, using labour on the 'battery' principle.

In the service of these Molochs we develop machine tools and all kinds of devices to carry out the innumerable bending, cutting, scraping and hammering operations which we find necessary in order to fabricate our primitive raw materials. One side effect of our factory system is that, visually, we have what must be the ugliest civilization in history and it seems to be getting uglier every day.

Of course any material must require some sort of fabrication process – unless we are to breed motor cars by biological means. What is wrong is that fabrication should absorb so much effort and yield so little satisfaction in the doing. With the introduction of plastics there is already a considerable tendency to reduce the complexity and the cost of fabrication. Most of the easily moulded plastics are fairly weak and flexible materials but it cannot be out of the question to extend the facility to stronger and stiffer substances. Many cheap moulding processes need at present a considerable capital expenditure on tools and dies but again I do not believe that this state of affairs is immutable.

If easy, cheap production of sufficient accuracy can be achieved by small units then we may be able to reverse some of the centralizing trends of the Industrial Revolution and perhaps, in part, to set ourselves free from the worst tyrannies of mass production. There may then be more room for individualistic skills and for individual tastes – perhaps we shall all feel better for it. However there is very little research going on along these lines at present and I am afraid that the Satanic Mills have still quite a long future before them.

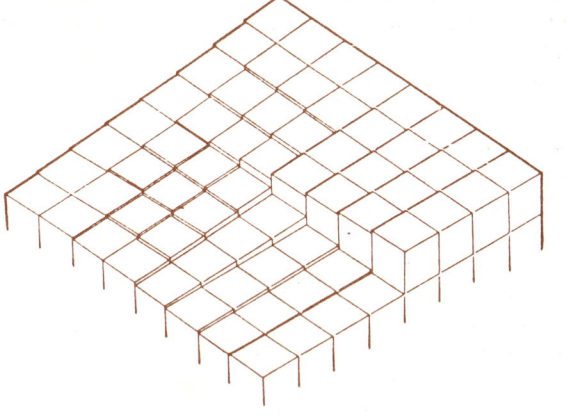

Schematic arrangement of screw dislocation.

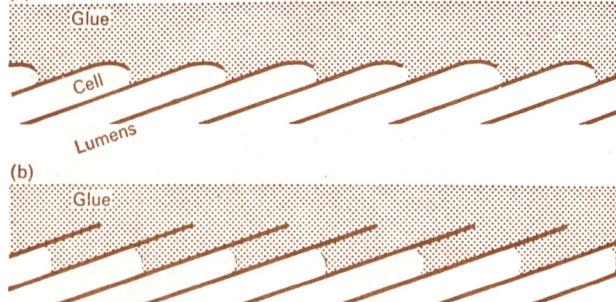

Figure 4. (a) 'Case-hardened' plywood. Emergent edges of cell walls are burred over during hot-pressing preventing adequate entry of glue into the tubes of the wood.
(b) Properly sanded plywood. Glue is enabled to enter cell lumens in considerable depth and thus to provide a reliable joint.

```
MATERIALS - Scientific American.
pp210; £1.20; W.H.Freeman 1967.

Another book-of-the-September-Scientific
American.
   Starts out by analysing materials in general,
goes on to materials in particular (metal, glass,
ceramics, etc.), then properties of materials
(thermal, electric, optical). Makes more
sense if you've read Gordon (above).
```

Silicate unit is a primary building block of many ceramics. It consists of a silicon atom surrounded by four oxygen atoms. This is the same tetrahedral arrangement as in beryllium oxide (see illustration on page 56). Since each of the silicon atoms has four valence electrons to give up, each of the surrounding oxygens gets one, leaving its outer shell one electron short. It can get that electron from another silicon atom by linking two groups (left). In this way a chain of silicate groups can be built up (right).

The most interesting and important structures are generated by silica (SiO_2). The silicon atom, like carbon, has four valence electrons, and it forms a tetrahedral grouping with oxygen: four oxygen atoms surrounding each silicon atom. These groups can link together in various ways [*see illustration above*].

Attached only end to end (by way of one of the oxygen atoms), they form a fiberlike chain, such as appears in asbestos. Built up in sheets, they produce layered minerals such as talc or mica. They can also be linked to produce a three-dimensional network— the quartz crystal. The versatility of the silica tetrahedrons in forming bonds with one another and with other groups explains how silica serves as the glue that cements the clay particles in bricks and earthenware and bonds the glaze to porcelain.

The Gramophone Record

The traditional rather brittle shellac composition record is now barely a memory, having been entirely replaced by synthetic polymer, usually a copolymer of P.V.C. and polyvinyl acetate, with appropriate flow properties to reproduce with exactitude the minutest variation in the track cut in the master. The production of these discs, like so many other plastic processes, is a simple one. Granules of copolymer are pre-heated and then spread as uniformly as possible on to a master metal disc in a special press. Another master metal disc is then lowered on to the top of the granules and pressure applied. Under heat the granules 'flow' and form a <u>soft</u> plastic <u>sheet</u>, which will accurately take the impression of the top and bottom master plates. Slightly more material than that required to make a record is loaded between the plates, so that a certain degree of 'flash' or 'un-wanted' material occurs around the outer edge of the finished disc; this is easily trimmed off, as already described in compression-moulding.

Plastics also play a vital part in the production of the master metal embossing discs. The sound is nowadays recorded first on magnetic tape, itself consisting largely of plastics, as described later, and the record in magnetic form on the tape is then used directly to control the cutting of a sound track on an aluminium sheet coated with a nitrocellulose composition.

The master record thus produced is then used to make metal moulds by a plating process, these moulds constituting the embossing discs referred to above. It is hardly necessary to emphasize the enormous outlet for vinyl polymers resulting from the production of millions of 'pop' records, as well as from the steady increase in 'L.P.' records for classical music.

For cheaper records, injection-moulding methods are being developed, as well as embossing of film in six and twelve mil thicknesses for single and double-sided records respectively; but long runs are necessary to make these processes economical.

METALS IN THE SERVICE OF MAN. A.Street & W.Alexander. pp346; 75p; Penguin 1972.(below). PLASTICS IN THE MODERN WORLD. E.Couzens & V.Yarsley pp386; 50p; Penguin 1969 (left).

Two textbook studies of their respective fields, with everything the layman would need to know presented in a well organized, slightly dull way.

FIG. 53. Hammer-welding

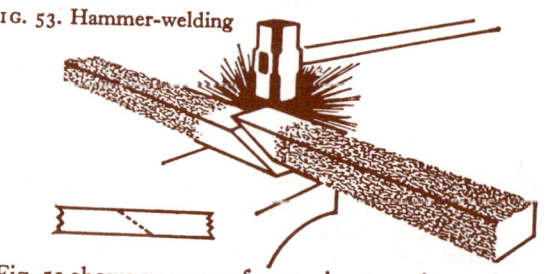

Fig. 53 shows one way of preparing two pieces of steel ready for hammer-welding. The two ends are thoroughly cleaned, heated to bright redness, and sprinkled with a flux such as fine sand which combines with the oxide on the surface and forms a liquid glaze over the metal, thus protecting the surface from oxidation. The ends are further heated, placed together, and the joint is rapidly hammered so that it becomes welded before the temperature falls unduly.

Each link in an iron chain is made from a length of wrought iron rod which is threaded through the preceding link, turned over and the ends hammer-welded together, usually automatically these days. The strength of each individual junction must be equal to that of each remaining link, and the reliability of such welds is demonstrated by the use of iron chains in ships' anchors and in lifting tackle.

MATERIALS HANDBOOK(10th. edn.) G.S.Brady pp 1045; £10.80 Mc.Graw Hill 1971

A huge catalogue of every material you ever heard of,plus plenty more. 'Material' is defined in the widest possible way, and everything is cross indexed in a way which makes it much more interesting than you'd think.

Sunflower Oil. A pale-yellow drying oil with a pleasant odor and taste obtained from the large seeds of the common sunflower plant, *Helianthus annuus,* of which there are many varieties. The plant is native to Peru but is now grown in many parts of the world, particularly in California, Canada, Argentina, Chile, Uruguay, and Russia. It requires boron in the soil. The specific gravity of the oil is 0.925. Sunflower oil is used in varnish and soap manufacture or as a food oil. The by-product cake is used chiefly for cattle feed, but **sunflower meal** is also blended with wheat flour or cornmeal in foods. It is higher in vitamin B than soybean flour. **Sunflower seeds** are also used as poultry feed. **Madia-seed oil** is quite similar to sunflower oil and has the same uses. It is obtained from the seeds of the plant *Madia sativa,* native to California. The seeds contain 35% oil, and the cold-pressed oil has a pleasant taste. **Watermelon-seed oil,** produced in Senegal as **bereff oil,** is an edible oil similar to sunflower. It contains about 43% linoleic acid, 27 oleic, 19.5 stearic, and 5 palmitic acid.

The leaves of selected varieties of some species of sunflower contain from 1 to 6% **sunflower rubber** and up to 8 resin. The *H. occidentalis, H. giganteus, H. maximiliani,* and *H. strumosus* are cultivated in Russia both for the oil seed and for the rubber in the leaves. These perennials yield leaves up to 10 years. A stand of 50,000 plants per hectare yields about 150 kilos of rubber and 325 kilos of resin. Another similar rubber-bearing plant of southern Russia is the *Asclepias cornuti,* known as **vatochnik.** It is a perennial, producing leaves for 10 to 15 years. The leaves yield 1 to 6.5% rubber and large percentages of resin.

WHAT WOOD IS THAT? H.L.Edlin pp160+wood samples; £2.10 Thames and Hudson 1969

This one's gimmick is about 40 samples of different woods, with a potted biography of each,plus general info. about wood and its processing. Useful if you're thinking of recycling the sideboard.

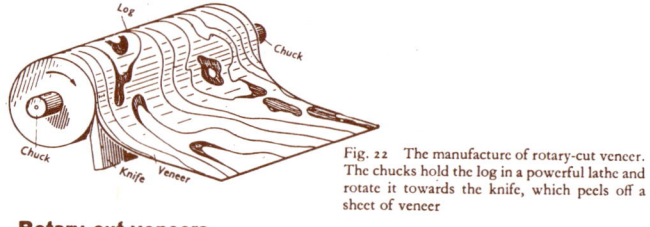

Fig. 22 The manufacture of rotary-cut veneer. The chucks hold the log in a powerful lathe and rotate it towards the knife, which peels off a sheet of veneer

Rotary-cut veneers

Another kind of veneer is produced, on an enormous scale, by the related, but quite distinct, process called 'rotary cutting' (Illustrated in Fig. 22). This is an entirely modern process, made possible only by the development of powerful machinery. Briefly, a large log is first steamed to make it soft and supple, and then fixed in a huge lathe which rotates it. As it turns, a long, sharp knife is pressed against it, so that a thin sheet of wood is peeled from its circumference. After each revolution this knife is automatically moved a bit closer to the heart of the tree, so that the peeling motion can continue. This results in a sheet of veneer that can be many yards long, and as wide as the log is long. In practice this thin sheet is cut into sections of convenient length as it emerges from the veneer lathe.

<u>A WORD FOR WOOD</u> Widely available, new and second hand, easily recycled, strong, worked with simple techniques, using low cost hand tools, and when you're through, a ready source of heat energy. Beat that.

TOOLS FOR WOODWORK Charles Hayward
pp 188; £1.75; Evans Bros. 1960

If you're a child of the Black and Decker age like me, the speed and ease of good hand tools is astounding. Have this book by you when you start to learn how to look after tools. It has details of dozens of tools, basic techniques, and the how and <u>why</u> of their maintenance.

Sharpening the axe. It must be sharpened properly to give good results. Many people have the curious illusion that an axe, because it does the rougher kind of work, does not need a really keen edge. The fact is that you should be able to sharpen your pencil with it. When first bought it is like a chisel, ground but not whetted on the oilstone. The simplest plan is to hold the axe flat on the bench with its edge overhanging ; then, holding the oilstone upside-down, work it across the bevel diagonally as in Fig. 14. Retain the ground bevel as far as possible, and rub equally over the entire width, sharpening both sides to the same extent. If this is not done the edge may become out of parallel with the shaft.

Never use an axe on the ground or on loose earth. It will rapidly blunt it. Use a chopping block and keep the top of this clean and free from grit. For such work as tapering the end of a post you can grasp the shaft near the end, giving greater leverage. The left hand, being well away from the part of the wood being

FIG. 14. SHARPENING THE AXE.
The edge should overhang the bench, and both sides should be rubbed down equally. Use a diagonal or circular movement.

cut, is out of danger. When cutting a plug, however, as in Fig. 12, the shaft should be grasped nearer the head. This gives greater control and is necessary because the left hand is near the cut. The slightest inaccuracy might result in a bad injury.

Never chop down directly at right angles with the grain. There is too much resistance (see A, Fig. 13), and the farther the axe penetrates the more resistance it meets owing to its wedge formation. Instead make the blow at an angle as at B. In this way the wood splits slightly and rises, so lessening the resistance. Of course, discretion must be used so that the split occurs on the side that does not matter.

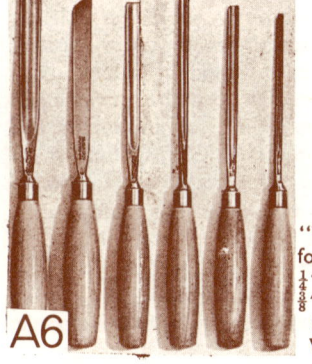

ASHLEY ILES
(EDGE TOOLS) LIMITED

Spilsby, Lincs.
List 3p.

Special tools for

wood carving.

"YORK" a kit of six professional tools for the beginner.
¼" No. 39, ¹⁄₁₆" No. 11, ⅝" No. 2, ¼" No. 9
⅜" No. 3, ⅝" No. 5.

SETS OF HAND FORGED WOODCARVING TOOLS

A6

PLANECRAFT
C.W.Hampton & E.Clifford.
pp255; 60p+10p post;
C&J Hampton Ltd 1959.
Record Works, Sheffield.

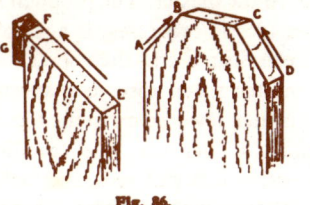

Fig. 86.

Dusty aprons, wood shavings on the floor, horny handed wisdom about types of planes, uses of planes, looking after planes, intricate techniques of plane-craft. The sort of stuff you should have learned at grandpa's knee.

(viii) To shoot an edge cut at any other angle than 90° to the length.

A consideration of the way of the grain (Fig. 86) will show that in (1) the plane must travel from E to F. The point at F can be saved from chipping off by cramping a small piece G there until the planing is finished. In example (2) B to C offers no difficulty, and is planed as in Section (v) on page 70. The grain will show that you must plane from A to B and then reverse the job and plane from D to C.

HOW TO WORK WITH TOOLS AND WOOD
R.Campbell & N.H.Mager
pp488; 30p+10p post
Stanley Works (GB) Ltd.
Parkside, Sheffield.

Beating out a mortise.
1. Start in the center.
2. Pry out the first chips.
3. Cut each way to end. Bevel to mortise.
4. Chisel out chips and repeat on opposite side.
5. Chisel out chips until through.
6. Finish by truing ends.

A book about how to work with tools and wood. Good basic stuff.

Mortises can be beaten out with the chisel alone. This done by driving the chisel, held squarely, with a mallet or hammer, starting in the center and working to each end. The back of the chisel faces the ends. The tenon should be tried in the mortise, and any part that binds noted and corrected. Glue can be spread evenly on all abutting surfaces and the work clamped together.

Sydney Evans Ltd.,
49, Berkley St.,
Birmingham B1 2LG.

Catalogues free
(Below) Crack clamp.

Tools, materials, fittings and equipment for making and playing musical instruments.

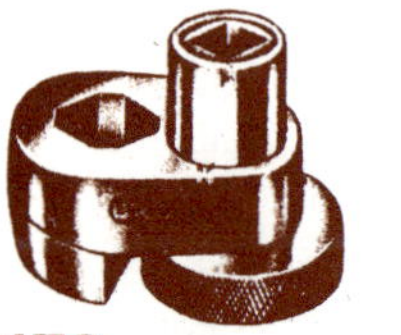

178 ELORA STUD EXTRACTOR
½″ CAPACITY Made from genuine chrome
vanadium steel, ½″ square drive.

LIGHT MACHINES FOR
WOODWORK C.H.Hayward.
pp 216; £1.75.
Evans Bros.
1963.

Another good book by Hayward,
with the pros and cons and
ins and outs of small scale
woodworking.

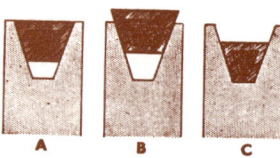

FIG. 10. SECTIONS THROUGH BELTS AND PULLEYS.
A. Correct fitting of belt.
B. Belt too large and liable to slip.
C. Belt too small so that it reaches groove bottom.

A.GATTO AND SON.
206-212, Garratt Lane,
Earlsfield, London SW18.
SAE for list.

DAVID HUNT LTD.,
Knowl Hill,
Reading, Berks. RG10 9VR.
Send 7½p for list.

Two sources for cut price tools,
Hunt selling quite a wide range
of stuff. Unfortunately neither
of them sell Bosch power tools,
generally agreed to be the best
around in terms of quality - i.e.
ability to take a lot of punish-
ment. If all you need is something to drill holes with, Black
and Decker will do, but if you
want a tool that won't
need a new motor every
time you overdo it-
Boschhh..... you know who.

**Model 267 1¼ hp
Heavy Duty Router**
Has the same quality
features as the 264,
but with a more powerful
1¼ hp motor for
tougher jobs.

**506 SELF GRIP ADJUSTABLE PIPE
WRENCH.** Polished drop forged steel jaws.

Capacity : 4″   Length : 11″.

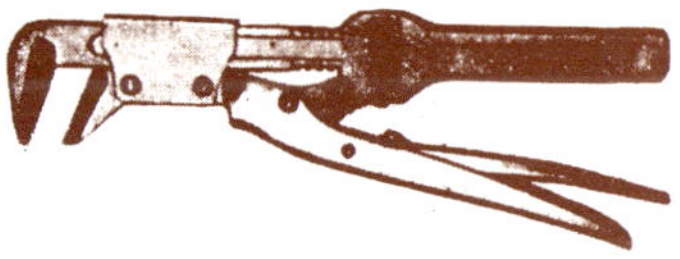

Speed and horsepower. We now come to a point not so
generally realized. A belt run at low speed will not transmit as much
power as when at high speed—in fact its efficiency may fall to a very
low level. Fortunately few woodworking machines are run at low
speed and the horsepower involved in light machines is small, but it
is a point to remember. It is because of this failure of single-groove
pulleys to transmit power at slow speed that pulleys are made with
twin, triple, and quadruple grooves. The increased area of contact
of the multiple belting raises the frictional grip and enables the
horsepower to be transmitted.

To sum up, the following points should be noted when installing
V-belting:

Calculate the sizes of pulleys required to give the correct speed at
motor and machine.

Avoid a larger ratio between the two than 7 : 1. If the difference in
speed between the two is greater install a countershaft.

When ordering pulleys give the *outside* diameter size and state
whether single, twin, triple, or quadruple grooves are needed.
(In most woodworking machines single-groove is sufficient,
because they are usually run at high speed.)

State the bore.

State whether a keyway is required, and state width and depth.

Arrange motor on pivoted platform so that tension to belt can be
adjusted (this also enables belt to be slipped on or off easily).

Size of belt is known by internal circumference. Imagine belt
opened as a circle. Size is the circumference of the inner edge.
To ascertain size tie string around pulleys, open flat, and
measure. Belt is slightly longer, as it does not reach to bottom
of groove. If distance between pulleys is adjustable, measure
when in closest relative position, thereby obtaining maximum
possible adjustment to take up wear.

J.SIMBLE AND SONS,
76, Queens Road,
Watford, Herts.
Catalogue 15p.

BEVERLEY POOLE & CO LTD.,
South Thorsby,
Alford, Lincs.
Calalogue 12p.

All the bits and pieces to make your own
woodworking equipment.

A HANDBOOK OF WOODCUTTING P.Harris.
pp44; 20p; HMSO 1946.

The theory of cutting and finishing wood
in quantity.

SAWING—CIRCULAR SAWS

Efficient operation of circular saw depends on the true running of the
saw spindle and collars, the quality of the steel from which the saw was made,
the correct rim speed and tension, proper packing, the shape and spacing of
the teeth, and careful sharpening and setting. For true running, the spindle
must be perfectly straight, with the faces of the collars square to its axis, and be
free from slackness in the bearings. Any defect at the spindle will be
magnified at the saw rim, widen the kerf and cause a rough sawn finish. Saws
of poor quality steel are likely to become blunt too rapidly and lose their
tension, resulting in irregular and poor sawing. They must be run at a correct
and uniform speed to ensure straight cutting, for a circular saw can only be
tensioned to suit a particular speed. A saw tensioned for a speed different from
that at which it is running will tend to deflect to one side or the other when
the wood is being fed to it. Insufficient rim speed causes extra resistance
to feeding and undue strain on the saw. Too high a speed induces tooth
vibration, especially in sawing the denser hardwoods, with consequent dulling
of the teeth, charring of the sawn surface, loss of tension, and deflection of the
saw blade. A suitable rim speed for circular plate saws for general conversion
and ripsawing is 10,000 ft. per minute. 11,000 ft. per minute can be used
with advantage in re-sawing softwoods and up to 13,000 ft. per minute for
swage saws, ground-off saws, and thin plate saws. The speed recommended
for inserted-tooth saws is from 8,000 ft. to 10,000 ft. per minute. Straight line
edger saws, dimension and travelling head cross-cutting machines usually have
the saw directly coupled to the motor. The speed of the latter, which is usually
run on 50-cycle alternating current, is 3,000 r.p.m. (nominal) and the maximum
diameter of saw used is 18 in., giving a rim speed of about 14,000 ft. per minute.
Such speed is suitable for cutting softwoods but rather high for cross-cutting
hardwoods, and may result in tooth vibration and charring if the saw is not
toothed correctly.

DRILL CHUCKS
3-Jaw Nickel Plated.
Self-Centring

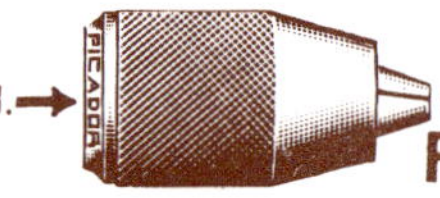

Thread
½″ × 24 T.P.I.

½″ Capacity
Fig. 111

MADE IN
ENGLAND

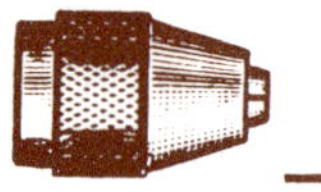

½″ × 24 T.P.I.

¼″ Capacity
Fig. 91

They are of the
correct Chucks
for spindles
Fig. 90 Fig. 75
Fig. 200
Fig. 200BB
Fig. 1200
Fig. 295 G C

For mounting on
Shaft of motor
Fitted with two
Hardened, Pointed
Grubscrews, a pair
of **PICADOR** 1⅝″ diameter
Flanges, and a Hex. nut.
Shank Bore ½ or ⅝

Fig. 125

For ½″ Bore Grinding Wheel Wire Brush
Calico Mop etc.

MADE IN ENGLAND

**STEEL SET
COLLARS Fig. 285**

Each fitted with Hardened
Cup Pointed Grub Screw.

RIP-SAW TEETH FOR DENSE HARDWOODS.

CROSS-CUT SAW.

A7

Glass Reinforced Plastics (GRP) or fibreglass is good intermediate technology- low on capital, heavy on labour and widely adaptable. Drawbacks are the energy used and shit churned out to make the stuff, and its relative indestructibility. If you don't mind that, away you go.

If you're new to it, the Strand and Glasplies info. is enough, but reading New Glassfibre Book won't hurt, and besides,they all have stuff the others haven't got.

GLASPLIES, 68, Park Road, Southport,Lancs.
List free.

. Glasplies' duplicated sheets may not be the slickest bit of graphics that you're ever going to see, but they're packed with working information, obviously written by someone who's used to cracking moulds open. They also carry some good lines (food grade resin,for example.)

(No extract from Glasplies lists is reproduced here.)

Plastics for Schools—recommendations for initial ordering quantities.
Cast Stock—machine and hand processes. Reinforcement for Trylon resins, including glass and carbon fibre.
GRP Chair—how to make a glass-reinforced plastics chair.
Anatomical Notes—the use of polyester resin for anatomical purposes in hospitals and for medical research

TRYLON LTD., Thrift St.,
Wollaston, Northants NN9 7QJ
SAE for lists.

Trylon is a member of the ICOM group, and you get a nice feeling that you're dealing with people.

They carry usual GRP lines, and are very good on information- lots of leaflets about plastics topics, many of them aimed at school/college users.

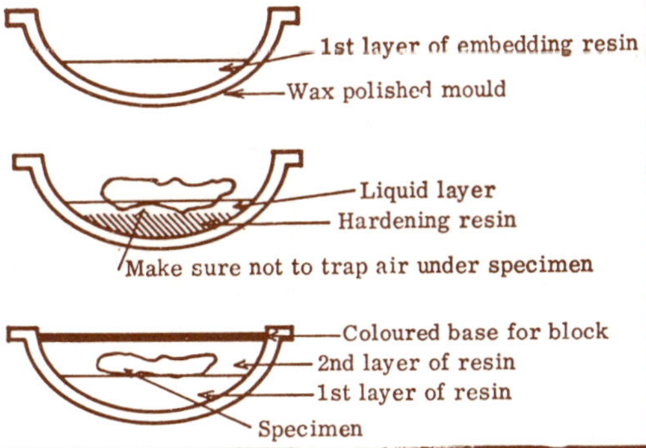

—1st layer of embedding resin
—Wax polished mould

—Liquid layer
—Hardening resin
Make sure not to trap air under specimen

—Coloured base for block
—2nd layer of resin
—1st layer of resin
Specimen

STRAND GLASS
Brentford,Middlesex.
Catalogue free.

Strand are the brand leaders. Their range is good, their catalogue pretty, with useful info.

Cleaning up

Brushes and tools are washed out in brush cleaner while the resin is liquid. Plastic gloves or barrier cream should be used on the hands and the special hand cleanser cream applied afterwards.

Resin Requirements

$1\frac{1}{2}$ lb of resin A is required for every square yard of 1 oz mat
2 lbs of resin A is required for every square yard of $1\frac{1}{2}$ oz mat
3 lbs of resin A is required for every square yard of 2 oz mat
$\frac{3}{4}$ lb of resin A is required for every square yard of 2 oz fabric
1 lb of resin A is required for every square yard of 5 oz fabric
$1\frac{1}{2}$ lbs of resin A is required for every square yard of 8 oz fabric
$4\frac{1}{2}$ lbs of resin A is required for every square yard of 24 oz fabric
$1\frac{1}{4}$ lbs of resin B is required for every square yard of mould surface
2 oz release agent is required for every square yard of mould surface
1 lb opaque pigment is required for every 14 lbs resin
1 lb translucent pigment is required for every 20 lbs resin
1 lb polychromatic pigment is required for every 10 lbs resin
1 lb vinamould or silicone rubber is approximately 20 cubic inches

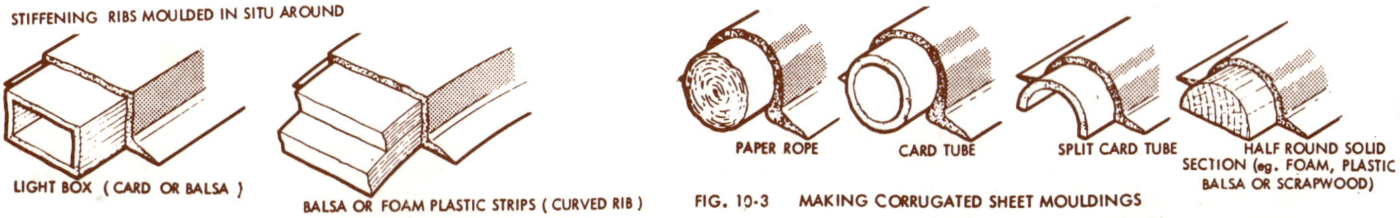

STIFFENING RIBS MOULDED IN SITU AROUND

LIGHT BOX (CARD OR BALSA)

BALSA OR FOAM PLASTIC STRIPS (CURVED RIB)

PAPER ROPE   CARD TUBE   SPLIT CARD TUBE   HALF ROUND SOLID SECTION (eg. FOAM, PLASTIC BALSA OR SCRAPWOOD)

FIG. 10-3   MAKING CORRUGATED SHEET MOULDINGS

THE NEW GLASSFIBRE BOOK
R.H.Warring
pp126; 75p
Model and Allied
Publications 1971

A good down to earth book about small scale use of GRP. Plenty of useful pictures and techniques.

Getting the Proportions Right

The majority of amateur constructions are done with pre-accelerated resins, leaving only the catalyst (hardener) to be added in recommended proportions. These proportions may range from 1 to 4 %. These proportions can be read as the *weight* of catalyst (hardener) required to mix with a given *weight* of resin. Where the catalyst is a liquid or paste, this involves translating weight into terms of liquid measure.

Where small quantities of resin are involved, the catalyst (hardener) can be added drop by drop, using the following count:

5   drops   equals   1% catalyst (hardener) per 1 ounce of resin
10   drops   equals   2% catalyst (hardener) per 1 ounce of resin
15   drops   equals   3% catalyst (hardener) per 1 ounce of resin
20   drops   equals   4% catalyst (hardener) per 1 ounce of resin

(1)
CORRUGATED SHEET (PATTERN)

(3) PAINT ON RESIN

(5) STIPPLE DOWN AND WET OUT

(7) LAY SECOND PIECE OF CORRUGATED SHEET IN PLACE AND PRESS DOWN UNIFORMLY

CELLOPHANE
(2)
DRAPE WITH CELLOPHANE

(4)
LAY GLASS MAT IN POSITION

(6) DRAPE WITH SECOND SHEET OF CELLOPHANE

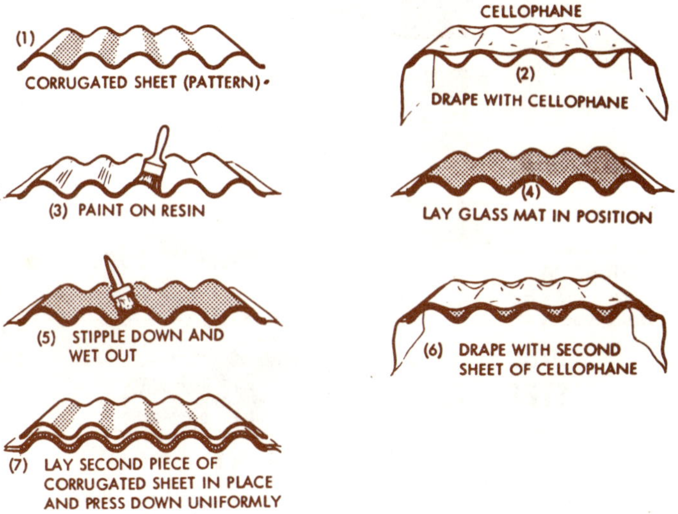

L.S.STARRETT CO LTD. Jedburgh, scotland.
Catalogue free.

Starrett are a big US outfit making
precision tools for engineering
measurement - micrometers, gauges etc.
They'll give you a nice catalogue listing
tools that will measure things you never
heard of.

Eyeglass Screwdriver
No. 554

A compact, streamlined screwdriver highly
useful for tightening ,and removing the many
extremely small screws found in radios, sewing
machines, electric razors, eyeglasses, etc. This
screwdriver is made with a chuck to hold the
blade firmly in a split socket when in use.

To carry in the pocket, or key-ring or watch
chain, the blade may be removed by slightly
loosening the chuck, then reversed and teles-
coped through the socket nearly full length, and
held safely by tightening the chuck. Chrome
plated. Blade width approximately $\frac{1}{16}$" (1·5 mm)

If you're using any sort of branded
product and you need some knowhow, try
sending off for the manufacturer's
technical information sheets. We were using
Perspex a while ago, and wrote off to ICI.
They sent us a set of very informative
glossy books filled with pics, tables and
techniques (below) that saved much
learning by experience/failure.

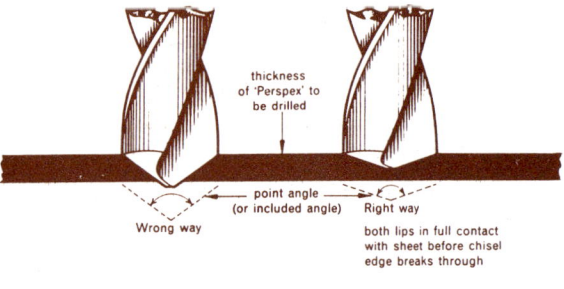

thickness
of 'Perspex' to
be drilled

point angle
(or included angle)

Wrong way

Right way

both lips in full contact
with sheet before chisel
edge breaks through

THE STARRETT BOOK FOR STUDENT MACHINISTS
pp 184; £1.10; L.S.Starrett Co.

Useful little book on the basics of
shaping metal. Plenty of working details
alongside the fundamentals.

A cone pointed drill of two or more cutting lips depends for
its efficient working upon four factors:

(1) All the cutting lips have the same inclination to the axis
of the drill.

(2) Cutting lips of exactly equal length.

(3) Surface back of the cutting edges having a proper lip
clearance.

(4) Correct angle of lip clearance.

After sharpening a drill freehand, use the hand-feed at first
and observe (a) the chips made by the cutting; (b) the size of the
hole. If the cutting lips are shaped to a proper clearance, the
chips will curl as they start from the cutting edge; but if the cutting lips lack a proper clearance the resulting chips have the appearance of being ground off rather than freely cut. If the cutting lips are of uneven length the hole will be enlarged over the
diameter of the drill. Drillings from cast iron should look as in
Fig. 35, and those from steel as in Fig. 36, if the drill is properly
sharpened.

FIG. 35. — Chips
produced from
cast iron.

FIG. 36. — Spiral
chips from steel.

Damascene inlay

Making the undercut groove

METAL TECHNIQUES FOR
CRAFTSMEN
Oppi Untracht
pp 500; £6.30;
Robert Hale.

Metal techniques for fine
working of metal. Very
comprehensive, with plenty
of handy little recipes
and examples of craftman-
ship.

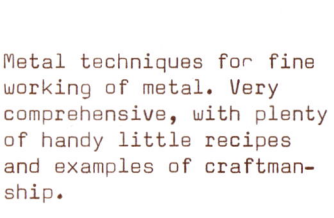

Hammering the wire in the groove

The finished inlay

Stripping is an electrochemical method of
cleaning and brightening platinum, gold, silver,
and copper articles after pickling and before
polishing. This step is commonly practiced by
production jewelers.

Stripping is the opposite of plating as the
metal is *removed* rather than deposited as in
plating (see pages 383–91). The article is
placed in the solution attached to a copper
wire and the source of current at the *positive*
or *anode* bar, while the stainless steel container
in which the electrolyte is placed becomes the
negative or cathode by attaching a wire with a

clip to it. When the current is applied, the
metal which is removed dissolves into the
electrolyte, and if separate containers are
maintained for each metal used, they can ultimately be collected and reclaimed as they ac-
cumulate at the bottom of the solution.

Stripping leaves the metal bright and makes
finishing simpler. A used solution is more efficient than a new one.

STRIPPING SOLUTION

¼ pound sodium cyanide
1 teaspoon sodium carbonate
added to 1 gallon of boiling water

Additional water and small amounts of
cyanide are added when replenishing is necessary. *Remember that these chemicals are
highly poisonous and should be handled with
care.* Breathing their fumes should be avoided,
and stripping should be done in the presence of
an exhaust fan. Commercially prepared stripping solutions are available.

Place the stainless steel container on an
electric hotplate and bring it to a boil. The
suggested voltage is 6 to 12 volts. Allow the
piece to remain for a few seconds and remove it
for observation. When it has reached the desired condition, rinse thoroughly with running
water, touching the surface as little as possible.
Dry in corn cob husk or sawdust and polish.

Wheel Classification

The Abrasive Industries Association have adopted a British Stand-ardised Marking System for grinding wheels. This will be of great benefit as previously the position was rather chaotic with different makers using their own symbols. The system, illustrated below, specifies the abrasive, the grain, the grade and the bond. The example given represents an aluminium oxide abrasive of 46 grit in a vitrified bond of medium hard-ness and structure. The Prefix, the Structure and the Suffix (shown in smaller print in the diagram) are optional in their use. The structure we have already discussed and the other two headings are for specifying individual manufacturer's abrasive and wheel types (e.g. W stands for white abrasive, etc.).

```
WORKSHOP TECHNOLOGY          The standard work on
W.Chapman.                   engineering metal,
Pt. 1 pp341 £1.20            starting at first-day-at-
Pt. 2 pp330 £1.40            work level and going
Pt. 3 pp 563 £2.25           through to the heights
Arnold 1961-3.               of the technology.
                             (Recommended by Austin
                             Carney)
```

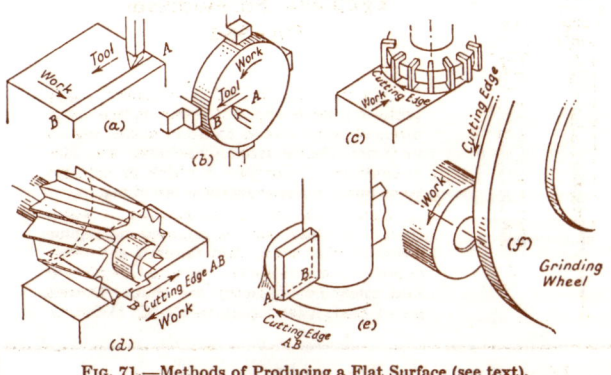

FIG. 71.—Methods of Producing a Flat Surface (see text).

```
WELDING CRAFT PRACTICE
N.Parkin, C.R.Flood
Part 1 Oxy-acetylene Gas Welding pp159; 90p.
Part 2 Electric Arc Welding pp102; 90p
Pergamon 1969.
Welding is fantastically useful low level technology,
as anyone trying to run a clapped out old banger will
testify. Main hangup is getting the energy to weld-
British Oxygen have got a monopoly of the gas supply,
and the initial deposit on the cylinders is large.
Electric arc needs expensive gear too, and a good
power supply. These books, like most textbooks for
City and Guilds training courses for apprentices,
give you a good solid grounding in the basics.
```

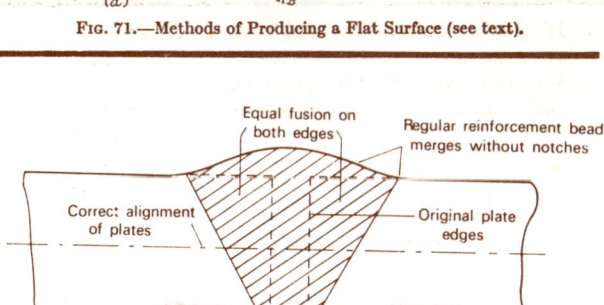

FIG. I.27. Features of a good butt weld.

Compressed Gas Cylinders

These may give rise to accidents from a variety of causes:

(a) Mechanical damage to the cylinder shell or outlet may be caused by careless or wrong use and may result in the leakage of gas.

(b) The gas may come into contact with some other substance, setting up a dangerous reaction, e.g. acetylene and copper, oxygen and oil.

(c) Heat may come into contact with the cylinder causing a dangerous increase in internal gas pressure, or weakening the cylinder shell.

(d) Gas leakages may occur, accumulating as explosive mixtures of air and gas in poorly ventilated or confined spaces, or the leakage may ignite at the source.

(e) The use of defective equipment may cause leakages, back-fires or flashbacks.

The recommended safety precautions aim at preventing such accidents; when they are properly applied and reinforced by the safety devices built in to the equipment they make welding a safe operation at all times.

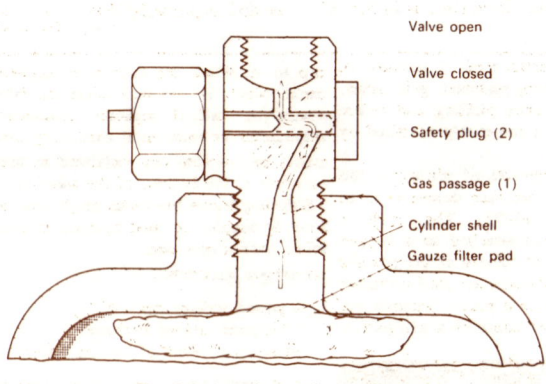

FIG. I.8. Acetylene cylinder outlet.

CORRODED PARTS

To repair eroded lands in a large diesel engine, Plastic Steel A was packed into the worn areas. The putty-type compound clung to the vertical areas without sagging. It has tremendous adhesion to metal. Once hardened, the built-up lands were ground to conform to the original machined surfaces. Over 250 diesel engines have been repaired by the U.S. Navy in this manner with Plastic Steel A. (Drawing and procedure covered by Bureau of Ships Instruction 9500.22, 27 Nov. 1957).

A10

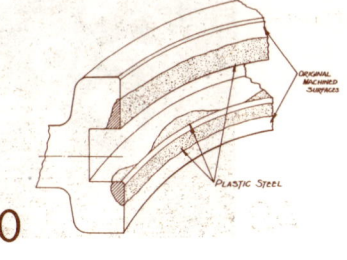

```
DEVCON LTD.,
Station Road, Theale, Reading.
RG7 4AB. Leaflets free.

A range of products based on epoxy
 resins and polyurethanes that sets
you thinking of ways you can use
them. Expensive , but just what you
want for that awkward job.
```

All by D.Rhodes.
CLAYS AND GLAZES. pp 220; £3.50; Pitman 1970.
KILNS - DESIGN, CONSTRUCTION, OPERATION
pp 240; £4.50; Pitman 1969.
STONEWARE AND PORCELAIN.
pp 228; £3.25; Pitman 1960.

Essential books of information to use day by
day.
        (Suggested by Margaret Bibby)

A version of the atmospheric gas burner can be made from pipe fittings, as shown in Figure 77. *A* is a 1½-inch pipe, into which a ½-inch pipe is fitted with reducing fittings at *B*. A pipe cap with a 1/32-inch hole drilled in it serves as an orifice at *C*, gas is controlled through valve *D*, and air is controlled through holes at *E*, fitted with a perforated slipping collar, which can widen or narrow the holes in the tube depending on its position. This burner lacks the venturi shape and does not entrain air as efficiently as a factory made burner, but it works quite satisfactorily, nevertheless. The orifice should be positioned just ahead of the air holes.

Figure 174 is a simple updraft kiln suitable for a camp or class project. It is very similar to early Mediterranean kilns such as are still in use in Crete. The drum shape of the kiln can be made of red brick, firebrick, or sandstone smeared with clay inside. The bricks can be layed in a circle for each course and the wedge-shaped spaces between bricks filled with clay. The kiln can be built right on the ground, with some sand placed in the bottom before firing. The fire mouth is made from a flue liner set at an upward slope. The bottom part of the kiln may be partially banked up with earth for additional insulation.

The pots are set up on a shelf arrangement to allow the fire to sweep in at the bottom of the cylinder. Plenty of space must be allowed for the upward circulation of the fire. The top of the kiln is closed over by corbeling in several courses of bricks, with a hole left at the top. A length of galvanized pipe placed over the hole forms a chimney to increase the draft.

A kiln of this sort will reach earthenware temperature with ease, although the bottom is sure to fire hotter than the top. It is certainly not good for exacting work with glazes, but a simple fritted glaze for cone 04, used, perhaps over slips, should work reasonably well. The kiln could easily be built in one day, and if scrap materials are used, the cost will be next to nothing.

The main pottery suppliers are,naturally enough, round Stoke. They will all send you curiously similiar free catalogues that look as though they have all been designed by the same bloke.
*HARRISON MAYER LTD.,Craft and Education Division, Meir,Stoke-on-Trent,ST3 7PX
*WENGERS LTD., Etruria, Stoke-on-Trent ST4 7BQ
*PODMORE & SONS LTD., Shelton, Stoke-on-Trent.
Also-FULHAM POTTERY, 210, Kings Rd.,London SW6 14NY
(Free catalogue)
(Suggested by Sunshine)

A POTTER'S BOOK
Bernard Leach
pp 294; £1.50
Faber 1945

Bernard Leach occupies a sort of high priesthood in British pottery. This book is his credo- roots, influences, activities.

Glazes are applied by *dipping, double dipping, pouring, spraying, painting, dripping, splashing* and *trailing.* For each

of these methods there is an appropriate technique which can be properly acquired only by observation and practice. I use double dipping whenever I can grip the pot by the foot sufficiently firmly. The drawing on page 145 will show how it is done better than words. By this method, which is much used in the Far East, the inside and outside of a pot are glazed with one movement. I possess a raw-glazed Sung pot with the finger marks of the old Chinese potter still showing in the glaze where he gripped it with three fingers and thumb in dipping.

The first instinct of the practical man in a 'new' district or country will be to set forth, armed with pick and shovel, to explore the countryside. This is a good beginning, but it should always be combined with the study of any available published (or unpublished) literature on the district, especially on the local geology and industries; and with meeting local people. If there are clays to be found at all, it is practically certain that they have already been found, and used, by somebody for some purpose. Valuable information can usually be got from people whose work involves making holes in the ground: well-sinkers, builders, makers of roads, dams, drains, watermains and even ordinary ditches; not forgetting gardeners and farmers, who are always interested in their soils and subsoils. As for local industries, it is surprising how often they use clay for some purpose, e.g. for holding candles in tin mines (Cornwall), or for investment moulding in *cire-perdue* brass casting (Ashanti). William Cookworthy (1705–80), discoverer of the Cornish china clay, remarks that the crude kaolin rock was already being used 'for mending the furnaces of the [tin-smelters'] Blowing-Houses, for which 'tis very proper'.

PIONEER POTTERY
Michael Cardew
pp 328; £5.00
Longmans 1969
Back to the fundamentals of pottery- earth, the chemistry of soil, firing,glazes and the manipulation of clay -in a deep and detailed way. The book has a peculiar air of ruggedness and simplicity.

All

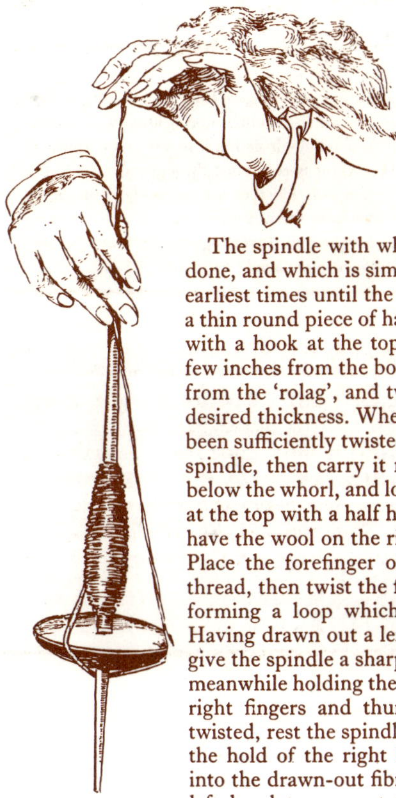

THE WEAVER'S CRAFT
L.E.Simpson & M.Weir.
pp221; £1.50;
Dryad 1969.

The spindle with which the first spinning will be done, and which is similar to the ones used from the earliest times until the sixteenth century, consists of a thin round piece of hardwood about 12 inches long with a hook at the top and a whorl of hardwood a few inches from the bottom. The fleece is drawn out from the 'rolag', and twisted with the fingers to the desired thickness. When a length of about 2 feet has been sufficiently twisted, tie it round the pillar of the spindle, then carry it round the end of the spindle below the whorl, and loop the thread round the hook at the top with a half hitch (see Fig. 41). To do this, have the wool on the right-hand side of the spindle. Place the forefinger of the right hand behind the thread, then twist the finger backwards over it, thus forming a loop which is slipped on to the hook. Having drawn out a length of fibre from the 'rolag', give the spindle a sharp outward twist and let it fall, meanwhile holding the wool near the 'rolag' with the right fingers and thumb. When the wool is well twisted, rest the spindle, draw out more fibres, relax the hold of the right hand, and the twist will run into the drawn-out fibre. Keep a firm hold with the left hand to prevent the twist extending into the 'rolag'. Repeat this process until the spun yarn is too long for further spinning, then wind this on to the shaft of the spindle above the whorl and start again

---

TIE AND DYE Anne Maile.
pp182; £1.50; Mills and Boon 1969.

Don't get ripped off by fashion punks - tie-dye it yourself (even tho' you are three years behind).

3. FOLDED SQUARES

3a. There are innumerable ways of folding, binding and dyeing a square of cloth, each giving interesting results. The squares may be large or small, but for the first experiments one approximately 8in. x 8in. is a suitable size.

Method

Fold into four, then again diagonally, so that a triangle is formed.

Finally, add binding to the corners or at convenient spots, and dye. Rinse and dry.

Before dyeing a second or third colour, rearrange the bindings. Rinse, dry and untie.

Other examples as :

113 A, B, C, D
114 A, B, C
115 A, B, C
116 A, B, C

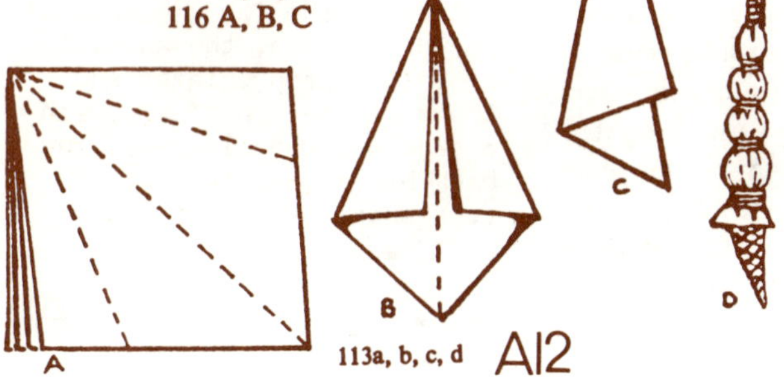

113a, b, c, d

SIMPLE WEAVING H.Chetwynd.
pp104; 62½p; Studio Vista 1969.

Simpson and Weir give the whole bag, from kids' stuff to processing and spinning your own wool. It's a golden oldie (11th. edition) and says it all in a nice staid gentle way.

'Simple Weaving' is a more general introduction with good illustrations.

(Suggested by Pip Richards).

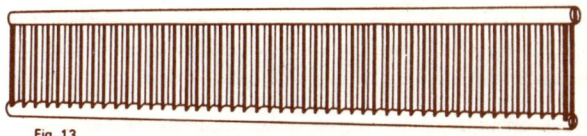

Fig. 13

J Reed consists of a number of wires closely set between two slats, and serves several purposes: separating the warp threads, guiding the shuttle, beating in the weft and, most important of all, determining the number of warp threads per inch. Reeds are bought to correspond with the width of the loom and with a number of dents desired per inch. A dent is the space between the wires, therefore an 8 reed has 8 spaces or dents per inch, a 10 reed has 10 dents per inch and so on. Since it is unnecessary to buy a whole range of different reeds to start weaving, begin with two reeds, an 8 and a 14, and continue buying as required. One reed will be supplied with the loom, usually an 8 or a 14 (Fig. 13).

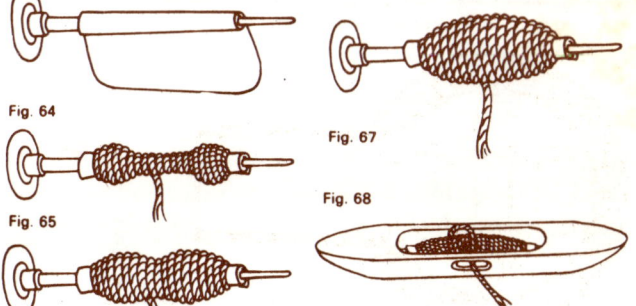

Fig. 64

Fig. 65

Fig. 66

Fig. 67

Fig. 68

Winding a bobbin

Cut some 3½" squares of medium thickness brown wrapping paper and round off the corners. Wind the paper tightly round the tapered spindle of the bobbin winder until approximately one inch of paper is left unwound (Fig. 64), then catch in the end of the yarn between the paper. Wind the handle of the bobbin winder with one hand, and hold the thread firmly between the finger and thumb of the other hand. Make a slight bump of yarn about ⅓" from each end of the paper (Fig. 65). Wind the yarn on to the bobbin backwards and forwards

with a sideways movement of the hand; always keep a bump of yarn at each end of the bobbin, never taking the yarn over the highest point of the bump (Figs 66, 67).

Do not wind so much yarn that the bobbin will not fit into the shuttle. Pull the bobbin off the winder and thread on to the spindle of the shuttle with the end of the yarn through the slot at the side of the shuttle (Fig. 68).

If the yarn slips off the bobbin and gets tangled in the shuttle when weaving, the bobbin is wound too loosely, too tightly or at some point wound beyond the bump at each end of the bobbin.

Single line of running stitches

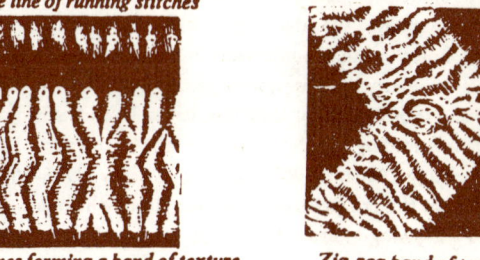

Several lines forming a band of texture

Zig-zag band of texture

THE USE OF VEGETABLE DYES - V.Thurstan.
pp48; 30p+15p handling from Dryad, Northgates,
Leicester.

Good organic colour book, with many useful from-
the·plant recipes.

13. ELDER (*Sambucus nigra*)

A large shrub very common all over England.
The leaves give a green colour with alum mordant (page 9).
The berries give a blue-lilac colour with alum mordant and salt,
a violet colour with alum mordant only. The bark gives a black
colour with iron mordant (page 12).
In each case 1 lb. to 1 lb. wool.

14. *GOLDEN ROD (*solidago spp.*)

A tall perennial with long flower heads made up of numerous
small yellow flowerets. Abundant in Great Britain, especially on
chalky soil. It should be picked just as the flower is coming into
bloom.
Mordant. Bichromate of potash, 2 oz. cream of tartar (page 12)
to 1 lb. wool.
Quantity. 1 lb.
Process. The plant and flower heads should be chopped into
small pieces and put in a pot of cold water. It should be brought
slowly up to the boil and simmered for two or three hours, and
then allowed to grow cold. The next day heated up again to just
below boiling-point, and the mordanted yarn entered and allowed to simmer until the required depth of colour is obtained.
It is suitable for wool, silk, and cotton.
Colour. Golden yellow. Alum may be used as a mordant
instead of chrome, and the colour is then lemon-yellow.

Two Methods of Dyeing with Lichens

1. Put the lichen into a large pot and fill up to the top with
cold water. About 1 lb. lichen to 1 lb. wool is required.
Bring this up to the boil very slowly and let it simmer for two
or three hours, and then get cold. Next day, put the wool, which
should be thoroughly wetted first, into the pot, and boil it all up
together until the required depth of colour is obtained. The
wool should not be taken out until it is cold. Then wash. The
loose lichen shakes off quite easily.

2. A layer of lichen at the bottom of the pot, then a layer of
wool, another layer of lichen, and so on until the pot is nearly
full. Fill up with cold water and put on the fire to simmer for
some hours, till the required depth of colour is reached. It can
be taken off at night and put on again next day. The colour
will be very fast. Wash well.

Two loom makers
Dryad, Northgates,
Leicester.
Catalogue free.

Harris Looms,
North Grove Road,
Hawkhurst, Kent.
Stamp for cat.
(extract left)

15 inch (38 cm.) 16 SHAFT TABLE LOOM WITH
TWO WARP BEAMS. also made 24 inch (60 cm.) wide

SUPPLIERS OF WOOL YARNS ETC. SAE for details.
Hugh Griffiths, 8, Frome Rd., Beckington, Bath,
Somerset.
    Excellent range of colours and textures,
including fine strings, and a wide variety of
yarns.
The Weavers' Shop, Wilton Royal Carpet Factory,
Wilton, Nr. Salisbury, Wilts.
    Good range for rugs.
Hand Loom Weavers, Fourways, Rockford, Ringwood,
Hants.
    Very nice textures in natural colours; good
range in heavy cottons - 18varieties, most
available in 35 colours.
J.Hyslop Bathgate, Galashields, Scotland.
    Standard fine wools and cottons.
Craftmans Mark, Trefnant, Denbeigh. N.Wales.
    Beoutiful natural wools in blacks, browns,
greys and whites. Wools for home spinning too.
T.M.Hunter Ltd., Station Sq., Broara, Sutherland.
    Tweed and Shetland wools.

    You can weave any old junk (almost), but for
knitting, hand or machine, you need lubricated
yarn. Suppliers -
The Direct Wool Group, 86a, Sunbridge Rd.,
Bradford 1.
A.K.Graupner, Corner House, Valley Rd., Bradford 1.
Hall Green Wools, Wakefield, Yorks.

Dye Suppliers
Comak Chemicals Ltd., Swinton Works, Moon St.,
London N1 SAE for list.
Skilbeck Bros. Ltd., 55-57, Glengall Rd., London
SE15. SAE for·list.
Candle Makers Supplies, 4, Beaconsfield Terrace,
London W14 OPP.
    Tie and dye, Batik and candle making supplies.
Users report good helpful people.
Informative catalogue 15p. ↓

These honeycombed, patterned beeswax
sheets offer the simplest way of candlemaking,
because they require no melting or casting.
They are available in sheets approximately
17" x 17" square
The basic principle is simple: you lay a wick
along one edge (see fig. 1). Fold and roll the
sheet as tight as possible (fig. 2). Many variations on this simple theme are possible. Although
you will find these sheets are pliable, in cold
weather it is a good idea to warm them slightly,
this will prevent fractures.
Always make sure you use a suitable wick (see
wick section in this book) 3/20's (2") wick is
used for a single sheet.

Beeswax Sheeting

TRADITIONAL COUNTRY CRAFTSMEN
J.G.Jenkins
pp236; £2.35 Routledge 1965

A general catalogue of crafts, craftsmen
and tools, solutions to problems of pre-mass
production. A book to give you general
knowledge- when you've read it,go and and find
your craftsman, if he's still around. Hurry.

Despite the fact that there are hundreds of local and trade variations in basket design, the process of weaving is basically the same throughout the world. Before he begins the day's work, enough willow rods have been soaked overnight to make them pliable and easy to handle, and the basket maker, seated on the floor with a lapboard in front of him, commences his task of weaving.

Fig. 9. 'Strokes' in Basket Making.

Whether a basket be round, square or oval, the base is almost invariably made first. If a rectangular or square basket is being made, the rods are first of all fixed in a small clamp made of two wooden blocks clipped bolted together and the finer rods woven between the upright sticks. If it is a round or oval basket, however, a start is made with the slath which consists of a number of rods overlapping crosswise. They are bound together and spread out to radiate from the centre like the spokes of a wheel. Finer rods are interwoven between the radiating stakes, and if the basket is large, more stakes are inserted as the work proceeds to make the base perfectly strong. When the base is complete, the edge being reinforced with a stouter weave, extra rods are inserted and bent up to form the side frame. A willow hoop is made and passed around the upright stakes to keep them in place as the work proceeds. Finer rods are woven round and round between the upright stakes from left to right, each rod being cut at the butt and inserted in the weave to overlap the end of the previous rod. The long ends of the stakes are finally woven along the rim to form a firm edge.

GRADING AND QUALITY

The main divisions of quality of centre canes are "Continental" and "Far East" or "Hong Kong". The buyer knows the grade by the colour of the string with which each pound bundle is tied. Continental is sold in Blue Tie and Red Tie, the latter being satisfactory for all but exhibition work. Far East is sold in Red Tie and White Tie, and occasionally Yellow and Black Tie. The quality is inferior to Continental cane, though a Far Eastern Red Tie can be used for class work and all grades are used commercially.

Since the war, West German processing firms have invented a method of bleaching the dark portions of the cane core which previously were unusable for basketry. This renders the cane very soft, more like macaroni when damp. This may be an advantage in therapy, but the resulting work is neither strong nor lively to look at and has a dead antiseptic air. It colours with age just as cream cane does, but it is cheaper.

PAPER MAKING AS AN ARTISTIC CRAFT J.Mason
pp96;   £1.95 with 2 samples of homemade paper.
        £3.20 "   6   "   "   "   "
12x8 Press 1963

Everyone who picked up this book while we
had it was grabbed by the idea of making
paper. All the basics are here.

(Suggested by Margaret Bibby)

Skeleton leaves, flower petals, grasses and coloured threads may be sandwiched between two layers of waterleaf. Some Japanese papers even incorporate butterflies

You may now prepare some raw material ready for beating. Towards the end of the summer or in the autumn you would do well to start with some wild plants such as nettle, cowparsley, leaves of rushes and coarse grasses, and several kinds may be mixed together, if you wish. Leaves of garden plants such as montbretia, gladiolus and iris, also make excellent paper. Surprisingly large quantities are needed to make even a small amount of pulp and so a good large sack should be filled and pressed down tightly. Later you will find that the fibres are separated more easily if the plants are placed for a time in a ditch or in a tank of water so that they partly rot, or they may be left in a wet mass on a concrete floor. This is similar to *retting* of flax in Ireland in preparation for the making of linen. At first, however, this process may be omitted.

BASKETS AND BASKETRY D.Wright
pp148; £1.95 David & Charles 1972

Baskets- useful, organic and craftmade- what
more could you want.Maybe make them yourself-
use this book. (We're not specially hung up on
baskets,by the way. Layouts happen that way.)

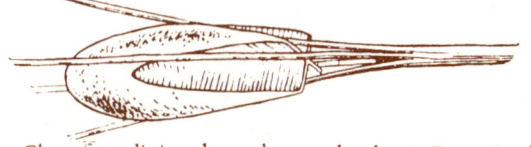

29. *Cleave* for splitting dry rods to make skeins. To make three clefts the cleave has three "fins". It is held in the right hand while the left hand guides the rod. The clefts run up through the fingers of the right hand.

Pitchers

Solid stone pitchers made of same quality steel as our standard stone and marble tools. Ideal for quick roughing out before using the heavy point. Available in mallet-head and hammer-head. In four sizes: 1", 1¼", 1½", 2".

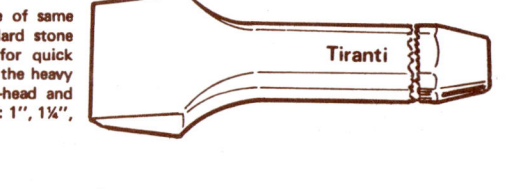

ALEC TIRANTI.
72, Charlotte St., London W1P 2AJ.
Catalogue 7½p post free.

Tools and materials for sculptors. Also supply a lot of books about art/design field.

The Scopas Chops

The perfect carver's vice. Made with heavy square-thread screw and bench screw; metal side plates. Overall length 18", height 9". Spare set of corks and buffs are available for the jaws.

CHARLES COOPER,
12, Hatton Garden Wall,
Hatton Garden, London EC1.
Cat. 30p (extract below)

E. GRAY & SON LTD.
12-16, Clerkenwell Rd.,
London EC1M 5PL.
Cat 25p.

Two suppliers of jewellers' bits and bobs.

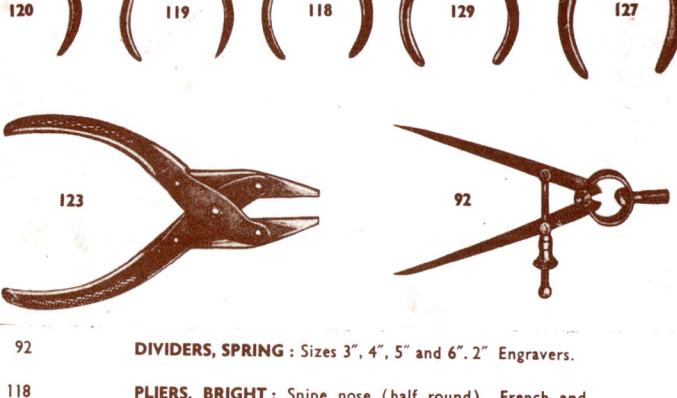

92	**DIVIDERS, SPRING** : Sizes 3", 4", 5" and 6". 2" Engravers.
118	**PLIERS, BRIGHT** : Snipe nose (half round). French and Swedish, all sizes.
119	**PLIERS, BRIGHT** : Round nose. French and Swedish, all sizes.
120	**PLIERS, BRIGHT** : Flat nose, French and Swedish, all sizes. Can be had with extra long jaws if required.
123	**PLIERS "BERNARD"** : Plated, parallel opening jaws. All shapes. Smooth or serrated jaws.
127	**CUTTERS (TOP NIPPERS)** : Best Swedish and French.
129	**CUTTERS (SIDE NIPPERS)** : Best Swedish and French.

A15

DRYAD.
Northgates, Leicester LE1 4QR.
Catalogue free.

Dryad - afternoons at school desks, sticky paper, Gloy paste, powder colour, bits of wool.

Now it means a good range of craft materials, equipment, books and leaflets. If you want a single source for a range of general craft stuff, this is it.

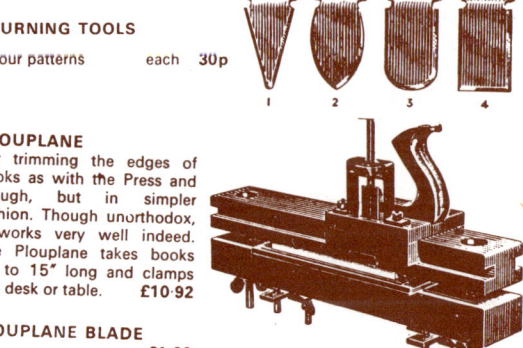

TURNING TOOLS

Four patterns   each   30p

PLOUPLANE

For trimming the edges of books as with the Press and Plough, but in simpler fashion. Though unorthodox, it works very well indeed. The Plouplane takes books up to 15" long and clamps to a desk or table. **£10·92**

PLOUPLANE BLADE
£1·36

SABLE LETTERING BRUSH

3 mm.	.	.	24p
5 mm.	.	.	41p
7 mm.	.	.	54p

T.N.LAWRENCE AND SON LTD.
2-4, Bleeding Heart Yard, Greville St., Hatton Gardens, London EC1N 8SL. 3p for list.

A visit here is better than a list, visitors say. Hand made papers, colours, books - all sorts.

TOOLS for ENGRAVING

Gravers, Lozenge	several sizes	...	45p each
„ Square	„ „	... ...	45p „
Spitstickers, Fine, Medium, Broad		... ...	45p „
Scorpers, round Nos. 1-12	...	...	45p „
„ square Nos. 1-12	...	...	45p „
Tint Tools, Nos. 1-6		... ...	45p „

(Low numbers of all Tools are fine)

Chisels, for borders 3, 4, 8 or 10 mm. wide	...	...	45p „
Multiples, various grades 2, 4, 6, 8, 10 and 14 lines	...	...	£1.50 „
American Square Gravers, for metal	...	...	60p „
Some superior quality Spitstickers, Tint Tools and Scorpers	... ...	...	55p to 85p „

All the above tools are sold in small graver handles and are shortened to required length, ground and sharpened ready for use.

Fitted with **Boxwood** handles	...	...	...	20p extra
Re-sharpening Tools	...	...	...	3p each
Green Baize Tool Cases	...	...	7 tools, 35p; 12 tools, 45p each
Sandbags	...	...	...	4" £1.50; 5" £1.60; 6" £1.80; 7" £2.00

BUCK AND HICKMAN TOOL BUYERS GUIDE 1971-72.
pp1220; £3.75;
From Buck and Hickman Ltd., PO Box 74,
2, Whitechapel Road, London E1 1EB.

The ultimate whole tool catalogue, of almost
every type of tool or machine that exists in
this country. Equipment for everything -
putting up telephone wires, cleaning drains,
fixing engines, tools for wood, metal, plastic,
leather, cloth. If you like browsing through
tool catalogues, fasten down your brain before
opening up.

It's a bit pricey (you thought catalogues
were free?) but if you want an inventory of
small scale technology three quarters of the
way through the twentieth century, this is it.

The guide is widely used by shops and firms,
and if you're friendly with your local tool
dealer, you can probably score a back copy.
(It's published about every two years.)

Bricklayers' Hammers
With Replaceable Scutching Points

Fig. 2370A
Dull Black Finish
Length of Head, 8 in.
Ash Handled
PRICE, 1·58 each

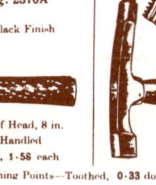
Fig. 2371A
Dull Black Finish
Length of Head, 7 in.
Ash Handled
PRICE, 1·49 each

Fig. 5039A
Best quality Ash Handles
Type A. All Bright Finish
Length of Head, 8 in.
PRICE, 1·40 each
Type B. Black and Bright
Length of Head, 11 in.
PRICE, 1·20 each

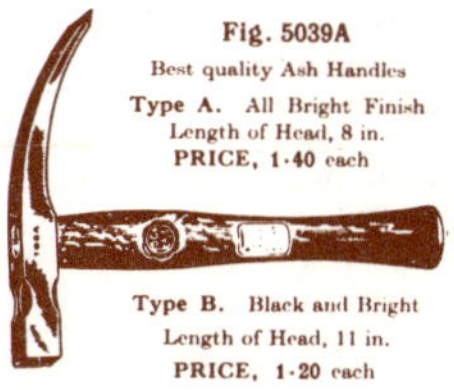

Extra Scutching Points—Toothed, 0·33 doz. Chisel Edged, 0·25 doz.

Patent Earthborers Fig. 461A

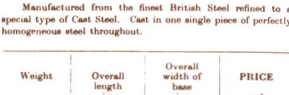

Indispensable to Architects, geologists, mining, prospecting, sanitary and electrical engineers, well borers, builders, farmers, etc.

Used extensively in tropical countries for making deep sanitary pits for checking ankylostomiasis.

HAND USE ONLY. Will bore from 1 to 200 ft. vertically, horizontally or at any angle, in any soil.

The hinged upper end of Drill allows the loosened soil or stones to rise upwards. When the Borer is raised the hinged flaps close the mouths, and the soil and stones rise with the Borer. The lower point (which is renewable on sizes from 3 inch upwards), has two grooved cutting edges.

The extension rods are of weldless cold-drawn steel tubing, and supplied in three different diameters. Rods 1¼ in. diam. are recommended for 6–10 in. Drills for depths greater than 15 ft. and for exceptionally hard or stony soil, in which case an Adaptor (see accessories) must be used.

Diam. of Drill ..	in.	2	3	4	6	8	10	12	14	16	18
PRICE, Drill only .. each		3·30	4·80	6·90	7·50	8·10	9·90	16·50	18·00	23·10	24·60
„ 3 ft. Extension Rods „		2·40	2·40	2·40	2·40	2·40	2·40	3·60	3·60	4·20	4·20
„ Handles .. „		1·50	1·50	1·50	1·50	1·50	1·50	3·30	3·30	3·30	3·30
„ 4 ft. Borer .. comp.		7·20	8·70	10·80	11·40	12·00	13·80	23·40	24·30	30·60	32·10

Accessories

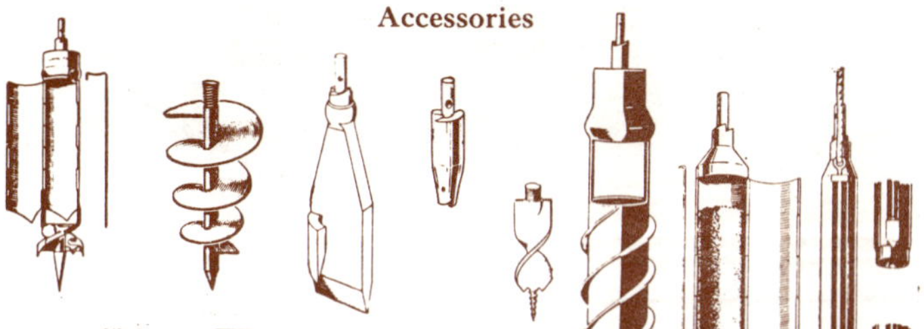

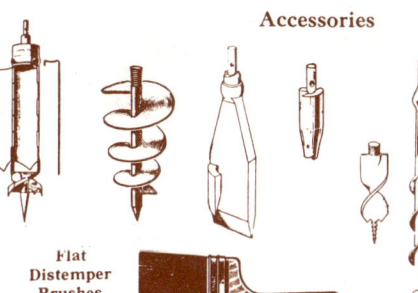

Flat Distemper Brushes
Fig. 5033A
Mixture Centres.
Bristle Capped.

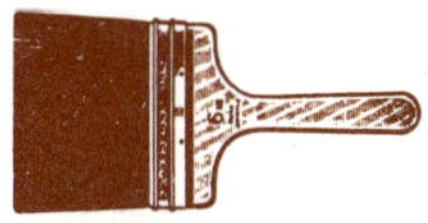

Size	5	6	7	in.
PRICE ..	1·80	2·10	3·10	each

Glue Brush
Fig. 8974A

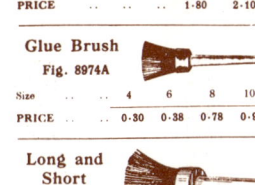

Size	4	6	8	10	12	
PRICE ..	0·30	0·38	0·78	0·93	1·10	doz.

Long and Short Tar Brushes

Fig. 9295A Long .. .. .. PRICE 0·38 each
„ 9296A Short .. .. .. „ 0·26 „

Hair Broom Fig. 9298A
Superior Quality

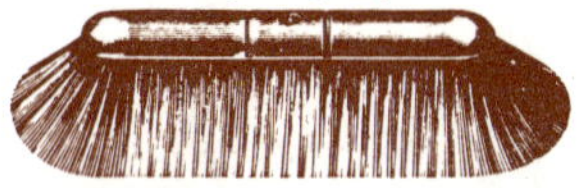

PRICE, Head only .. .. .. 0·99

Bass Broom Fig. 9299A
Superior Quality

PRICE, Head only .. .. .. 0·36

All-Steel Anvils
Fig. 7767A 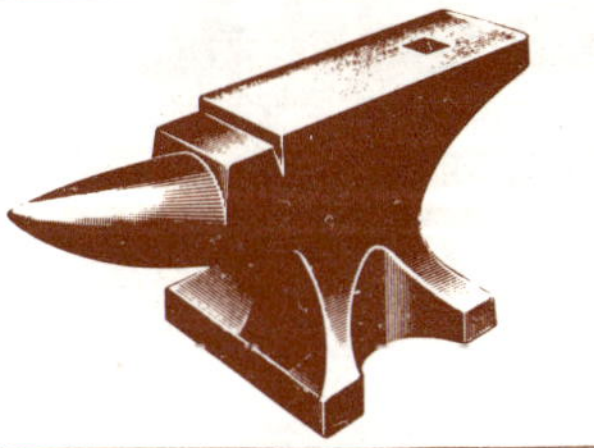

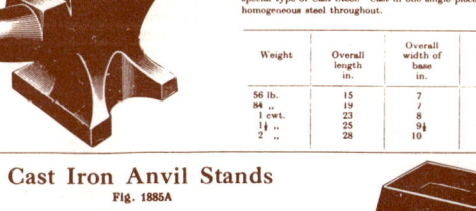

Manufactured from the finest British Steel refined to a special type of Cast Steel. Cast in one single piece of perfectly homogeneous steel throughout.

Weight	Overall length in.	Overall width of base in.	PRICE each
56 lb.	15	7	14·70
84 „	19	7	21·15
1 cwt.	23	8	26·50
1½ „	25	9½	34·50
2 „	28	10	45·00

Cast Iron Anvil Stands
Fig. 1885A
To Suit Above

To suit Anvils .. .. Weight, lb.	56	84	112	168	224
Weight of Stand .. .. lb.	87	87	91	107	125
PRICE .. .. .. each	10·50	10·50	10·50	13·00	18·75

Cast Iron Swage Blocks and Stands
Blocks, Fig. 1887A.   Stands, Fig. 1888A.

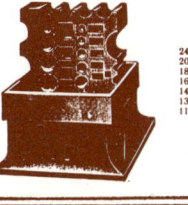

Size of Block	Approx. Weight of Block	Approx. Weight of Stand
24 in. × 24 in. × 7 in. ..	713 lb.	478 lb.
20 „ × 20 „ × 7 „ ..	490 „	410 „
18 „ × 18 „ × 6 „ ..	340 „	350 „
16 „ × 16 „ × 6 „ ..	260 „	258 „
14 „ × 14 „ × 5 „ ..	184 „	231 „
13 „ × 13 „ × 5 „ ..	140 „	196 „
11 „ × 11 „ × 5 „ ..	102 „	168 „

Price on application

SMITHS' LEATHER APRONS, Fig. 1340A
PRICE, 2·10 each. Plus P.T.

TOOL CATALOGUE.
pp118; Published by the National Feder-
ation of Ironmongers, Hagbourne Road,
Birmingham 3.

A handy free catalogue of all sorts of
tools, hardware and materials. If your local
dealer is a member of the NFI, he'll get you
a copy of this catalogue, (or the next one
when it comes out sometime early '73.) If
you're desparate for one, and can't find it
locally write to NFI.

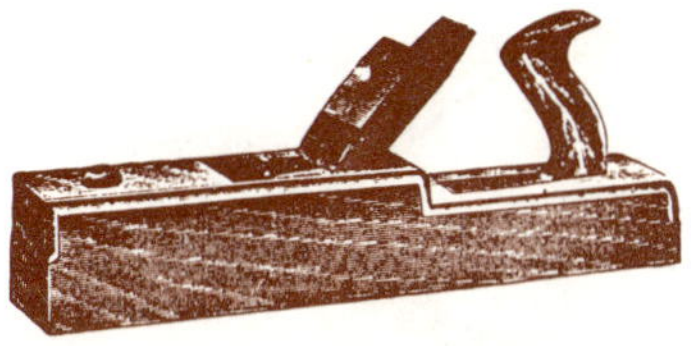

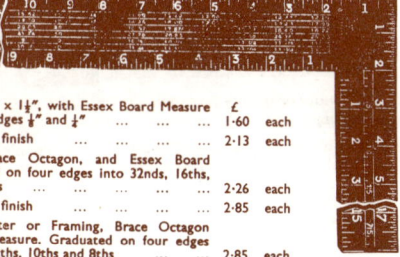

No. 380.	Size 24″ × 2″ × 18″ × 1½″, with Essex Board Measure graduated on four edges ⅛″ and ¼″ .. .. .. £ 1·60	each
No. 380B.	As above, but blued finish .. .. .. 2·13	each
No. 381.	Polished, with Brace Octagon, and Essex Board Measure. Graduated on four edges into 32nds, 16ths, 12ths, 10ths and 8ths .. .. .. 2·26	each
No. 381B.	As above, but blued finish .. .. .. 2·85	each
No. 383.	Polished, with Rafter or Framing, Brace Octagon and Essex Board Measure. Graduated on four edges into 32nds, 16ths, 12ths, 10ths and 8ths .. .. 2·85	each

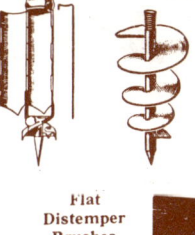

46	Beech Smoothing Planes	...	...	...		2 £2·50	2¼ —	ins. each
49	Beech Jack Planes	...	...	...		£3·25	3·75	each
51	Beech Technical Jack Planes	...	...		2 £3·54		ins. each
53	Beech Trying Plane 22″ × 2½″	...	...		£4·35		each
56	Beech Skew Rebate Planes ...			1 £2·50	1½ 2·90	ins. each
57	Spare Wedges 1⅜″ to 2¼″	...	26p each	Striking Knob	... 8p each

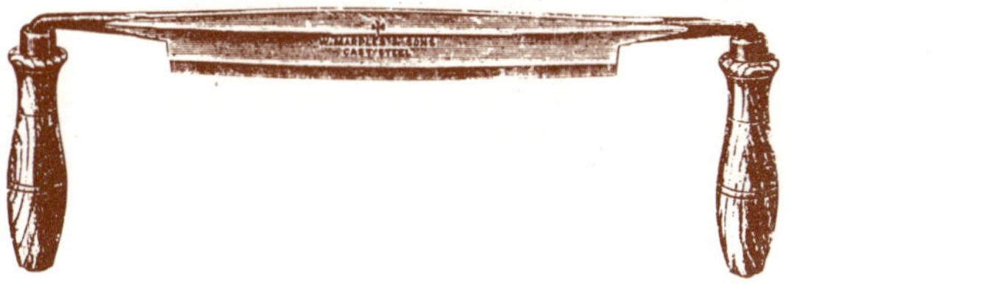

Carpenters' Drawing Knives ... ... 10 ins. £2·29 each

If you've always enjoyed rooting round second-hand dealers, or saving things because they may be useful some day, you can now feel smug because you're recycling resources. There's a huge amount of stuff around that's junk to the owner, but solid gold to someone else. Here are a few second-hand dealers who do lists or catalogues.

Maybe a local information exchange would work- a monthly sheet listing unwanted stuff from firms and organizations going free or for a small price. That's what NIMRA (see below) are doing on a national scale, but local friendly info. would be more immediately useful.

H.W.English, 469, Rayleigh Rd., Hutton, BRENTWOOD, Essex. 3p stamp for 47 page catlogue.

Optics- telescopes, binoculars, lenses, stuff for building your own telescopes, enlargers, etc. Also publish info. on using their material.

E17

E.17*. 26½mm focal length Kelner. Field of view 52 degrees. Weight 12 oz. In high quality focussing mount of German manufacture (usually Zeiss or Leitz). New condition, £4.
E.20. 44mm focal length 6 lens Erfle. Field of view 60 degrees. Weight 2 lb. 4 oz. Of American manufacture, this eyepiece is used on the Mount Palomar telescope. In focussing mount. To obtain maximum field of view requires the use of a drawtube not less than 2″ in diameter. New condition £12. Secondhand condition (as E.3) £7.

E20

ARTIFICIAL TEETH-New ex Gov't stock,on cards.Asst'd. types & shades.16 teeth for 13p .P&P 9p per card.
GLASS LIGATURE REELS & STANDS-New ex W.D. 1p to 5p stands (glass) various sizes.

DEAF AID BATTERIES:Mallory RM.401.(mercury) 5p + P&P
Flex Retriever   LISTON SPLINTS-53"x2½"- 4p each.
coin catcher & probang 45p Stirrup pin Bohler 6"x4m.m. & 8¼"x 6mm S.S. new 8p .Nozzles Urethral 13p Torniquet with stick 5p .Directors Hernia key 10p Perineal staff 23p   CLIPS ext. finger 3p
MANOMETER-Spinal needle. Barker with stopcock 13p
Troc & Art F.G.35 53p .leg bone splint back only 48p . set.

Laurence Corner, 62-4, Hampstead Rd., London NW1 Catalogue 12p

Weird paste-up catalogue, heavy on colours and pictures, light on solid info. about what's being sold. Clothes, army surplus, tools etc.

Valley Agricultural Engineering Co. Ltd. 83,Prestbury Rd., Cheltenham, Gloucs. List 10p.

Farmers' hardware- fence posts, baling wire, big nuts and bolts.

Spirax Flowmeters for Steam or Air £3.50

Tin Mens Funnel Stakes Approx 20 lb £2
Grease Guns Rom Pom Handy Grip High
                              Pressure £2.15

All Leather Tool Bags Metal Insert with carrying handles 13 x 5 x 7 New £1.75

Carpenters Tool Bags New 39"   £1.25

Desoutter Mighty Atom Air Drills ¼" Chuck
                                        £6

Pneumatic Screwdrivers by Thor New £10

Leytool Universally Jointed Socket Spanners 7/16 AF 30p, 9/16 AF 30p, 11/16 AF 30p

Thomas Foulkes,Lansdowne Rd., Leytonstone, London E11 3HB Large SAE for free catalogue.

Just bought a parachute from Foulkes, to skin a dome with. Their main trade is boats and yachting, but the catalogue has lots of interesting ' I bet I could find a use for that' stuff in it.

STIRRUP PUMPS
Yes, the genuine 1939 issue, complete with 30ft. hose. £2. p. & p. 40p.
ANTI GAS EYESHIELDS
Most useful when sailing, in dusty conditions, have many other uses too, thank goodness! Per packet of 6, 15p, p. & p. 10p.

MIXED THIN CORD AND THREAD
Assorted Synthetic cords and threads, suitable for Sewing, net making, Fishing, whipping ropes, etc., each bag contains 4 to 6 spools assorted. 1 lb. minimum. Ask for Bag B. 75p p. & p. 25p on any number.
EX RAF BOX KITES
Unused, with many potential applications afloat, packed in small tubular container, size 17in. × 17in. × 36in. when erected. Bright Orange. £2.25. p. & p. 25p.
NEW NYLON PAINTER LINE
Breaking Strain 1 ton. A flat tubular braid, soft and supple, approx. ½in. wide laid flat. Originally intended to secure Life Rafts to Oil Rigs, many uses afloat and ashore. Send S.A.E. for sample. 2p per foot. p. & p. 25p. per order.
NYLON BRAID
1in. wide, a flat tubular braid of great strength. I have always used a length of this as a car tow rope. It is a flat webbing type material somewhat akin to pyjama cord. 7p per yard, p. & p. 10p.
FUEL CAN AND POURER
Solidly constructed from steel, interior coated with petrol resisting paint, outside finished in red primer. Capacity 1.3 gallons. Dimensions 12in. × 12in. × 4in. Price 75p, detachable spout 50p. p. & p. 30p.

PETROL JERRICANS
Capacity 4¼ galls. good condition, used and suggest swilling out before refilling. Ex. W.D. and well worth £1.25 each, carr. 50p. Pourer spout 50p extra.

PETROL CANS
2 gall. brand new, bright red, £1.25 each, p. & p. 25p. 2 for £2.50 plus p. & p. 40p. 6 for £6.95 plus carr. 75p. Flexible pourer 12in. long ex. W.D. and may be stock soiled, 25p.
ALUMINIUM TANKS
Capacity 35 gallons, totally enclosed. Size 39in. × 28in. × 14in. deep. Weight 20lb. Inlet 2½in. screw cap located on 39in. × 28in. topside outlet ½in. located underside £8.75, plus carriage 60p.

David Green & Son, Albert St., Lytham,Lancs. List free.

All sorts that you'd find useful on a desert island. Farm/garden emphasis.

AI7

WATERPROOF COVERS. Birkmyre quality. Heavy green proofed sheets. Strong and long lasting. Hemmed, eyeletted and roped. Size approx. 9ft x 6ft ... £4-72; 12ft. x 9ft. ... £9-45; 15ft. x 12ft. ... £15-75. Prices for other sizes can be quoted on request.

LIGHT SACK TRUCKS. (Capacity 1½ cwts.) All steel welded construction with angle steel frame and 5" deep bevelled steel foot. Tubular handles, rubber grips, cushion tyred wheels 8" x 1¼". Height 41", width 14". Weight 18 lbs. £4-40 each.

CASE TRUCKS. (Capacity 4 cwts.) All steel electrically welded construction with angle steel frame and dished cross runners. Solid steel axle welded into foot and cradle supports. Tubular handle bars. Rubber grips, steel wheel guards. Alert orange finish. Height 48", width between handles 15", 12" foot. Plain bearing solid rubber wheels 8" x 2". ...... £8-80 carriage paid.

Tarpaulin and Tent Maunufacturing Co. Ltd.,
101-3, Brixton Hill, London SW2
Catalogue 15p

Camping and outdoor equipment, some new, some second hand.

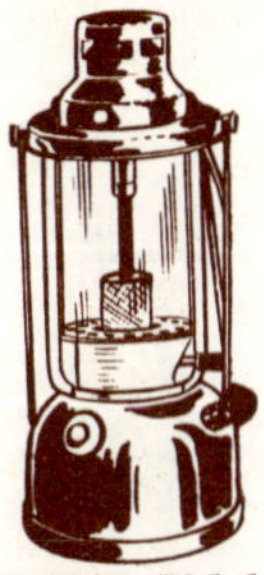

Ex-W.D. Bialaddin Lamp (Model 305)

A brilliant portable paraffin lamp with a brass tank. A real bargain offer for only ~~69/6~~ DISCONTINUED

As new ~~89/6~~

P. & P. 6/-

Ex-W.D. Paraffin FLOODLIGHT

For your camp area or marquee. 5,000 mean reflected candle power. Fitted with built-in pump, completely stormproof, portable and independent of cables or generating plant. Armour plated glass and 14" reflector. ~~£10-10-0~~ £12.50 Carriage 20/-

CONVERTIBLE BUNKS

Fully sprung collapsible steel frames, designed for use as single or bunk beds. Ideal for homes, hotels and hostels. Used, but in very good condition. Size 6' 6" x 2' 6". £6.00

Price Single ~~50/~~ £3.00 Double ~~100/-~~ £2.50

Carriage ~~20/-~~ £1.25 Carriage ~~30/-~~

National Industrial Materials Recovery Association (NIMRA).
Secretary A.W.V.Holden, PO Box 8,
9, Sea Rd., Bexhill-on-Sea, Sussex.
Subscription £5 per annum.

NIMRA is an information exchange between members who want to get rid of stuff, and members who want to get hold of things. Definitely a Good Idea, and if you're into any sort of production, I bet you'd save your sub, every year. They publish a magazine which carries the info., which is available to members only (extract below.)

PAN LIDS
426—9in. dia. aluminium, with hole for knob of which 282 are red anodised and 144 are in bright polished condition.

VACUUM CLEANER BRUSHES
2,700 approx.—Vactric No. 1 with 2 stripping slots, clear lacquered, at £3.00 per 100. Samples available.
Jones Textilaties Ltd., Audley Range Works, Blackburn. BB1 1TQ. Lancashire.
Tel. 0254-57145. (Mr. A .So

DIESEL GENERATOR
Make. Taylor. Ford diesel engine. New batteries and starter. Mounted on steel chassis. Price: £120 o.n.o.
The Leeds Welding Co. Ltd., Laneside Mills, Churwell, Nr. Leeds.
Tel. Modley 4100 (Mr. Archer)

ELECTRIC MOTORS
430—1/3 h.p. for vertical mounting G.E.C. 1425 r.p.m. 415/3/50. 8 amp.
Neil & Spencer Ltd., Argosy Works, Kingston Road, Leatherhead, Surrey.
Tel. 75441. (Mr. A. D. Allman)

ELECTRIC MOTORS
12 units.—UDHE out of balance type. Model S40/1. 240v. 3.3 amps. 50 cycles. 1.5 KW.
The United Sulphuric Acid Corporation Ltd., Greenoaks Works, Tanhouse Lane, Widnes, Lancashire.
Tel. 051-424 4161. (Mr. G. H. Yealand)

GENERATOR
1—G.E.C. motor and alternator, with control panel to suit, DC. motor 2½ h.p. 10.9 amp. 220v. Alternator 1.26 KVA 3 ph.
Westinghouse Brake and Signal Co. Ltd., Chippenham, Wiltshire.
Tel.4141. (Mr. L. S. Clifford)

PRINTER
Multilith Model 1250, year 1961.

ADDRESSING MACHINE
Addressograph Model 831, year 1966.

TIME CLOCKS/RECORDERS
National and Gledhill Brook office staff type.

FORUMS BURSTER
Uarco continuous stationery Model 1741 - 1, year 1964.

PRINT MACHINES
Ozalid One Step Ozoprinter, year 1961.
Ozorapid Reflex-Diazo Photo Unit Model OR 510/336.

DIAZO MATRIC
Hall Harding, year 1966.
Rolls-Royce (1971) Ltd., Nightingale Road, Derby.
Tel. 42424, Extn. 488. (Mr. N. F. Wrigl

LARGE LIBRARY BOOKCASE
Magnificent curl mahogany, for disposal. 6ft. high x 6ft. wide. Double carcass. Break front. As new. Would cost £200 today. Will accept £90 for quick sale. Can deliver if required.
George Serlin & Sons Ltd., 121/133 Church Walk, off Albion Road, London, N.16.
Tel. 01-254 2000. (Mr. Morris)

WOODEN DESKS & BENCHES
Various sizes, types and condition, offers please.
Smiths Industries Ltd., 13/15 Carlisle Road, Colindale, London, N.W.9.
Tel. 01-205 7011, Extn. 52. (Mr. R. E. Grey)

COPIER
1—3M's model 209. New Aug. 1968. Cost £357. Offers?

A.E.KING (TOOLS) LTD, 3, Central Parade, Station Parade, Sidcup, Kent. SAE for list.

Mainly engineering tools, a lot of them specialised.

EYELET PLIERS Large size with three punches & dies, sizes 3/32, 1/8" & 1/4".
WORTH OVER £3.00 each..........OUR PRICE 90p each.

B.A. SOCKET SETS in 9/32" square drive, one socket each size, 0,1,2,3,4,5,6,7B.A. with a 4" EXTENSION BAR, SLIDING TEE-BAR, UNIVERSAL JOINT, SPINNER HANDLE, complete in fitted box.
WORTH OVER £4.20 a Set.............OUR PRICE £2.20 a Set.

SIZE 9 B.A. DIES Standard split circular type 13/16" o.d. to suit Lot 153.
USUAL PRICE 49p each......................OUR PRICE 20p ea.

PARALLEL PIN PUNCHES size 1/16" diameter length 4½".
OUR PRICE 7p. each.

CHESTERMAN 6" Precision steel Rules......OUR PRICE 15p each.

CHESTERMAN 12" Precision steel Rules.....OUR PRICE 27p each.

H.S.S. PARTING OFF TOOL BLADES four assorted.
OUR PRICE £1.00 for four

LEFT HAND 4B.A. TAPS one each TAPER & PLUG.
LIST PRICE 45p a pair...........OUR PRICE 15p a pair.

HEXAGON SOCKET CAP SCREWS

B.S.F. OR WHITWORTH THREAD

L'th	½" Dia. Per 10	½" Dia. Per 100	7/16" Dia. Per 10	7/16" Dia. Per 100	⅜" Dia. Per 10	⅜" Dia. Per 100	5/16" Dia. Per 10	5/16" Dia. Per 100	¼" Dia. Per 10	¼" Dia. Per 100	3/16" Dia. Per 10	3/16" Dia. Per 100	L'th
2"	£1.27	£9.34	£1.27	£9.24	77p	£5.74	75p	£5.40	64p	£4.52	64p	£4.52	2"
1¾"	£1.24	£8.96	£1.12	£8.12	73p	£5.22	65p	£4.58	55p	£3.88	—	—	1¾"
1½"	£1.05	£7.62	£1.08	£7.80	67p	£4.80	57p	£4.00	53p	£3.66	53p	£3.58	1½"
1¼"	£1.00	£7.56	£1.05	£7.58	57p	£3.97	55p	£3.76	48p	£3.32	—	—	1¼"
1"	89p	£6.46	96p	£6.88	55p	£3.91	46p	£3.09	41p	£2.68	43p	£2.88	1"
⅞"	—	—	—	—	—	—	—	—	41p	£2.70	40p	£2.65	⅞"
¾"	£1.23	£8.92	94p	£6.78	52p	£3.52	43p	£2.86	37p	£2.40	39p	£2.53	¾"
⅝"	—	—	—	—	—	—	—	—	36p	£2.30	37p	£2.36	⅝"
½"	—	—	—	—	50p	£3.36	43p	£2.80	35p	£2.20	33p	£2.10	½"
⅜"	—	—	—	—	—	—	—	—	35p	£2.24	34p	£2.18	⅜"
¼"	—	—	—	—	—	—	—	—	—	—	34p	£2.18	¼"

⅜" A/F Wrench 5/16" A/F Wrench 5/16" A/F Wrench 7/32" A/F Wrench 3/16" A/F Wrench 5/32" A/F Wrench

K.R.WHISTON, New Mills, Stockport. SAE for list.

Nuts and bolts, fixing hardware etc. Also sell useful bundles of miscellaneous metal.

H.FRANKS
58/60, New Oxford St.,
London WC1A 1ES.
Catalogue 10p.

Mainly control and measurement - meters,
motors, servos, relays, WD cameras etc etc.

THERMOSTATS AND THERMOMETERS

D.324

D.324—Pastorelli & Rapkin Ltd. London Thermometer, Temperature range 20° to 100° Fahrenheit. Fitted with 5inch long stem capillary with ¾in. diam. fixing ferrule. Diam. of dial 3½in.
New £3.15 each p.p.

D.325

D.325—'Satchwell' Thermostat type SA10, temperature range adjustable 80° to 130° Fahrenheit, contacts 15 amp. 250 v.a.c. non-inductive load, size 3½in. x 1¾ x 2½in.—new   75p each p.p.

D.326

D.326—'Elka' Variable Thermostats temperature range 38° to 80° Fahrenheit, contacts 6 amps to 250 volts A.C. baseboard mounting, spindle ¾in. long ½in. diam., size excluding spindle 2½in. x 1in. x ¾in.   45p each p.p.

D.327

D.327—'Sunvic' small one-hole fixing Air Thermostats, variable 30 to 80°F., contacts 10 amp., 240-volts A.C., overall length 3in., maximum width 1½in., depth 1in.—unused   50p each p.p.

Surplus Electronic Trading,
Drivers End Lane,
Codicote, Hitchin, Herts SG4 8TP.
List 25p

Radio, mostly communications gear, and
associated equipment.

R 10   R 11   R 12   R 13

R 14   R 15   R 16   R 17

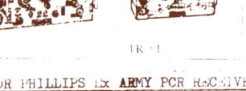

R 55   R 18   R 19   R 20

R 30   R 31   R 32   R 98

R.17 PYE OR PHILLIPS EX ARMY PCR RECEIVERS. PCR 2 covers 850-2000 metres 190-550 metres 6-28 MHz outputs for 'phone and speaker. PCR 3 covers 150-155 metres 2-7 and 7-22MHz Separate PSU.
  Price (Used Serviceable) PCR 2 from   £9.50p   Carr. 30.0 (£1.50)
                           PCR 3 from   £10.50p   Carr. 30.0 (£1.50)
                           Mains PSU £3.10.0 (£3.50) Carr. £1.25p
                           12V DC PSU £1.15.0 (£1.75) Carr.   £1.25p

TR.55 MURPHY Design Ex ARMY B.4.. Transmitter/Receiver portable/mobile VHF Radio Telephone Xtal controlled 3 channel covers 60-70 Hz. 50kHz bandwith intermediate frequency 5. kHz, modern 12 valve superhet employs 170 valves amplitude modulation, cast aluminium case size 14x11x7" weight 31 lbs, built-in 5" speaker, output, volts meter, microphone and 'phone sockets, internal Sync. vibrator 12V DC PSU.
  Price (Used Serviceable) from   £3.50p   Carr. 30.0 (£1.50)
       Moving Coil Mic.   £1.10.0 (£1.50), Post 20p
       Rod and Dipole Aerial £2.10.0 (£2.50)   Carr 50p

R.18 COLLINS (USA) NAVAL RECEIVER. 7 valve international octal valves, covers 1.5 - 12 MHz tuneable RF/AF Gain BFO etc. 'phone outputs, excellent receiver Requires power 240 DC 80mA 12V heaters 1.25A.
  Price (Used Serviceable   £11.50p   Carr. £2.00p

C.W.Wheelhouse,
9/13, Bell Road, Hounslow, Midd'x.
Large SAE for free catalogue.

Electric motors, fans, refrigeration
equipment.

RADIATORS

Designed for refrigerator evaporator coils. Suitable for making car heaters and oil coolers and hot water radiators, etc.
New as illustrated, surplus stock Suitable for up to 100 PSI. Four banks aluminium tube set in aluminium fins and end brackets with two ½" SAE connections, one male one female flare nut. Size 11" x 6¼" x 2½" thick.

Price 98p each
P.P. 32p
Price in half doz. lots 75p pp. 50p

AIR RECEIVERS

With gauge Smiths 0 to 160 p.s.i. Safety valve adjustable 0 to 100 p.s.i. Inlet and outlet connections ¼" BSP. and one hose union. Fitted with mounting platform in heavy gauge steel ready for mounting compressor and motor.
Secondhand ex oxygen cylinder as illustrated suitable for working up to 150 p.s.i. Overall size 7" x 8" x 17" long plus approx. 3" for pipe fittings, gauge etc.

Price £4.00 Carriage 60p

P.Harris,
Organford, Dorset.
List free.

Cornucopia of all things
radio and electronic.

MORSE CODE PAPER TAPE in 8" dia. rolls 950 feet (5000 words). Standard centre perforation parchment paper for 3 unit machines. 17½np. a rool (12½np). (2T/4727/F).

EXCLUSIVE OFFER, AMERICAN ALL CHROME POLICE CAR SIRENS Mayor's large size model 15" dia. x 7" on pedestal mount Torpedo shape with flashing headlight built into front. A most attractive article of finest quality. Complete with relay. 6 volt supply required. Price in U.S.A. £58.00, our price in maker's carton £10.50. (paid U.K.). Alternative finished in red enamel £7.50, otherwise as above. (7M/4570/F). These sirens if fitted to road vehicles are prohibited for use in British Isles.

MORSE PRACTICE TAPES Type OP-15A. A series of fifteen printed 16m/m film spools forming lessons in code. These tapes operate an electronic keyer in wood cabinet. £4.50. (75np.). (2T/2785/F).

AMERICAN HAND GENERATORS ON TRIPOD STANDS WITH OPERATOR'S SEAT Four outputs with filters and regulator built in (1) 425v. 115 m/A. (2) 105v. 32m/a. (3) 6v. 250 m/a. (4) 1.4v. 450 m/a. £3.50. (75np.) (5P/2219/B).

AMERICAN HAND GENERATORS as above, but outputs - (1) 420v. 70 m/A. (2) 365v. 100 m/A. (3) 10v. 1.25 amps. £3.50. (75np.). (5P/2223/H).

AMERICAN CLARION 25 WATT MODULATED POWER AMPLIFIERS In grey crackle cases with chrome handles. 12" x 6" x 6". Output 2-6L6 in p/p. 4, 8 and 16 ohms. Input 100/120v. A.C. Oscillator provides 1000 cycle note with volume control if required. Price £5.50. (£1.00). /- (2A/1127/B).

Lately I've been thinking about a ferro cement dome on a wooden frame. I've always liked the idea of a monolithic shell, no separate components to piece together, no leaks.

It will be used lumber, with washer connectors.

I'll have to check first to see that the connectors are strong enough to hold the weight of wet cement.

This summer when I put together the cardboard model of the aluminum triacon dome, I noticed that with the first ten diamonds together it formed a pentagonal flower shape, touching the ground at five points with arches in between. It suggested a low dome, sculptural ferro cement flowing into the ground at five points.

DOMEBOOK 2

p128; £2.50; (distributed by A.D.) Pacific Domes 1971

Aw shit you'll never get planning permission, and anyway who can afford the land. Those lucky bastards in the States, land going for grabs just about, thats something else –

Domes are domes wherever you build them. This book is illustrated summarized experience of hundreds of dome builders in North Amerika, working details, problems – everything for rolling your own.

Balls to the planners – build them, infest the country with them. (How about a summer dome farm in a hired field somewhere – groove all summer long, tear 'em down when the frosts come, away for another year?)

Think spherical.

We've lived for two years now in a dome without easy access to *outside*. To be able to move in and out more freely, to be able to have large sections open I'd build walls inside the shell, using the ferro skin as an umbrella.

The arches would be curved, would need extra steel to carry weight down to the ground. An engineer's help would probably be needed. The weight of the dome could rest on the five points, rather than on the wood frame, steel carrying the weight onto five large concrete footings. If it's strong enough, grass could grow up along some of the touch points. The lower the dome, the easier is a sod roof.

ferro skin over interior walls

build up at edge, so water drains down to 5 points

Somewhere in the middle of taking all these pictures we realized that we were showing the best side of things: a dome in the forest, sunlight shining through tree branches, rather than the junk underneath the dome. A plastic dome glowing in the field at night, rather than the poisonous gases produced in converting petroleum to plastic. After realizing this I looked at Life, Newsweek, realizing that they're doing the same thing, writers, photographers show one side. We're still doing pretty much the same with this book. Taking the best pictures, using what's most beautiful and instructive. What most closely corresponds with the vision. As you read, keep in mind it's not as pristine, simple, clean as it appears. There's a danger in the hype, overromanticizing domes.

bubble-dome cluster

$r = 2x$

if $x = 8'$

black:
$\pi(2x)^2 = 804$ sq.ft.

white:
$2\pi x^2 = 402$ sq.'

DIVIDING BOARD into EQUAL PIECES

1 SLANT RULE WITH DESIRED NUMBER OF DIVISIONS ACROSS BOARD

2 REPEAT AT OTHER END

3 JOIN MARKS WITH STRAIGHTEDGE

THE ORGANIC DOME

I plan on building a few more domes in the spring and next summer. My big dream idea is still to use paper mache. Paper mache houses have been built in the Orient for thousands of years using wheat paste and persimmon juice for waterproofing.

Laminated newspaper soaked with wallpaper paste is plenty strong enough if it can be waterproofed.

Another way to do it would be (and this is the way I will try in the spring) to make a mixer like a cement mixer for paper mache. The newspaper would be shredded and mixed with a waterproof glue then poured into panel forms along with willow branches or cattail reeds from the swamps and then pressed with heavy weights into a light, strong, porous panel of paper mache. Then to cinch it and seal it, a laminated paper mache face would be applied to front and backside of the panel. This would also add a great deal of strength.

The paper mache panel would hopefully bring the price of a dome down into a reasonable range. There aren't too many people that I know who can come up with the $Grande it takes to build these domes in the ways they've been built so far, flaunting industrial gimmicks on $200 whims.

Another system would be simply boards and stucco. Tear down an old building get all the 2 X 4's and wallboards and floorboards. Build a dome, cover it with boards then stucco it or put mud on it or shit on it. That would probably cost $100. for a 10 meter dome. There would be a little extra work involved, but what are we living for. What a gas!

I can't say enough about what I call "organic" houses. That is houses made of material that doesn't come through the system, or material which the system has discarded.

1. Principles of Joint Design

Expansion-contraction difficulties are minimized by designing joints that are wide and shallow:

caulk   plywood   use thin bead

extended

The *depth* of the sealant should be less than ½ its width. A shallow joint can cut the amount of caulk in half, and a thin bead will allow more stretching than a thick bead. The joint *width* should be at least four times the calculated maximum joint movement. Some builders use a router over dome seams after plywood is nailed on, routing out ¼" groove, then installing a back-up strip before caulking. Recommend depth for GE silicone sealants is 1/8"-3/8".

ARCHITECTURAL DESIGN.
26, Bloomsbury Road,
London WC1A 2SS.
Monthly 40p.

Hip mag. out in front in picking what's coming in eco-building.

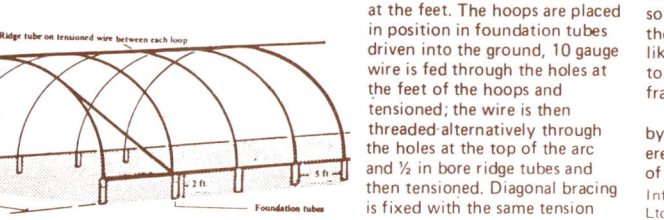

A very simple greenhouse structure consists of a simple hand made hoop system of galvanised tubing, separated by a ridge piece and intermediate bracing, and covered with 500 gauge (125 micron) polythene ultra-violet inhibited film.

The ½ in bore tube is bent easily on a jig of stakes placed in the ground; holes are then drilled at the top of the arc and at the feet. The hoops are placed in position in foundation tubes driven into the ground, 10 gauge wire is fed through the holes at the feet of the hoops and tensioned; the wire is then threaded alternatively through the holes at the top of the arc and ½ in bore ridge tubes and then tensioned. Diagonal bracing is fixed with the same tension

FORMER FOR BENDING TUBE

system, the amount of diagonal bracing used depending on the sort of wind loads expected. Polythene should be stretched over when the weather is warm so that a tighter fit is obtained; the tauter the skin the less likelihood there is of wear due to excessive flapping against the framework.

The overall cost of the 14 ft by 135 ft house including erection labour was £77; a cost of approximately 4p per sq ft.
Information: British Visqueen Ltd, Stevenage, Herts.

Sandbag

Low-key technology freaks may be interested in Edward Dicker's ideas for the do-it-yourself housebuilder. Porous containers filled with a mixture of sand, gravel and cement are stacked in position and when a suitable configuration is obtained the whole thing is sprayed with water thus binding the structure and effecting the setting of the cement. Alternatively, in wet climates the structure can be left to harden in the rain.

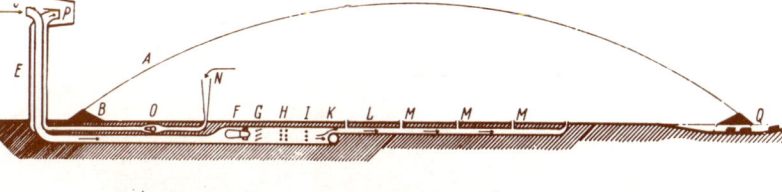

A Membrane of heavy fabric or wire with transparent plastic coating.

B Annular foundation.

C Air inlet in air-conditioning tower having rotatable cap.

D Guide-vane annulus to adjust position of cap.

E Heat exchange in air-conditioning tower. In winter the used air heats the fresh air in a counter-flow arrangement.

F Blower.

G Air baffles.

H Heating and cooling plant.

I Humidifier.

K Ring main.

L Underground distribution line, serves also to heat ground.

M Warm air discharge.

N Used air extraction

O Pressure regulation valve.

P Exhaust discharge.

Q Air lock accessible to trucks.

TENSILE STRUCTURES
pp 320; £10.50.
PRIMATIVE STRUCTURES
pp 171; £5.85.
Frei Otto; MIT 1967.

Ideas and theory book from the old wizard of nets and blow-ups - heavy on maths and little doodles, light on practical small scale techniques. Books for the design stage.

The economics of power and heat are important in the maintenance of pressure and climate inside large envelopes. New problems in air conditioning arise in large envelopes (Fig. 1) since air currents and the possibility of condensation give rise to zones having different inner climates. This effect can be considerable in spaces exceeding 500 m in span.

These demands benefit most from the peculiar qualities of air structuring which can be summarized thus:
— Universal availability of air.
— Lightness of structure.
— Resultant high portability value of such a structure.
— Calculable life of constituent parts.
— Ease of control and variation of major structural element – air.
— Rapid structuring and controlled collapse.
— Ease of re-use, re-location, storage and transportation.
— Avoidance of structural complexity due to size.
— Reduction in importance of site conditions in comparison with load bearing structures.
— Inherent multi-purpose usefulness of major structuring element – air; e.g. ventilation, heating, etc.
— Economy achieved as air energy can be varied for periods of particular loading.

AIR STRUCTURES C.Price & F.Newby.
pp   £4.25; HMSO 1971.

Detailed well illustrated survey of the state of the art in air structures - what's being done by the firms in the business, theories, practical problems.

Also by Price & Newby -
LIGHTWEIGHT ENCLOSURES UNIT BIBLIOGRAPHY ON AIR STRUCTURES.
£1.50 from LEU, 38, Alfred Place, London WC1E 7DP.

LONGITUDINAL SECTION OF FABRIDAM

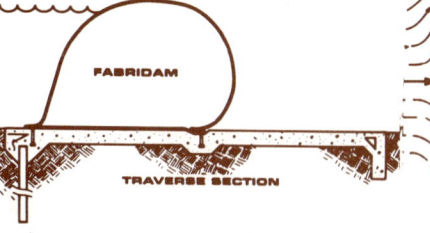

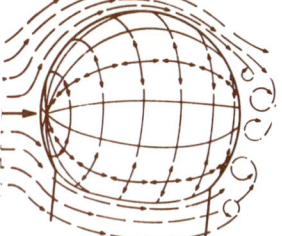

MAIN COMPONENTS OF AN AIR-SUPPORTED STRUCTURE (DIAGRAM 3.2)

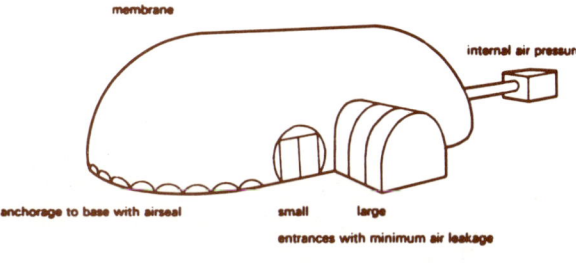

membrane

internal air pressure control unit

anchorage to base with airseal   small   large

entrances with minimum air leakage

(B) WIND LOAD
The distribution of wind pressure over the surface of an air-supported structure is complex. A few wind tunnel tests on models have been carried out (Ref 9, 12, 29). As the wind loads are greater than any other loads it is important to estimate their magnitude as closely as possible. Failures of air-supported structures in very high winds have been recorded.
The distribution of wind pressure over a cylinder is shown

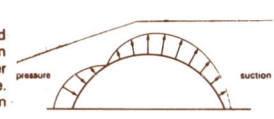

STRUCTURES: Circus Tents, Oldies but goldies.
The Welfare State, theatre group and wierdness by appointment, spent the summer of '72 travelling around using a circus tent as part of its performing area.

Having watched the Earth Star Dome people (Glastonbury) put up a scaffolding dome and talked to Welfare State veterans, I think there are very great advantages to the tent.

Once you've used the routine, five (one pole) or nine(two poles) people can put the tent up in four hours and take it down in two. The structure is strong and will take a remarkable amount of blustery wind although its a bit unsettling psychologically in these conditions. With standard circus seating you can get between 400 (one pole) and 700 (two pole) people in. Without the seating the shapes are lovely, particularly if you play around with them a little.

They do need attention both in relation to the weather and day to day maintainance. You need someone who knows how to handle rope and patch canvas and assess the amount of tension the canvas needs for different conditions.

We (the Welfare State) bought the tent through 'Worlds Fair' (which is a gas of a paper anyway). I haven't seen any books on the subject. Perhaps someone can help here.

John Quail.

```
HANDBOOK OF SEAMANS ROPEWORK
Sam Svensson  pp 192; £2.50
Adlard Coles Ltd., 1970

   Nitty gritty knots for when they've really
got to stay tied. How to choose and use ropes,
bend 'em and mend 'em, with authentic sea air.
```

Fig. 66 Timber hitch and half-hitch   Fig. 67 Fisherman's bend—Left: correct Right: incorrect

The *timber hitch* (Fig. 66) is also suitable for use on large objects. Make a round turn around the object and then snake the end of the rope four to six times around the standing part. Where a long spar is to be hoisted a half-hitch is often made at the end of the spar.

The *fisherman's bend* (Fig. 67) is one of the best hitches for tying a line to a thin object. It is important that the half-hitch, which is made

under the two round turns, is correctly laid. If it is made forwards, in the same direction as the turns, the hitch will not hold at all. Nor will it hold on large objects, but it is ideal for tying a line to a bucket or paint pot or fastening the end of a boom guy in a ring bolt. It can be made in a second, stands any amount of strain and is always easy to undo, even if it has been used in hoisting operations.

```
READERS DIGEST COMPLETE DO-IT-YOURSELF
MANUAL
Readers Digest Association, 25, Berkely
Square, London W1
2nd. edition, 1969 £4.50
   Good for basic simple jobs, but be
ready to look around if things get
complicated.
```

Cutting a groove with a half-round chisel

Fault: too great an allowance producing a mis-shapen head.

Fault: gaps between the plates caused by not removing burr.

Fault: plate not set down properly—rivet forced into gap.

Removing round-head: file or chisel off head and punch out.

Removing countersunk type: centre-punch the head. Drill out head with a countersink bit and punch out the remainder of the rivet.

```
MITCHELL'S BUILDING CONSTRUCTION
Vol 1 Environment and Services
Vol 2 Materials
Vol 3 Components and Finishes
Vol 4+5 Structure and Fabric
£1.60 Or £2.50   Batsford 1971

   Standard basic books about the techniques and resources
of conventional construction.
```

Red bricks Red, caused by iron oxide, is perhaps the typical clay brick colour, produced in most parts of the country.

White bricks are made from chalky clays including *gault* clay found in South East England. *Gaults* shaped either by wire cutting or by pressing are available almost white and also *flushed* pink.

Yellow bricks include London Stocks which are made from the brickearth and chalk found in Kent and Essex. Fuel added to the clay before firing leaves characteristic voids and burnt particles in the fired brick.

Brown bricks in various shades from light to dark.

Blue bricks result from a high content of iron compounds and firing in reducing (low oxygen) conditions as in the Staffordshire blue engineering brick.

Superficial colour results from a surface treatment such as *sand facing*, from oxide pigments applied before firing, or from control of the atmosphere in the kiln. Damage in handling, or at a later stage, exposes the body of the brick the appearance of which may be quite different from that of the thin facing.

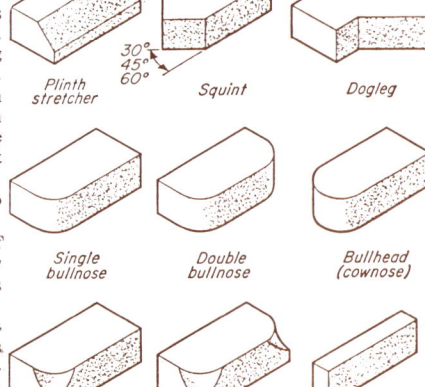
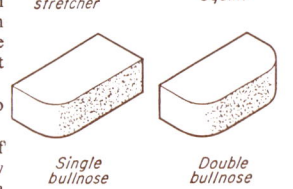

Plinth stretcher   Squint   Dogleg

Single bullnose   Double bullnose   Bullhead (cownose)

Single bullnose stop   Double bullnose stop   Slip tiles

```
SPECIFICATION 1972
ed. Dex Harrison
Vol 1 pp528
Vol 2 pp621
2 vols. £4.00
Architectural Press annually

   Huge inventory of products and
sevices currently available to
architects and builders. Lots
of inside dope on specialised
products that could well fit
the job you're doing. Besides
all the technical stuff, there's
general comment on the
basics of each area covered (see
below for example.)
```

The Right Adhesive

Whichever of the above theories is responsible for the formation of an adhesive bond, it can be seen that the nature of the surface of the materials to be joined as well as the surface of the adhesive itself is of vital importance. The strength of the bond is the strength of this surface interaction even though the nature of the interaction is not fully understood. Because the nature of the bonding surface is so important it can be appreciated that it is easier to bond the same material together than to bond two dissimilar materials. When bonding metal to itself for example the adhesive/surface interaction is the same for both sides of the joint. On the other hand, when bonding rubber to metal the adhesive/surface interaction is different on the two dissimilar surfaces. Thus it is possible to achieve shear strengths of 1,000 p.s.i. when bonding metal to metal, but only 100 p.s.i. when bonding rubber to metal using the same adhesive.

To bond dissimilar surfaces a compromise must be made between the ideal adhesive/surface interaction for each surface. The more dissimilar the nature of the two surfaces the more difficult will be this compromise and, in general, the lower the strength of bond obtainable. For this reason most examples of the structural use of adhesives involve the bonding of the same material on either side of the joint, e.g. wood/wood, metal/metal, concrete/concrete.

Again, all the theories of adhesion require a condition of close contact between the adhesive and the adherend. That is to say the adhesive must wet out the surface so that molecular contact can be obtained. The ease of obtaining this condition varies widely with different surfaces. It is well known that whilst water will not wet a polythene surface, wetting can be obtained with organic solvents. This difference between wetting and non-wetting is the extreme case of the phenomenon: the degree of wetting can vary between these limits. This lack of complete molecular contact results in a lower bond strength than is to be expected from a consideration of the surface interaction and the components of the adhesive must be chosen so that this reduction in strength is as small as possible. When bonding two dissimilar surfaces a compromise may need to be made in this property, sacrificing some adhesion to one surface to obtain adhesion to its partner in the joint.

These compromises from the ideal situation for both adhesive/surface interaction and for wetting out are the reason for choosing different adhesives for bonding various materials to one given surface. For example, an epoxy adhesive may be chosen for bonding wood to metal, a reclaimed rubber/resin adhesive for bonding rubber to metal and a nitrile synthetic rubber adhesive for bonding PVC to metal.

B3

Running the cable along the joists to feed a socket-outlet fixed above the skirting board. The joists should be drilled. Illustration shows a flush box sunk in the wall. The cable is shown as uncut but in practice it is usually necessary to cut it.

Q. What type of sockets are available for the ring circuit, and which is preferable?

A. There are three principal types of 13 amp socket. (i) unswitched socket; (ii) switched socket; and (iii) switched socket with pilot light. It is not compulsory to use a switched socket. In fact, the unswitched socket, which is the least expensive, is most commonly used. A disadvantage of the unswitched socket is that the plug has to be removed from the socket to switch off the appliance, unless the appliance has its own switch; when an appliance has its own switch and the plug is left in the socket this too is a disadvantage because the flexible cord is 'live' at all times. A typical example is the radio or television receiver. It is dangerous to leave this permanently in circuit and fires have been caused by this practice. If unswitched sockets are preferred a good rule is to use unswitched sockets for occasional appliances and to use switched sockets for those which are 'permanent' standing appliances, such as the TV receiver, table lamp, and standard lamp, portable heaters standing in the fireplace, and so on.

Sockets with pilot light are usually suitable where the appliance is unlikely to be switched off unless there is a pilot light to indicate it is on or off. Bedwarmers and convector fires not fitted with a luminous device are typical examples.

```
RING CIRCUITS 48pp;25p.
REWIRING A HOUSE 96pp; 40p.
Geoffrey Arnold  Burdett Workbooks 1967
```

Two good books for DIY electricians, as long as you're not too ambitious.

```
GKN HANDYBOOK FOR HOUSEHOLDERS  free from-
GKN Screws and Fasteners, Heath St. Division,
PO Box 61 Heath St., Smethwick, Warley, Worcs.
```

Basically a book about GKN wood-screws, self-tapping screws and machine screws, with lots of data about sizes, fittings etc., as well as a lot of practical hints about their use.

(Suggested by Paul Simpson)

The Pozidriv Twinfast Wood Screw has a parallel, two start thread. This screw is particularly suitable for use in low density chipboard, block board, fibre and soft woods, offering up to 25% greater holding power than the conventional thread wood screw when fixing thin attachments.

The shorter lengths, up to ¾" long, of Twinfast Wood Screws are threaded to head. The longer screws with their relieved shank can also be driven more deeply into thin sections of soft wood, or the edge of chipboard, than conventional wood screws of the same size, before splitting occurs.

Because they bury two thread pitches per turn of the screw thread Twinfast Wood Screws can be inserted almost twice as quickly as the conventional screw.

```
HANDBOOK OF FIXINGS AND FASTENINGS
Bill Launchbury  pp81; £1.00
Architectural Press 1971
```
Once you've got it together, here's how to keep it that way. Theory and general practice of fixing methods, aimed at architects, but generally informative.

7.03 Minimum spacing of screws is shown in **14** (from BS CP 112 table 24) but may vary slightly according to type.

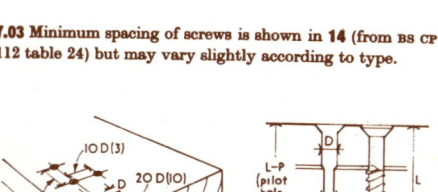

14 *Minimum spacing of screws shown by number of diameters* (D). *Bracketed figures show spacing if holes are predrilled*

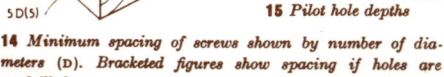

15 *Pilot hole depths*

7.04 Pilot holes should be long enough to ensure that seven diameters of thread engage in base material (absolute minimum is four diameters). For fixing a wood component, length should be three times the thickness of the component **15**.

7.05 Diameter of the pilot hole should not exceed one-tenth of width of wood into which it is fixed. Pilot holes in softwood should be 70 per cent of screw diameter, and in hardwood, 90 per cent. In chipboard, double spiral screws are preferable, with pilot holes 60 to 90 per cent of screw diameter, depending on chipboard density.
Pilot holes are essential when fixing to chipboard. Screws driven directly into chipboard retain loosened chips within the thread. This considerably lowers holding efficiency.

Grooved pop rivets are designed for use in soft or brittle materials eg hardboard, plywood, glass fibre, asbestos. This rivet is inserted into a drilled hole, and expands sideways. Available in 3·2 mm, 4·0 mm and 4·8 mm diameters.
Examples: Serrex (Geo Tucker Eyelet Co Ltd)

mushroom

fillister

cheese

pan

binder pan

round

raised countersunk

countersunk

```
BUILDING ADVISORY LEAFLETS
Dept. of the Environment 4p.
BUILDING RESEARCH STATION
DIGESTS. 5p.  Both HMSO.
```

The DOE leaflets give you cheap basic bumf on plenty of the problems you meet building or repairing. (extract right.)
The BRS ones are more specialised, but they do some interesting titles.

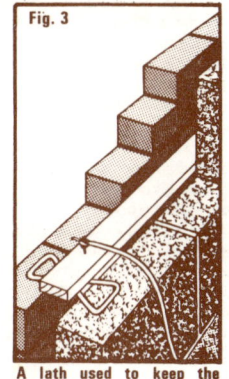

Fig. 2

Shell-bedding to resist rain penetration at joints

LAYING LIGHTWEIGHT CONCRETE BLOCKS

Before using lightweight concrete blocks below damp course level check with the manufacturer that they are suitable and have adequate resistance to frost and to damage from aggressive ground conditions.

Lightweight concrete blocks should not be wetted before use.

They should normally be laid on a full bed of mortar but when a single skin of blocks is used for external walling 'shell-bedding' is recommended. This gives greater resistence to rain penetration although the wall will be less strong than one with a full mortar bed. In shell-bedding mortar is laid only on the edges of the inner and outer faces of the blocks, see Fig. 2. Blocks must be laid true to line and the faces plumbed every course. Lightweight blocks can be cut with a bolster and some types can also be cut with a coarse-toothed saw.

Fig. 3

A lath used to keep the cavity clean

COMPOSTING H. Gotaas
pp205; World Health Organization
(out of print)

The book for making gas from shit. If
you aren't a member of your local library, try to
get hold of Mother Earth News No 3, which had an
article about methane production largely based on
Gotaas, as well as other stuff about crap power.

Digester tanks with gas collection are particularly advantageous in
areas which are short of fuel and where animal dung is burned for cooking,
thereby wasting the valuable nitrogen and other nutrients needed for
fertilizer. The nitrogen, phosphorus, potash, and other nutrients are
retained in the tank as humus and liquid while much of the carbon and
hydrogen are evolved as methane, for collection and use as fuel. The
quality of the humus is similar to that obtained from aerobic composting,
and when the liquid is utilized together with the solids for fertilizer, practically all of the fertilizer nutrients are reclaimed.

The evolved gas, which is approximately two-thirds methane and one-
third carbon-dioxide, may contain 4500 to 6000 calories per cubic metre,
thus providing a convenient source of heat at a low cost. One cubic metre
of the gas at 6000 calories is equivalent to the following quantities of other
fuels : 1.100 litres of alcohol ; 0.800 litres of petrol ; 0.600 litres of crude
oil ; 1.500 m³ of commonly manufactured city gas ; 1.400 kg of charcoal ;
and 2.2 kilowatt-hours of electrical energy.

The gas can be stored in the gas-holder and piped into the house to
provide clean fuel for cooking and lighting. It has a slight barn-yard odour
by which any leaks can be readily detected, and a very low toxicity since
it contains very little carbon monoxide—the toxic constituent of most city
gas. It burns with a violet flame without smoke. Since a considerable
amount of CO_2 is mixed with the methane, the risk of fire or explosion
is somewhat less than it is in the case of city gas. However, every
precaution should be taken to avoid obtaining a mixture of methane
and air, except when the methane is burned as an open flame. Mixtures of 5%-14% methane in air are explosive when large quantities are
ignited.

FIG. 44. CROSS-SECTION OF GAS-HOLDER FOR MANURE GAS PLANT

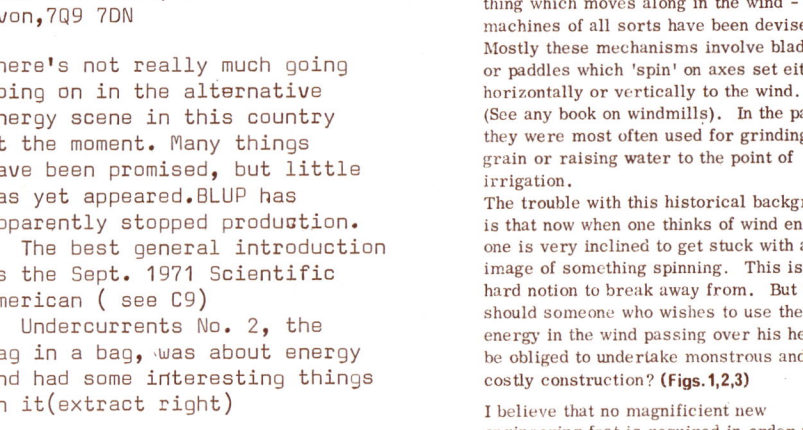

All measurements are in centimetres.

*The proportion of height to diameter of cover may be changed, but the equivalent volume
should be maintained.*

Other methods of collecting methane besides Gotaas' methods
are possible.
    To use your methane(or propane or whatever) you need
a device to convert your engine. Solex(write Zenith
Carburettors, Honeypot Lane, Stanmore, Middlesex) or
Calor Gas (local phone book) do them, as well as Harold
Bate, Mr. Chickenshit, who supplies very basic plans for
gas digester and autogas device for £2.50, the device
itself for £6.50, the device and plans for £7.50, from
Pennyrowden, Blackawton, Totnes, Devon,7Q9 7DN

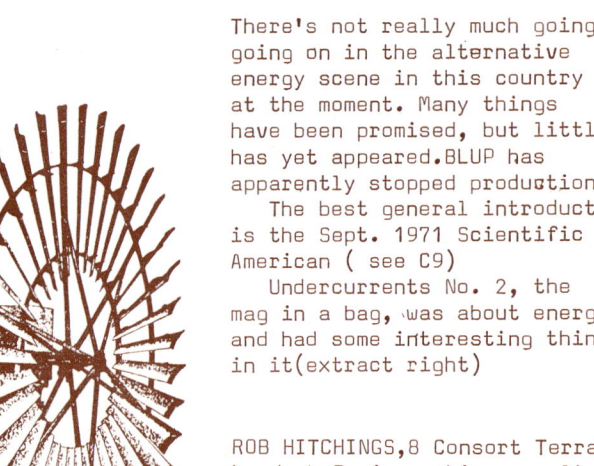

There's not really much going
going on in the alternative
energy scene in this country
at the moment. Many things
have been promised, but little
has yet appeared.BLUP has
apparently stopped production.
    The best general introduction
is the Sept. 1971 Scientific
American (see C9)
    Undercurrents No. 2, the
mag in a bag, was about energy
and had some interesting things
in it(extract right)

ROB HITCHINGS,8 Consort Terrace,
Leeds L 3, is working on alternative power sources, and has
information and plans on methane
generation, and collection from
septic tanks. Will exchange notes
with anyone working on similiar
projects, or send SAE for details.

Air in movement can be made to do work.
In order to harness the power of the wind
to a fixed position - as opposed to something which moves along in the wind -
machines of all sorts have been devised.
Mostly these mechanisms involve blades
or paddles which 'spin' on axes set either
horizontally or vertically to the wind.
(See any book on windmills). In the past,
they were most often used for grinding
grain or raising water to the point of
irrigation.
The trouble with this historical background
is that now when one thinks of wind energy,
one is very inclined to get stuck with an
image of something spinning. This is a
hard notion to break away from. But why
should someone who wishes to use the
energy in the wind passing over his head
be obliged to undertake monstrous and
costly construction? (Figs.1,2,3)

I believe that no magnificient new
engineering feat is required in order to
harness the wind's power cheaply - only a
simple re-examination of the "means of
access" to that power. By this I mean
tapping potentials which are already
available if one could but see them.
For example, architects in future could
produce custom-designed tower blocks
with fancy styling or ducting at some
suitable point, to pick up the wind being
spilled off the buildings' surfaces.

AN AGRICULTURAL TESTAMENT
Sir Albert Howard
pp 210; £1.10 OUP 1940

Sir Albert Howard was a pioneer of the organic
method. From his work in India,he came to the
conclusion that organic matter was the most
important factor in crop success, and developed
the Indore method of composting.
A classic book, and very readable.

Since the Great War the factories then engaged in the fixation of atmospheric nitrogen for the manu facture of the vast quantities of explosives, needed to defend and to destroy armies well entrenched, have had to find a new market. This was provided by the large area of land impoverished by the over-cropping of the war period. A demand was created by the low price at which the mass-produced unit of nitrogen could be put on the market and by the reliability of the product. Phosphates and potash fell into line. Ingenious mixtures of artificial manures, containing everything supposed to be needed by the various crops, could be purchased all over the world. Sales increased rapidly; the majority of farmers and market gardeners soon based their manurial programme on the cheapest forms of nitrogen, phosphorus, and potash or on the cheapest mixtures. During the last twenty years the progress of the artificial manure industry has been phenomenal; the age of the manure bag has arrived; the Liebig tradition returned in full force.

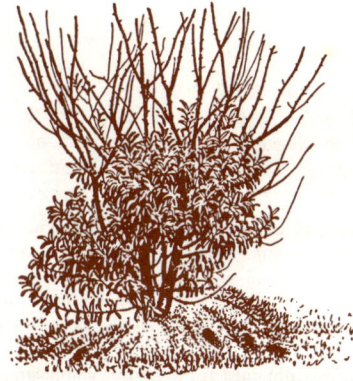

FIG. 4. The effect of burrowing rats on the growth of the plum under grass   In July 1923 burrowing rats took up their quarters under one of the limes and one of the loquats, in each case on the southern side. Shortly afterwards the leaves just above the rat holes became very much darker in colour than the rest. Examination of the soil immediately round the burrows showed a copious development of new active rootlets, far greater even than in the surface soil of the cultivated plot. The extra aeration had a wonderfully stimulating effect on the development of active roots, even under grass. The appearance of the leaves suggested an application of nitrogenous manure. Similar observations were made in the case of the plum (Fig. 4). Here the burrows caused a dying tree to produce new growth.

ORGANIC GARDENING AND FARMING MAGAZINE
Rodale Press. Monthly 15p
Magazine produced in cooperation
with the Soil Association. Lots of
useful articles.

6"LAYER OF GREEN MATTER

SPRINKLING OF
TOPSOIL & LIME

2" LAYER OF MANURE

6" LAYER OF
GREEN MATTER

LOOSE WASTE

*The Indore method of composting was perfected by Sir Albert Howard.
The heap is made in layers to ensure that it heaps up quickly and doesn't putrefy.
Remember, if certain materials are not available, use others that are.*

The first organized plan for composting, perfected by Sir Albert Howard, became so popular and widely used that it generated the organic method itself. His Indore method was successful ·because it assured that the heap would heat up and not putrefy.

Sir Albert's method is to assure that the proper amounts of the different materials get incorporated in the heap. You can make just as good a heap without layering if you are sure to put in the green matter, maure and earth in the same proportions.

CHASE ORGANIC SEEDS, Benhall, Saxmundham, Suffolk
All Chase's seeds are grown by organic methods
and they claim that the resulting plants ' have
more vigour, a greater resistance to disease and
a better flavour' than plants from seeds grown
by other methods. Besides seeds, they also supply
compost activators,comfrey plants, organic
fertilizers and sprays. Send 3p for catalogue.
More in the agriculture line, HUNTERS OF CHESTER,
Chester, give away a comprehensive catalogue, and
sell   a book called 'Hunters' Guide to Grasses,
Clovers and Weeds' for 62½p, plus 10p post.

PYRETHRUM is a safe, non-poisonous general purpose insecticide, grown in Africa. It is for use against aphids, green fly, black fly, thrips, capsid bugs, woodlice and earwigs. It can also be used with the utmost confidence and with complete safety in dwelling houses against ants, fleas and silverfish. It is a powder supplied in a shaker tin.

DERRIS is also a powder, supplied as a dust in puffer cans and is a non-poisonous, non-toxic general purpose insecticide for controlling a wide range of leaf-eating and fruit-eating pests such as flea-beetle, caterpillars, sawfly and other beetles. It is particularly useful against attacks by cabbage butterflies on brassicas as these can strip the leaves off in a short time if left unmolested. It can be used with the utmost confidence by the organic gardener and should be used by all gardeners not only to repel but to protect.

Fig. 8. The root tip of a broad bean seedling marked off with Indian ink (a). After a period of growth the marks became separated as in (b), showing that elongation is mainly confined to a region just behind the tip. (After Sachs, 1887.)

THE GROWTH OF PLANTS
G.E.Fogg
pp302; 50p; Penguin 1970

All you need to know
about how plants grow.
Gets rather heavy
towards the end, with some
chemistry and maths even.

THE WORLD OF THE SOIL Sir. E.J.Russell
pp285; 50p Fontana New Naturalist 1957
Understand the ground beneath you.
This book tells what's going for the
first two feet down, with bugs and
creepy crawlies by the million.

Centipedes are carnivorous and feed on small insects and other animals, killing them first by poison which they inject through a pair of special organs. The name is a complete misnomer : most species have not got 100 legs nor anything like that number. Their bodies are long, flattened and segmented, each segment has one pair of legs. Six families are represented in Britain. In one of the two commonest, the glistening red-brown *Lithobiidae*, there are 14 segments; when disturbed these animals can move very rapidly. In the other common family, the *Geophilidae*, the bodies are longer and pale yellow and the movements sinuous; some of this group have at times taken to strawberries and become rather a pest.

Centipede families : a, *Lithobiidae*
b, *Cryptopsidae* ; c, *Geophilidae*.

GROW YOUR OWN FRUIT AND VEGETABLES. L.D.Hills.
£2.50; Faber 1971.

An organic gardening book which, unlike many, is
written for the British gardener. Describes in
detail how to grow both fruit and vegetables -
as well as more general chapters on how to keep your
soil in good nick without the aid of artificial
stimulants. Some good illustrations too. A good
book to start with.

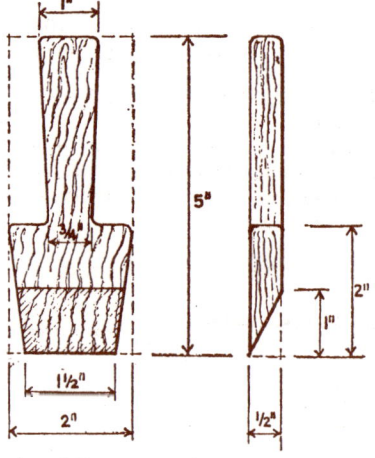

18. The 'Man' Tool Cleaner, as used by the 'navvies' who bought their
own picks and shovels, unlike modern bulldozer drivers

The soil in fact is rather like the Bradford wool trade. It is full of determined individualists doing unusual jobs on a basic commodity and taking a nice little profit for their trouble. Where there's muck there's money and if we give them 'nowt' of 'owt' we shall have to do their jobs ourselves, or leave the work undone, with serious consequences for our soils. Hydroponics is impossibly complex and costly in labour and materials except for certain specialized crops like carnations under glass, or vegetables for desert airports, apart altogether from the loss of vitamins, minerals and taste substances there would be if ever we have to do the whole job of growing our own food, instead of leaving the difficult jobs to our microscopic 'under-gardeners', for they do their gardening under the soil.

If we rely on chemical fertilizers alone, our soil will run out of fuel and the chemicals will lock each other up till we have a complete shut-down. If we use chemicals and peat we shall only get the mechanical qualities of humus which hold on to moisture and our soil will be underpowered because the energy foods will be locked up by humic acids, including tannins. If we rely on comfrey and green manures *alone* we can run short on energy material as well as the moisture-holding capacity of humus. A soil needs a balance and there is no substitute for good manure and good compost.

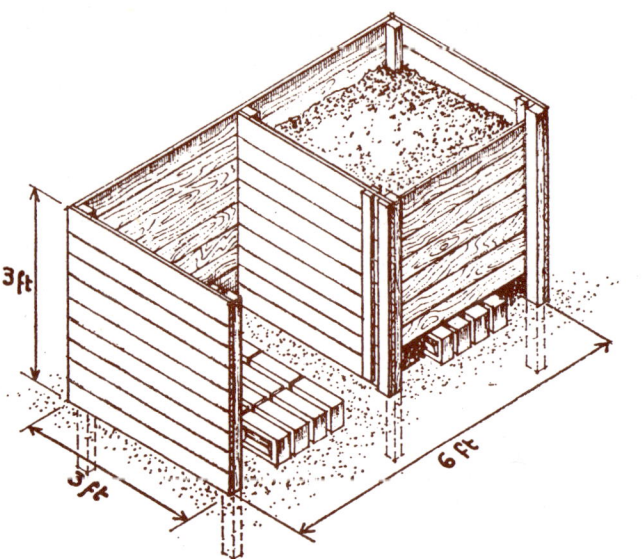

1. A two-compartment compost box: note removable board front and brick air
channels for air supply from below

GARDENING WITHOUT POISONS. Beatrice Trum Hunter.
pp294; Hamish Hamilton 1965.
(At the moment this is out of print but possibly
being reprinted in the States)

One of the earlier advocates of gardening without
the use of pestisides. How to deal with all those
animals and creepy crawlies which are the scourge
of the gardener. Written for the US but we've got
lots of pests in common.

COMPLETE GUIDE TO GARDEN-
ING. Morton and Mannering.
pp256; 22½p; Fpulsham.

Written by gardeners of
the old school, great
believers in the benefits
of a barrowful of 'muck'.
Tells you what to do week
by week throughout the
year. Good for beginners
and its a good price too.

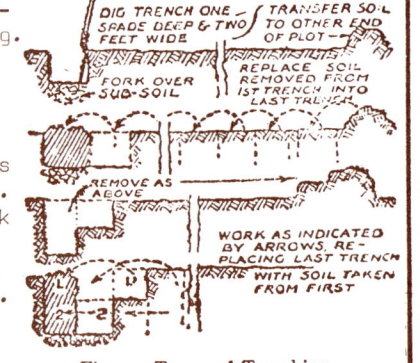

Fig. 1.—Types of Trenching.

COMBATTING PLANT DISEASES WITH OTHER PLANTS

Scientists are now discovering that many plants produce actual plant medicines which are natural bactericides and fungicides. For instance, a few drops of an extract from cauliflower seeds has been found to inactivate the bacteria causing black rot, and radish seeds also contain an antibacterial substance. In Helsinki, Professor A. I. Virtanen, testing nearly 1300 plants, found that 305 of them contained antibiotic substances which were especially high in the cruciferae (*mustard family*).

Folklore has credited garlic and onions with medicinal properties which are now being established experimentally. Researchers, using garlic juice or commercial liquid and powdered extracts, and disguising the odor with a deodorizing agent, found it to contain a powerful antibacterial agent. It is an effective destroyer of diseases that damage stone fruits, cucumbers, radishes, spinach, beans, tomatoes, and nuts.

T. A. Tovstoles, a Russian biologist, experimented with a water solution of onion skin. Used as a spray three times daily at five-day intervals, the solution gave an almost complete kill of hemiptera, a parasite which attacks more than a hundred different species of plants.

Onion spray will also serve as a nontoxic fumigant. In one experiment, a water solution of onion skin and crushed onion was sprayed on apples as they were packed in boxes. Within two to three weeks, the onion odor had disappeared and the damage to fruit in treated boxes was significantly lower than in untreated boxes.

ENCYCLOPEDIA OF ORGANIC GARDENING ed.J.I.Rodale.
pp1145; £2.90; Rodale Press 1959.

Written by the staff of Organic Gardening and
Farming Magazine, this is the organic gardener's
bible. Covers the whole field:- vegetables,fruit
flowers, greenhouse, soil, composting etc.
Written for the American gardener but most of it
is applicable to Britain.

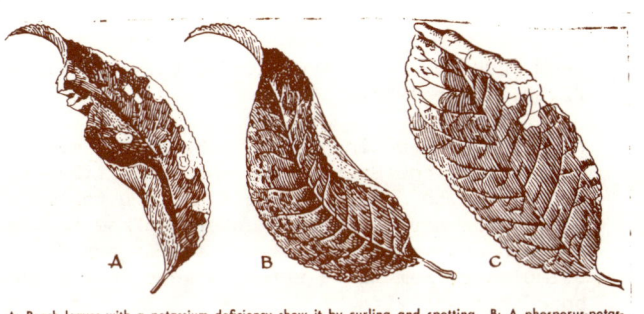

A: Peach leaves with a potassium deficiency show it by curling and spotting. B: A phosporus-potassium deficiency gives added curling and spotting. C: A lack of calcium kills tissues of mature leaf.

INSECT CONTROL, BIOLOGICAL: Biological control is the practice of reducing the numbers of a pest by the use of natural agencies such as parasites, predators and diseases. The aim of biological control is to achieve the most practical means of pest control. The fundamental basis of such control is the fact that life in nature exists in a state of balance which is maintained by the competitive interaction of various forces. However, man through, his diverse activities frequently disturbs this natural balance, often with disastrous results to his own well-being.

For example, plant-feeding insects are seldom serious pests in their native environment where they have natural enemies that prey upon them. However, when such plant-feeding insects are transported to new areas, and their natural enemies are left behind, they may become extremely numerous and cause serious damage to agricultural crops. For this reason introduced species probably comprise more than ⅔ of the major insect pests of agricultural crops in the United States.

When such a change occurs in the natural balance of an insect it becomes the business of those concerned with biological control to re-establish a satisfactory balance through the introduction of such control agencies as may be available regionally.

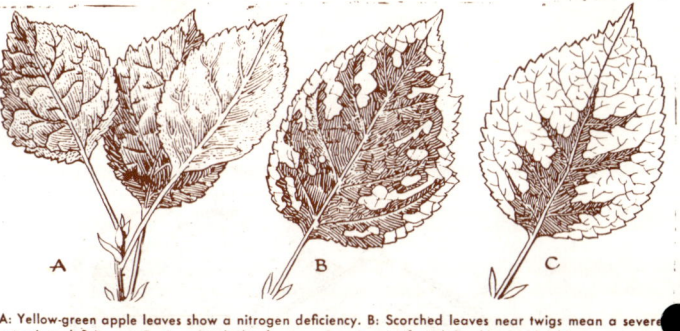

A: Yellow-green apple leaves show a nitrogen deficiency. B: Scorched leaves near twigs mean a severe potassium deficiency. C: A great lack of magnesium is manifested by heavy blotching near vein.

SOIL ASSOCIATION
New Bells Farm, Haughley,
Suffolk; annual sub. £3
SAE for details of pubns.

HENRY DOUBLEDAY RESEARCH
ASSOCIATION.
Sec. Lawrence D.Hills,
Bocking, Braintree, Essex.
Sub. £2p.a. SAE for pubns.

Propoganda and pressure groups on behalf of the soil,
engaged in research on all aspects of organic
gardening and farming. The general raison d'etre of
Doubleday is to promote the cultivation of russian
comfrey - a prodigious growing, deep rooted, huge
leaved plant - ideal for composting and mulching.
Both produce newsletters and a wide range of leaflets
covering biological pest control, composting etc.
Doubleday particularly acts as a sort of clearing
house for research done by gardeners all over the world.

From 'Pest Control Without Poisons' HDRA 15p.

The traditional slug trap is a basin sunk level with the soil surface and filled with sweetened beer or milk, which attracts the slugs who fall in and drown. Beer was cheaper when the trap was invented and a 50-50 mixture of milk and water is a modern economy mixture; but tipping away several basinfuls of drowned slugs every morning is a less attractive job for housewives than it was to the garden boys who are now Park Superintendents.

One part powdered alum to seven of slaked lime scattered on warm summer evenings produces a kill by contact, rather more effective than surrounding the lettuces with soot.

The Metaldehyde baits have the disadvantage of allowing many slugs to recover in wet summers, when infestation is worst. Very large quantities of small slugs are eaten by Centipedes, Devil's-Coach-Horse beetles, and Violet Ground beetles and their larvae, and the cumulative effect of poisonous metaldehyde (see 'Chemicals in Food' by Dr. Franklin Bicknell, Faber & Faber, 12s. 6d. for notes on a British poisoning case) kills predators. In their official capacity as garden scavengers slugs eat a great many creatures killed by chemicals, and their high resistance to chlorinated hydrocarbons means that anything eating them, especially birds, has an accumulating dose.

In America our two-spot ladybird is bred and sold to control scale insects in orange groves, and aphides, but we have this useful creature free. It would not be possible to breed enough to control blackfly on broad beans entirely, but with the help of other predators, however, they can go further towards keeping pace than we think.

Both the familiar beetle (there are nineteen kinds, of which the two-spot is the most efficient) and its larvae, rather like tiny six-legged crocodiles, eat aphides in quantity. So do the slug-like larvae of the large hover fly (like a slim grey wasp hovering round flowers) and the larvae of the lacewing fly, which cover themselves with sucked empty aphides.

The H.D.R.A. have begun work on the most promising aspect of this control method, which is finding ways to increase the survival rate of our native predators. A way for ladybirds may lie in providing better hibernation quarters, for another 5 per cent surviving each winter would make more difference than breeding and releasing by the hundredweight where there was not food enough to keep them going.

The attempt to domesticate glow-worms (*Lamphyris noctuleuca*) as slug controllers and charming garden pets failed for lack of hard knowledge of how to breed them. This beetle (of which only the males are winged), and its larvae, eat quantities of slugs and snails but they appear to be dying out, and are as worth saving as any Osprey.

The hedgehog is an excellent slug and snail controller, but the motor-car is deadly at night to a creature whose sole defence is to roll in a prickly ball. The report 'Slugs and the Gardener' gives some guidance on hedgehog feeding, on how to keep them safe in gardens (with milk, especially in the breeding season and in towns), for those who feed birds could just as easily feed hedgehogs, which are purely pest eaters without bud or fruit pecking on the other side of the ledger.

**EARTH
is a
space-ship**

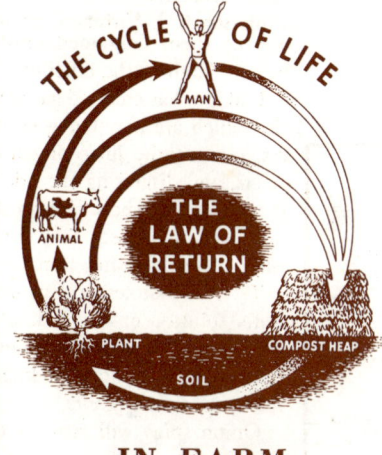

COMPOST MAKING

THE CYCLE OF LIFE

MAN

ANIMAL

THE
LAW OF
RETURN

PLANT   COMPOST HEAP

SOIL

**IN FARM
ALLOTMENT
AND GARDEN**

The customary dates for turning out rams in various flocks are usually closely adhered to from year to year, and vary from the end of July (early Hampshires) to mid-September (Lincolns), mid-October (Half-breds), 10th November (average Mountain Cheviots), and 22nd November (Blackface Mountain). Rams are left in the flock for about six weeks, which is ordinarily long enough to ensure that practically all the ewes will conceive. The period of œstrus in the ewe lasts about twenty seven hours and recurs, if she does not conceive, after about sixteen days. A six weeks' breeding season thus covers at least two and, in a majority of cases, three œstrous periods. In lowland flocks, where the ewes will have close attention at lambing, it is necessary to record the dates of service. To this end the ram is smeared between his forelegs with colouring matter so that he leaves a mark on each ewe that he serves. At the end of, say, each week, the ewes that have taken the ram are given a distinguishing mark, which remains till spring as an indication of the date of lambing. At the end of sixteen days the colour on the ram is changed to a darker one, so that the ewes not holding to the first service can be immediately known by the fact that they are marked with two colours. Any such should be examined, and if necessary, clipped about the tail and inside of the thighs. The longer wooled breeds are generally so clipped before tupping begins. Occasional ewes that have failed to hold to the first service should be placed with another ram in case the second service should also have proved ineffective. If many ewes are being twice marked another ram should be procured; in large flocks it is best to run two or three rams together with a combined allotment of ewes, as the accident of one ram proving infertile will then cause comparatively little loss. If, however, the rams fight, this plan must be abandoned; also, the method is not applicable in pure bred flocks, where matings are made with close regard to individual merits and faults. Under ordinarily good conditions and on low ground the proportion of barren or "eild" ewes should not exceed 1 or at most 2 per cent., in hill flocks it may reach 3 or 4 per cent. in ordinary seasons

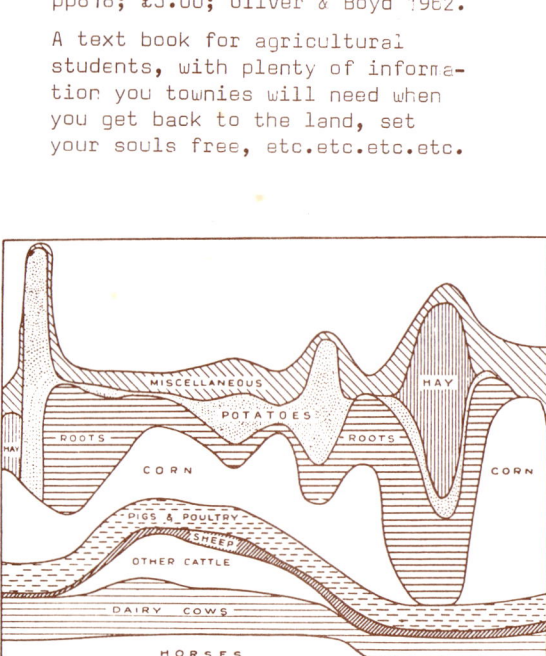

FIG. 9.—Horse-drawn Mower

AGRICULTURE J.Watson &J.A.Moore
pp818; £3.00; Oliver & Boyd 1962.

A text book for agricultural
students, with plenty of information you townies will need when
you get back to the land, set
your souls free, etc.etc.etc.etc.

FIG. 37.—Labour distribution on a mixed farm.

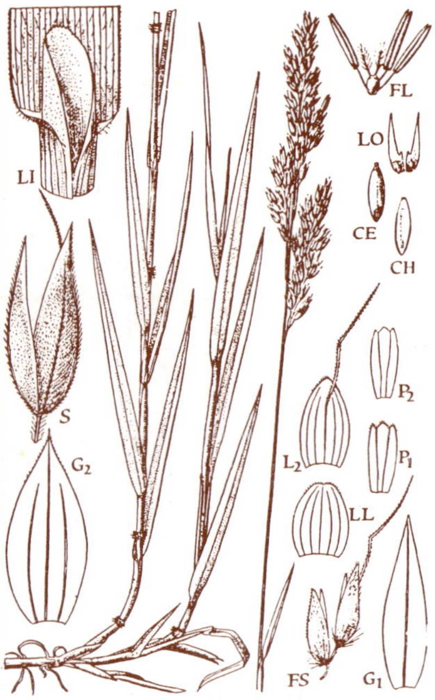

Holcus mollis. Common; shaded places and arable land.

GRASSES C. E. Hubbard
pp463; 60p;
Penguin 1968.

I bet you never
knew there were as
many grasses as this.
Beautiful illust-
rations, incredible
factual details. Once
you've mastered this
one, you will be
able to recognise
every type of grass
in Britain. Wow.

By means of its extensively creeping rhizomes, this grass has become a troublesome weed in sandy fields. It is most difficult to eradicate, as each small piece is capable of developing into a fresh plant. Investigations have shown that within 6–8 in. of the surface, a square foot of infested sandy soil may contain up to 110 ft of its rhizomes, whilst the weight of roots and rhizomes in such cases has been estimated at over 7½ tons per acre.

MINISTRY OF AGRICUL-
TURE PUBLICATIONS.
Catalogue free from
HMSO.
Every topic in agri-
culture covered from
Foot Rot in Sheep
(AL 567) to Dysentry
in Bees(AL 566). Some
free and some priced.
Hardly organic but
definitely worth a
browse.

= FREE PUBLICATIONS =

Clotted Cream. A.L. 438.
§Cream. A.L. 495.
Cream Cheese. A.L. 222.
Home Freezing of Fruit and Vegetables. A.L. 434
Home Storage of Apples and Pears. A.L. 181.
Soft Cheese. A.L. 458.
Starters for Cheesemaking. A.L. 302
§Beekeeping—Making Increase. A.L. 574.
Bees for Fruit Pollination. A.L. 328.
Beeswax from the Apiary. A.L. 347.
British National Hive. A.L. 367.
Dysentery in Bees. A.L. 566.
European Foul Brood Disease. U.L.
Examination of Bees for Acarine. A.L. 362.
Feeding Bees. A.L. 412.
Foul Brood. A.L. 306.
Acarine. A.L. 330.
Advice to Intending Beekeepers. A.L. 283.

PRICED PUBLICATIONS

Asparagus. Bull. 60. 5th edition, 1969. Reprinted 1971. 27½p (*30p*) (SBN 11 240360 3) Contains the latest and most up-to-date information on this crop. Illustrated. (20 pp.)

Beans. Bull. 87. 3rd edition, 1962. 15p (*17½p*) This publication takes into account developments in the cultivation of beans, particularly for canning and freezing, and includes notes on diseases and pest control. Illustrated. (24 pp.)

Horticulture in Britain. Part 1. Vegetables. 1st published 1967. £2·87½ (*£3·11½*)

Peas. Bull. 81. 4th edition, 1969. 35p (*39½p*) (SBN 11 240381 6) Covers all aspects of pea culture including growing, weed control, harvesting (and the part played by mechanization) and pests and diseases. Also contains sections on varieties and marketing of: green peas for canning, freezing and dehydration; dry harvested peas for canning and packeting; and green peas for market. Illustrated. (58 pp.)

Soils and Manures for Vegetables. Bull. 71. 4th edition, 1968. 31p (*35½p*) Covers all aspects of vegetable growing. Among these are soils, mineral nutrition, types of fertilizers and their placement and use, and a section on recommendations for particular vegetable crops. (75 pp.)

Watercress Growing. Bull. 136. 3rd edition, 1967. Reprinted with minor corrns. 1968. 27½p (*30p*) (SBN 11 240436 7) The various methods of cultivation employed throughout the country have been studied and a system devised and described in detail. Illustrated. (35 pp.)

FOXWARREN MACHINERY SERVICES LTD.
Jessamy Road, Weybridge, Surrey.

If you send a stamped addressed envelope they
will send you their current list of second hand
small scale farm machinery - a lot of mowers
but also cultivators etc.

```
HOW TO ENJOY YOUR WEEDS.
A.W.Hatfield.
pp116; £1.50; Muller 1969.


If you see a weed  don't rush for
the poison sprays, look it up in
this book and see if you can eat
it. Recipes on how to cook them too.
```

I have experienced unmistakable instances of this plant
symbiosis, and I have heard of and read about others, which
I can easily accept, and though these happenings apply
equally to weeds, the wild ones, they are perhaps easier to
appreciate with cultivated plants. For instance, the *Alliums*,
members of the onion tribe, are so rich in their sulphur
secretions, excretions and 'breath' that they can greatly in-
fluence other plants. Garlic, chives and shallots appear to be
good neighbours to most garden plants except peas and
beans, who hate them and are noticeably retarded when
oniony plants are near by. My broad beans are usually excellent, but they failed twice when grown near shallots. Peas
and beans prefer carrots and turnips as neighbours and
broad beans are happy, too, near early potatoes, and,
curiously, they will tolerate leeks. Carrots are so encouraged
by the friendly chives and shallots that they grow larger,
stronger and more flavorous when near them. Carrots and
leeks do well together and the leeks discourage the carrot-fly
pest.

STINGING-NETTLE

A complete plant food liquid can be made by soaking a
sheaf of nettles in a vessel of rainwater for two or three weeks,
when the water will contain all the plants' virtues.

A liquid fertiliser made from nettles either fresh or dried,
by the usual method (page 20), is not only a good folia feed
but also an effective spray against mildew, black fly, aphis
and plant lice, in the greenhouse or outside.

The nettle's good points are nowadays often obscured by
its stinging ones, but as the venom, which is said to be harm-
less bicarbonate of ammonia, is dispelled by heat, the plant's
medicinal and culinary properties may be as comfortably
enjoyed when cooked as they used to be. The nettle can be of
great help to remedy deficiencies in the human diet, since it
contains most of the elements we require. As a source of iron
it exceeds spinach and other recommended vegetables; it can
give us our necessary vitamin C, to mitigate our chances of
suffering colds or worse debilities.

Creamed Nettles. Wear gloves to gather a quantity of young
nettle tops. Wash them and shake off the excess water. Strip
off the leaves and put them into a pan with a large lump of
butter or margarine. Place the pan on a slow heat and
occasionally lift the nettles up from the bottom so that the
leaves will all be buttered and equally cooked. As the juices
begin to flow, add a light seasoning of salt and pepper. When
the leaves are cooked and tender, strain them well and save
the juices to make a delicious soup. Reheat the nettles,
stirring a little more butter and some cream or top-milk. This
vegetable is also very good when cooked with a few chopped
chives, shallots or spring onions.

	Water	Nitrogen	Phosphoric Acid	Potash	Organic Matter
Corporation Sludges	%	%	%	%	%
Birmingham	0·0	2·15	3·51	trace	43·7
Bolton	8·0	2·8	1·5	trace	45·0
Bradford	17·30	2·08	0·54	trace	39·0
Chesterfield	15·0	3·0	2·25	trace	50·0
Chorley	37·5	2·0	0·96	trace	31·5
Colchester	10·0	3·0	2·0	trace	30·0
Croydon	50·0	1·5	1·5	trace	30·0
Dagenham	55·1	1·07	2·68	trace	25·1
Denton	37·23	1·39	1·58	trace	27·54
Derby	50·0	2·2	—	—	44·0
Easthampstead	34·9	1·2	2·9	0·16	18·3
Halifax-'Organifax'	20·0	2·5	0·9	trace	49·0
Halifax 'Fibrefree'	20·0	2·0	5·0	—	45·0
Huddersfield No. 1	25·0	4·05	0·89	trace	61·5
Huddersfield No. 2	25·0	3·42	2·81	trace	61·2
Huyton	12·4	2·25	2·65	0·2	37·1
Isleworth	10·0	3·0	2·0	trace	50·0
Kingston-on-Thames	33·0	1·17	1·56	trace	27·1
Llanelly	43·72	1·25	0·92	0·06	21·1
Manchester	50·0	1·64	1·45	trace	31·1
Rickmansworth 'Covanic'	5·4	7·01	5·10	trace	68·9
Rickmansworth 'Air-dried'	50·0	3·0	2·0	trace	30·0
Rotherham	25·0	3·5	2·0	trace	50·0
Stoke-on-Trent	13·30	2·04	3·16	0·16	37·80
Stroud	34·0	1·92	0·46	0·16	63·4
Ware	33·0	1·8	3·2	0·1	35·0
West Kent	36·1	1·74	1·80	0·04	32·5
Wigan	35·0	1·5	1·8	0·2	28·0

```
FERTILITY FINDER - Lawrence Hills.
pp28; 10p plus postage; Henry
Doubleday Research Association.


This is a really useful booklet on
sources of sludge, compost, and
leaf mould from local authorities.
Hills says that the government
spends 31million pounds a year on
subsidizing the chemical industry
on the pretext of helping agric-
ulture. 'The subsidy enables farm-
ers to buy chemical fertilizers
rather more cheaply. Organic man-
ures such as dried sludge and
municipal compost recieve no
subsidy at all'.
Other sources of organic compost-
ing materials are riding schools,
(ring round for the cheapest)
breweries (spent hops).
Alternatively if you live in a
horsey area keep a dustpan and
brush handy.
```

BIO

```
ABOUT ORGANIC GARDEN-
ING G.J.Binding.
pp64; 25p; Thorson 1970.



At only 25p you can't go
far wrong. Its a good
general introduction.
One of a series which
include basic facts
about:-
wheat germ, yoghurt,
honey, dried fruits
and nuts etc.
```

Worm Casts and Soil

An interesting insight into the value of worm casts is shown
when we compare them with soil.

Worm casts contain 7 times more nitrogen than soil

	6	„	„	magnesium	„	„
	3	„	„	potash	„	„
	2	„	„	phosphorus	„	„
	2	„	„	lime	„	„

Worms are known to exist mainly beneath the earth for
periods up to about fourteen years. The worm will reproduce
itself hundreds of times each year, which is wonderful for the
organic gardener or farmer. In good organic soils rich in
humus, hundreds of thousands of worms provide up to ten
tons of worm casts each year per acre. They not only produce
these casts, but do extensive tunnelling, allowing rain and air
to penetrate the soil. There is a saying, 'breeding like rabbits',
but worms excel this. Under ideal conditions, one thousand of
them will produce forty million in two years. A good aim for
the creation of ideal garden and farmland is to produce one
million worms per acre. These will prove to be good and faithful servants, returning to each acre some two hundred tons of
digested soil each year.

```
THE ORGANIC GARDENER - Catherine Osgood.
Foster.  pp234; £1.45; Vintage 1972. (US)


An American book, but still very useful.
Begins at the beginning. There are some
really nice illustrations and the
bibliography is good.
```

Blanching

Cauliflower

Celery

Go easy ordering seeds for this vegetable, because a packet
will yield 150 plants, and for best nutrition and taste the
head should be eaten as soon as picked; or frozen for use
a little later. For varieties, choose Snowball or Snow King
for white; and Royal Purple or Purple Head for the dark
ones (which do not cook purple, but green). Quick growers
are Snow King Hybrid, Early Snowball, and Snowball Imperial. Start seeds in the cold frame and plant in succession
so they won't all mature at once. They are a delicate vegetable, or rather flower, and you need to keep watch for cut-
worms, cabbage loopers, maggots, and club root. Dust freely
with wood ashes, and some of your troubles are under control. Have a very good soil, rich and loose, with plenty of
nitrogenous materials such as blood meal or cottonseed meal.
These plants can endure cold, so can be put out in the garden
quite early.

Place the plants 2 feet apart, or 15 inches if small,
but discard all that have stunted leaves, for you need the
leaves later to tie over the head as soon as it appears. Cut
early, or when the head is about 6 inches wide and florets
are still compact and tight.

In favour of goats:

* The cow is basically a wholesaler whereas a goat's production is much more geared to a small family's needs
* Goats will eat just about anything; they can survive on land where a cow would starve; they will tackle nettles and even thistles quite happily
* The goat is proven in experiments to be a more efficient converter of food into milk - for every 10-stone bag of dairy-cake fed, the average goat produces 2 gallons more milk than the average cow.
* A goat is much cheaper to buy to make your start in dairying - you can always 'move up' to a cow later.
* A goat needs far less area for grazing
* The facilities and equipment needed are smaller.
* With a small trailer, goats can be taken along if you go on trips, whereas there always has to be someone at home to milk a cow.
* Goat's milk is easier to digest and better for you.
* A goat generally needs to be mated less often.
* Goat's milk can be frozen.
* You don't need a licence in the UK to sell goat's milk.

What it boils down to is this. Cows are far better in size for commercial dairy production and although their food-to-milk conversion rate is lower, the labour cost of cow's milk is far lower. This is what counts to the commercial farmer. Cows might also be preferable for a commune or large family with at least one acre of grazing land available. For a start on a smaller scale than this we would definitely recommend goats.

Unless you have a lot of mouths to feed, the cow's output of upwards of 15 pints per day can become more of a nuisance than a benefit. The 2-7 pints you get from a goat are far more realistic for most people reading this.

The trouble is that goat's milk *is* different. It has a slightly sweeter taste than cow's milk. Some goats give a more distinctive-tasting milk than others. And as with a cow, if you don't operate a good clean dairy, the quality and taste of the milk will definitely suffer. Before you decide definitely on a goat, try goat's milk from barious sources for a while and see if you can get used to it. It sounds an effort, but the point is that the effort could certainly be worthwhile. Children may be persuaded to accept the changeover more easily if the milk is sweetened in the early stages

Figure 2.—Modern hive with Standard frames for production of extracted honey Between super and hive-body should be a queen-excluder. (Deep extracting-super identical with hive-body may be substituted for shallow extracting super.)

STARTING RIGHT WITH BEES
14TH. Edition.
pp100; 55p; A.I.Root Co
1967.
From Mt. Grey (rt.) post 8p.
or Landsman's Bookshop.

Don't get stung, start
right with Root. (hoho).

Perhaps the most wonderful of the special characteristics of the queen is her ability to lay at will either worker or drone eggs, and so produce either worker or drone bees. The male elements within her are contained in a sac known as the spermatheca. Many of these male cells are received from a number of mating flights and render her fertile for life. The eggs deposited in a worker-cell are fertilized from this and produce workers; those deposited in drone-cells are not fertilized and produce drones. So it is that the drone or male bee is really a bee without a father. An infertile queen can lay eggs but these unfertilized eggs will produce drones and drones only. This is a reproductive power known as parthenogenesis, and possessed by only a very few other insects. The queen mother may live for a term of three or four years and perform her duty of laying during this time, and possibly be the single mother of a half million workers and drone bees. But, ordinarily a queen older than one year begins to fail, and for this reason many beekeepers replace all their queens as often as every year.

Only one queen, under normal conditions, is found in the hive at one time. The workers might tolerate more than one queen, but queens themselves are jealous of each other, and, when they meet, a mortal combat follows, during which one of them receives a fatal sting from the other and dies at once. Sometimes a queen mother and her daughter will get along together in the same hive during the summer, but ordinarily toward the fall and winter season, when the busy time is past, the mother disappears.

It is well for the beginner to remember that, as the queen is, so is the whole colony. Her blood is the blood of all the members of the hive, and the faults or virtues of her strain will be the faults or virtues of her progeny. So it is all-important that the colony have a good queen mother.

THE BACKYARD DAIRY BOOK.
Len Street & Andrew Singer
pp47; 40p; Whole Earth Tools 1972.
or from - Mill Cottage, Swaffham Road
Bottisham, Cambs.

All about milk production (from cows and goats)
and what to do with the milk once you've got it.
(e.g. making cheese, butter, yoghurt etc.).
Not intended to be too detailed but it directs
you to the right sources. It's the first in a
series of small books which will include info.
on methane gas generation, vegetable production
etc.

SMOKERS	
Popular Type complete ...	1.88
Spare Tinware Nozzles for same	65p
Bent-Nosed Tinware complete (as illustrated)	2.20
Bent-Nosed Copperware complete	3.30
Bellows for Popular Type ...	1.00
Bellows for Bent-Nosed Type	1.00

QUEENS

Reared in our own apiaries and tested that they are properly mated and laying normal worker brood before being sent out.

M.G. Select Fertile Caucasian Queens (available early July onwards)
or each 1.50
Select Fertile dark Hybrid ... ... each 1.45

MOUNTAIN GREY APIARIES
Holme on Spalding Moor,
E.Yorks YO4 4EZ. Cat. 3p.
Country Bizarre No. 7 also
listed the following firms
who supply equipment.
E.H.Taylor Ltd., Welwyn, Herts.
E.H.Thorne Ltd., Beehive Works,
Wragby, Lincs.
Robt. Lee Ltd., Beehive Works,
George St., Uxbridge, Middlesex
Burtt and Son, Stroud Rd.,
Gloucester.
Birdwood Apiaries, Hawkers Lane
Wells, Somerset.
No details about cats. - write
and ask if you're interested.

Flake Test

HOME PRESERVATION OF FRUIT &
VEGETABLES.
pp135; 47½p; 1968.
ABC OF PRESERVING. pp32; 15p
1969. Both HMSO.
First published in the days
of rationing, so the emphasis
is on the best methods by which
fruit and vegetables can be
preserved for use when fresh
produce isn't available. Still
relevant if you grow surpluses
or want to save by buying in
bulk in season. Both cover the
same ground, but the larger one
has a section on home freezing.

A wooden spoon is dipped into the jam, removed and turned horizontally in the hand until the adhering jam is slightly cooled. The jam is then allowed to drop from the edge and if it has been sufficiently boiled, so that it partly sets on the spoon, the drops will run together forming flakes which break off in a clean, sharp manner

Salting is another very old method of preserving food. If salt is used in large enough quantities it prevents the growth of bacteria, yeasts and moulds. In other words, it prevents the food from decaying. For good results, you must use young, fresh beans—it is a waste of time to salt old, stringy ones. Wash and dry the beans, then string and slice them in the usual way. French and very small beans can be left whole.

Allow 1 lb *household* salt for every 3 lb beans.

Use large stone or glass jars if possible. Put a good layer of salt in the bottom, then alternate layers of beans and salt, pressing them down well and finishing with a layer of salt.

After a few days when the beans have shrunk, fill the jars with more beans and salt. You will find that the salt draws moisture from the beans and makes a brine. When refilling always finish with a good layer of salt on top.

Close each jar with a cork, stone stopper, plastic material or a piece of calico dipped in melted paraffin wax. These covers will prevent the salt taking up moisture from the air. If using glass jars, store in the dark or wrap in paper to prevent fading.

How to use Salted Beans

Wash them thoroughly, changing the water several times. Then soak them in warm water for 2 hours, but not for longer or toughness may result. Cook the beans in boiling water, without salt, until they are tender, which will take about 25–30 minutes.

Causes of failure in Salting Beans

If the beans become black or slimy, this may be caused by:

1. Using too little salt.
2. Excessive moisture in the beans.
3. Failure to press the beans well down, so leaving air spaces.

If the beans are tough, it is because:

1. They were old.
2. Table salt was used.

The Tassajara Bread Book

THE TASSAJARA BREAD BOOK
E.Brown   pp146; £1.00
Shambala Publications,
Barn Cottage, Stert,
Devizes, Wilts. 1967
    Recipes from Zen Buddhist
monastery in California.
Advocates something called the
'sponge method' which they say
does new things for your dough.
Not just bread alone, other
goodies too.

TASSAJARA YEASTED BREAD

The fundamental Tassajara Yeasted Bread recipe.
(Four loaves)

I. *6 c lukewarm water (85–105°)*
   2 T yeast (2 packages)
   ½–¾ c sweetening (honey, molasses, brown sugar)
   2 c dry milk (optional)
   7–9 c whole wheat flour (substitute 2 or more cups
     unbleached white flour if desired)

II. *2½ T salt*
   ½–1 c oil (or butter, margarine, etc.)
   6–8 c additional whole wheat flour
   2–3 c whole wheat flour (for kneading)

(For detailed explanation of directions, see the GENERAL
DIRECTIONS FOR TASSAJARA YEASTED BREAD,
page 19.)

Dissolve yeast in water.

Stir in sweetening and dry milk.

Stir in whole wheat flour until thick batter is formed.

Beat well with spoon (100 strokes).

Let rise 60 minutes.

Fold in salt and oil.

Fold in additional flour until dough comes away from sides
   of bowl.

Knead on floured board, using more flour as needed to keep
   dough from sticking to board, about 10–15 minutes
   until dough is smooth.

Let rise 50 minutes.

Punch down.

Let rise 40 minutes.

Shape into loaves.

Let rise 20 minutes.

Bake in 350° oven for one hour.

Remove from pans and let cool, or eat right away.

HOME FREEZING OF PORK

To Home Freeze Pork

INSTEAD of pig-curing today many farmer's wives get a
pig killed and put the meat into the deep freezer. Here are
some short notes on packaging the meat after cutting up,
which is best done by the butcher.

Packaging.
  Use only special quality moisture-vapour-proof polythene
paper and bags.

1. Select best cuts of meat, hung for the required time.
2. Freeze joints of sizes suitable for use on one occasion.
3. If convenient, freeze boned joints—they take up less
   space. If bones are not removed, wrap any sharp ends
   with several thicknesses of greaseproof paper to avoid the
   wrapping being pierced.
4. Wipe meat with a clean cloth.
5. Wrap in polythene paper or bag—exclude as much air
   as possible.
6. Seal and label.
7. Chops or steak. Wrap each separately in polythene or
   transparent paper and place in polythene bag, then the
   required number can be easily removed.
8. Thaw joints of meat slowly if possible, in refrigerator
   overnight—as there is less loss of juices. Cook immediately. On no account should thawed meat be refrozen,
   unless it has been cooked.
9. Pork will keep up to 4 months in a home cabinet but it
   should be looked at occasionally and if the fat is going
   at all yellow it should be used at once.
10. Pork offal can be deep frozen but should be used within
    2 months.

FARMHOUSE FARE
Farmers' Weekly
pp 336; 40p;
Agricultural Press Ltd
1971
    Collection of recipes
from country housewives.
Many of them date from war
years, so the emphasis is
on thrift, or using natural
ingredients

CORNISH CHEESE

TO make our good Cornish cheese, first clean out your bath
or pan and place in it on the stove, to bring to a milk
temperature of 94 degrees. Then put in a cool place to lower
the temperature to 88 degrees for renneting. You will need the
special cheese rennet in the following proportions: 1 dram of
rennet to 2 gallons of milk, 2 drams to 5 gallons, 3 drams to
9 gallons, 4 drams to 12 gallons.
  Put every 2 drams of rennet into four times as much water
and pour into the milk when the latter is at 88 degrees. Deep
stir for 3 minutes; then top stir till set. Take count of the time
the curd takes to set (counting from the time it starts to turn),
and when it has set, leave exactly 4 times as long for the whey
to rise. If setting has taken 10 minutes, for example, leave for
40 minutes.
  Now cut the curd into ½-in. cubes, and leave for 10 minutes.
Next, put on the stove and bring to a temperature of 98
degrees, stirring till this has been reached. Leave for another
10 minutes. Then dip off the whey, take up the curd and
squeeze it in strainer-cloth; fix on a plate, and put a heavy
weight on top. Squeeze like this for 15 minutes, and then cut
into 6 large pieces. Squeeze again 3 times, for 15 minutes at a
time, and keep turning the pieces in between.
  After this, break into small pieces and once more get the
temperature up to 78 degrees. Now mix salt in thoroughly,
using 1 oz. salt to every 4 lbs. curd.
  Put into strainer-cloth, and keep in a mould for 2 hours. Then
put into muslin, and leave for 24 hours. After this, butter the
outside of the cheese, bandage, and keep in a cool place;
turning every day. It will take 6 weeks to ripen.

From Mrs. Stuart Hicks, Cornwall.

NATURAL FOOD COOK BOOK
Beatrice Trum Hunter
pp369; 47p; Pyramid 1967(US)

    How to conserve the
goodness in your food when
you cook it. Good section
on bean shoots too.
(Suggested by Jenny Headley)
    There are loads of
cookery books around.
The ones here are our
favourites. Penguin do
some good ones too;
INDIAN COOKERY byDharamjit
Singh, and MODERN VEGETARIAN
COOKERY by W.&J.Fleiss both
seem good. **B12**

17 • Sprouts

Seeds contain the elements necessary to grow new plants.
When given heat and moisture, they become rich in vitamins, particularly B-complex.
  The following seeds, whole grains, dried beans and peas
(*untreated*) can be sprouted successfully:
SEEDS—alfalfas, unhulled sesame, unhulled sunflower, radishes, mustard, red clover, fenugreek.
WHOLE GRAINS—wheat, rye, oats, corn, barley.
WHOLE DRIED BEANS AND PEAS—soybeans, lentils, green
peas, lima beans, mung beans, chick peas, marrow beans,
kidney beans, pinto beans, cranberry beans, fava beans

METHOD OF SPROUTING

1. Select clean, whole seeds, grains or beans. Remove any
   debris and broken seeds. Soak a small quantity at a
   time—remember that ¼ cup dried seeds, grains or beans
   will swell to ½ cup after soaking and to 2 cups after
   sprouting. Soak overnight.
2. Next morning, drain off water and reserve as stock.
   Put seeds in sprouting container (see below). Be sure
   cover fits loosely; sprouts need ventilation to develop.
3. Keep sprouts moist, warm and dark. A kitchen cupboard
   usually assures even warm heat. Sprouts will be ready to
   eat in 3 to 6 days, depending on variety of plant as well
   as on temperature.

SPECIAL HINTS FOR SOYBEANS

Soybeans are sometimes difficult to sprout, especially in
warm weather. The varieties that sprout best are Chief,
Ebony, Illini, Lincoln and Richland. Beans older than one
year will not germinate well. Try to use only those from
the current year's crop. As they germinate, remove any
that are decaying.

SPROUTS ARE READY TO EAT WHEN:

  the wheat sprout is the length of the seed;
  the mung bean sprout is 1½ to 3 inches long;
  the alfalfa sprout is 1 to 2 inches long;
  the lentil sprout is 1 inch long;
  the soybean or pea sprout is 2 inches long.
  Use sprouts as soon as they are ready, if possible. They
are best served raw. If not used immediately, they should
be stored in a covered container in the refrigerator and
used within a few days, as any fresh food. To preserve their
crispness and nutritive value, add them to any hot dish
immediately before serving. Use both the bean and the
sprout. The skins of mung beans may also be eaten.

WINE

'First Steps in Winemaking' and 'Making Wines Like Those You Buy' are both very useful books for the beginner. With modern recipes, often incorporating concentrated grape juice, you can make anything from plonk to claret.'Recipes for Prizewinning Wines' also is good and clearly set out. With a little experience you can move on to 'Progressive Winemaking' which is the most comprehensive source of information available. Some useful points -

* Bulk buying of ingredients such as honey, grape juice, dried fruit, and fruit and vegetables in season from wholesale markets, will save a lot over a year.
* Making wine in bulk (5-10 gallons) is just as easy as small amounts and actually gives better results. (One gallon only makes 6bottles!) 5 gallon carboys are expensive and hard to get, but large polythene containers are much cheaper. Make sure that all polythene is food grade or has been used for food, ie. wine or fruit juice containers. Be very careful with round glass carboys - they may have held chemicals which have contaminated the glass.
* Don't ever buy wine bottles. Ask nicely at your local big hotel and you can help yourself from their mounds of empties. Wash them!
* One good equipment buy - the 'Vinty' plastic hand corker, vastly superior to any other. Doesn't warp or rust like the wooden ones do.
* A wine acid test kit is useful once you're into it, but the constituents could be bought separately much cheaper.
* The quality of grape concentrate varies - you get what you pay for. But if you are adding it to other ingredients, the cheaper brands are OK.
* Cheaper still are the ingredients from the countryside. Elderberries (in October) make a good dry table wine.

The basic winemaking ingredients and equipment are widely available, but a much wider range can be obtained through mail order firms. Free catalogues can be from :-
SEMPLEX Old Hall Works, Stuart Road, Birkenhead.
W.R.LOFTUS LTD. 16, The Terrace, Torquay.
A&B TEMPLE 62-4, High St., Newton-le-Willows, Lancs.
VINA LTD. 63-5, St. Johns Rd., Waterloo, Liverpool. L22 9QB.

There are many books available on beermaking. We like Ken Shales' 'Brewing Better Beers' - covers the basics and the details too. If you're in a hurry to get pissed beer is ready much quicker than wine.   John Comer

In view of the fact that prevention is much better than cure, winemakers are well advised to add a small amount of sulphite to the must prior to its inoculation with the yeast starter as already recommended and as a further precaution to add another 50 p.p.m. sulphur dioxide immediately after the first few rackings (except a preliminary first racking).

Apart from helping to keep a wine free from spoilage, sulphite added after racking also performs several other useful functions. Thus, it aids the stabilisation and clarification of a wine by discouraging the growth of a new yeast colony (the conditions here are already rather unfavourable for further yeast growth and the presence of fresh sulphite merely aggravates matters). By neutralising the electrical charges on suspended colloidal particles, sulphite promotes their coagulation and settling and consequently assists clarification. Moreover, sulphite has anti-oxidant properties so that a proportion of the oxygen absorbed by wines during racking will preferentially combine with the sulphite rather than with certain constituents of the wine itself, and overoxidation due to excessive aeration during racking should therefore be largely prevented. Certain wines, notably those prepared from over-ripe fruits, are also susceptible to oxidative browning which is caused by the presence of unduly large amounts of certain enzymes (o-polyphenyloxidases) catalysing the oxidation of complex substances in the wine to brown oxidation products. Sulphite will also prevent this enzymic browning, known as oxidative casse, by acting as an anti-oxidant and combining with any dissolved oxygen before it can be utilised by these enzymes.

PROGRESSIVE WINE-MAKING.
P.Duncan& B.Acton.
pp 425; 75p.
Amateur Winemaker 1967.

Polyethylene bulk storage vessel

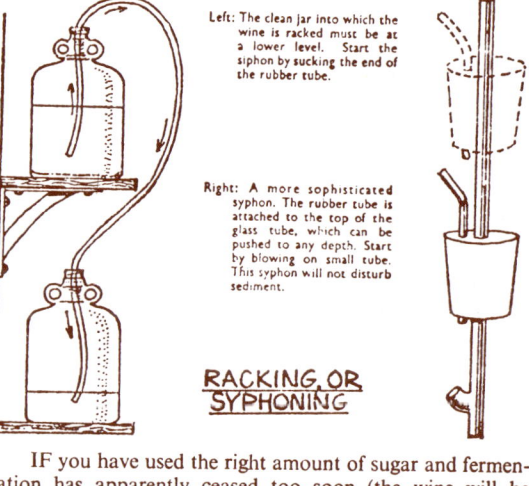

Left: The clean jar into which the wine is racked must be at a lower level. Start the siphon by sucking the end of the rubber tube.

Right: A more sophisticated syphon. The rubber tube is attached to the top of the glass tube, which can be pushed to any depth. Start by blowing on small tube. This syphon will not disturb sediment.

RACKING, OR SYPHONING

IF you have used the right amount of sugar and fermentation has apparently ceased too soon (the wine will be oversweet and its specific gravity too high) the fermentation is said to have "stuck". Possible causes: Too high or too low a temperature; the yeast has reached its limit of alcohol tolerance (i.e., the wine is finished); the sugar has all been utilised (add more); too much sugar (dilute slightly); insufficient nutrient or acid (add more); insufficient oxygen (aerate by stirring and pouring); too much carbon dioxide (uncork and stir). If these and all other remedies fail make up half a pint starter with the juice of three oranges, water, 1 level dessertspoon sugar, yeast, and a pinch of nutrient. Get it going well, then add an equal quantity of the "stuck" wine. When all this is fermenting, again add an equal quantity of the wine and continue "doubling up" in this way until all is fermenting once more.

FIRST STEPS IN WINEMAKING C.J.Berry
pp143; 30p; Amateur Winemaker 1968.

MAKING WINES LIKE THOSE YOU BUY
B.Acton and P.Duncan.
pp145; 30p; Amateur Winemaker 1968.

Basic Procedure

1. Process fruit, etc., and commence fermentation as outlined under each individual recipe.
2. When fermentation is *almost* complete (gravity down to 1.000) rack carefully without splashing into fresh jars, and sulphite 100 p.p.m.—two Campden tablets per gallon. It is very important not to carry over any fruit pulp at this racking and if by any chance this does occur, it will tend to sink to the bottom of the jar in about 10 days, whereupon the wine should be racked again carefully and a further one Campden tablet per gallon added (50 p.p.m.). This sulphite will have disappeared by the time of the next racking.
3. A light yeast sediment should form, and the wine can be safely left on this for four months, after which the wine should again be racked and once more sulphited at two Campden tablets per gallon (100 p.p.m.).
4. The wine should then be bottled immediately after this racking and sulphiting and a further few months in bottle will mature it. These wines improve up to 2—3 years, but after that will not normally attain further improvement unless of exceptional merit.

RECIPE No. 3
(Moselle)

Ingredients:

4 lbs. green gooseberries	½ oz. pectozyme
1 pt. white grape concentrate	Nutrients
¾ pt. elderflowers	Zeltinger yeast starter
1 lb. honey	Water to 1 gallon

Method:

Top and tail and wash the gooseberries. Scald with six pints boiling water and add the honey and nutrients. When cool crush the fruit by hand then add the elderflowers, pectozyme and yeast starter. Ferment on the pulp for two days, then strain off and press the pulp lightly. Add the grape concentrate and sufficient water to make the volume up to one gallon. Thereafter proceed as instructed in the basic procedure.

- Companies House, 55 City Road, London, E.C.1., 253-9393, is the official depository for information that all but the smallest companies are required to file. Members of the public are entitled to use these records, and there is a search fee of 1/- per company. (Many companies will send you their annual report for free, particularly if they think you are interested in their shares.) Using Companies House effectively may take some practice, as not all the material in a file comes up on the first request. Ideally, you should get (for a public company):

- A list of the current directors, their addresses, and perhaps some personal details and information on their other directorships.
- A list of all subsidiary companies
- A recent list of shareholders
- The last annual report

If you don't get all this, it may be because the company has neglected to keep the information up-t-date, but it is worth asking the staff.

WHICH?
Monthly, plus quarterly supplements Handyman's Which, Money Which, Motoring Which, also books.
Details from - Consumer's Association, Caxton Hill, Hertford.
As Spaceship Earth plunges into the eco-crisis, Which? will be there, with earnest reports on the best buy in gas masks, value for money in water purifiers, and which of six medium size family saloons gave off least toxic exhaust emissions.
    For the present, it does contain many reports on things that you think you need, both in the magazine, and in the books (Contraceptives et al.) Best buy is to ask for them at the library.

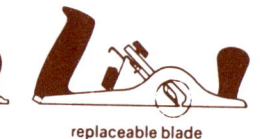

jack plane   smoothing plane   replaceable blade plane

PLANES

	price £	spare blades p
SMOOTHING PLANES		
Record 04 ⌁	3.05	45
Salmens 004	3.00	45
Stanley No 4	3.15	45
Talco No 4	2.50	45
Whitmore No 4[1]	2.75	45
JACK PLANES		
Record 05 ⌁	3.75	45
Salmens 005	3.60	45
Stanley No 5 ⌁	3.85	45
Whitmore No 5[1]	3.15	45
REPLACEABLE BLADE PLANES		
Paramo Plane:master No 10[2] ⌁	3.25	16½[3]
Stanley RB10 ⌁	3.30	19[3]

[1] Also available with plain lever cap assembly (25p less).
[2] Also available in 12 in. length (£3.95).
[3] For five blades.
⌁ In Council of Industrial Design's Index.

VALUE FOR MONEY

In our tests, the two most expensive brands of conventional plane, Record and Stanley, came out best. They were well finished, performed best in the hands of our expert carpenter and our users found them easy to use and the easiest to adjust and set. We pick then as:

JOINT BEST BUYS
- Record 04 (smoothing) £3.05
- Stanley No 4 (smoothing) £3.15
- Record 05 (jack) £3.75
- Stanley No 5 (jack) £3.85

You can get other sizes of all these planes.

    We do not think that a replaceable blade plane is a good substitute for a smoothing plane. Our non-expert users could not get good results with them, and both had other disadvantages too.
    The job you most need a plane for is smoothing. So we do not think it is an important advantage that the replaceable blade planes will rebate as well – particularly as the beginner will probably find it easier to make rebates by sticking two bits of wood together rather than by cutting them out with a plane.
    There are in fact many types of plane for specialist jobs, like cutting rebates. We shall tell you about them in the future.

POWER RESEARCH GUIDE
Vic Schoenbach
pp30; 10p;
Europe/Africa Research Project 1970
(Available from Agitprop)

An excellent guide to digging out the working details of money and power.

LIBRARIES

    Nearly every book recommended here can be obtained through the public library system. When we were compiling this catalogue, we constantly found that the local library (admittedly a big one) had books which we never expected to find. (Mind you, they refused to buy the Last Whole Earth Catalogue. Maybe they couldn't catalogue it).

    Most people know that libraries will get almost any book if it's available, either through other libraries, or by buying it. They can also get back copies of magazines, and stuff from the National Lending Library. In fact if it's printed on paper there's a good chance they'll get it.

    ASLIB   is an organization dealing exclusively in information (membership is mainly , as they put it, 'for corporate bodies'. Further details from Aslib, 3, Belgrave Square, London SW1.) They publish a directory of information sources listing specialized libraries, and Aslib Booklist (monthly) which briefly reviews new scientific and technical books. (Both in major libraries).

    If you want to check out details of a book try 'Books in Print' and 'Paperbacks in Print', but don't count on them as being a very accurate guide. Ask the local bookshop if you can look at their copy.

    Kelly's Directories are a suprising thing. They have a volume for each major town, and have much useful information arranged in strange ways - such as where people live, or what businesses are in particular streets, rather like a reshuffled phone book. Again major libraries have reference copies.

    Check out library shelves for weird and wonderful bibliographies of this and that, record books, registers of all sorts, trade directories, telephone books from all corners of the world- it goes on and on.........

C1

BOOKSHOPS

Nearly all titles listed are available through
any bookshop.
Detailed below are various shops specializing
in particular fields, some in general
alternative/left/underground stuff, others
in technical areas.

AGITPROP, 248, Bethnal Green Road, London E2.
Agitprop is about political information - not
just an ordinary bookshop, but a clearing
house for material about all levels of
political activity from all over the country.
They also supply groups with material. The only
real political bookshop in the country.

BOOKS, 84, Woodhouse Lane, Leeds 2.
Fairly new shop with a big stock of
alternative socio-political material,
including many difficult to obtain titles.

COMPENDIUM, 240, Camden High St., London NW1.
Still the poetry/arts shop, but now into
mysticism, yoga et al. as well.

UNICORN BOOKSHOP, 50, Gloucester Road,
Brighton, Sussex.

SPECIALIST BOOKSHOPS

LONDON ECOLOGY BOOKSHOP. 45, Lower Belgrave St.,
London SW1.
Catalogue 10p.
Books about wildlife, zoology, botany etc.
agriculture, ecology and environment.

STOBART & SON LTD. 67-73, Worship St., London EC2.
Lists free. State area of interest.
Building and related subjects, such as .
carpentry, electrical installations etc. They
supply books on approval.

PRINT ABOUT PRINT.
65, Beak St., London W1.
Lists and catalogue - write for details.
Printing, graphic design and related subjects.

J.WATKINS LTD.
21, Cecil Court, London WC2.
Glastonbury type material. Stone circles,
mysticism etc.

CHILDREN'S BOOK CENTRE
140, Kensington Church St.,
London W8 4BN.
Children's books, but also a newsletter
reviewing new titles.

****

BLACKWELLS, Broad St., Oxford.
Big fat Blackwells - not so much use over
here as it is to the Americans who can get books
cheaper, but still just about the major bookshop
in Britain. Publish lists under various subject
headings.

****

HMSO
Free catalogues of the publications of
Government, most of which are totally boring,
some of which are interesting, and a few very
useful.
Catalogues of Unesco, World Health
Organization and United Nations publications
are available through HMSO agents.

LANDSMANS BOOKSHOP LTD.
Buckenhill, Bromyard, Herefordshire.
Catalogue 10p.

An exceptional service. Landsmans is a
shop specializing in books on
farming, gardening, forestry, and
related topics, like beekeeping,
natural history etc.
    The catalogue is very comprehensive,
but the service doesn't stop there.
They also publish monthly reports on
new titles, operate a second hand and
part exchange scheme, and are prepared
to offer specialist advice on the merits
of books. Really good.

C2 (Suggested by Rob Lavender)

The Golden Dolly. LAMBETH. '69. £1.50. (making of corn dollies - well illustrated).
Oxford Book of Invertebrates. D.NICHOLSON. '71. £5.00.
Shell Book of Country Crafts. '68. £1.50. (miscellaneous articles, well illustrated).
Nature Conservation in Britain. Sir D.STAMP. '69. £1.80.
Young Specialist Looks at Molluscs. H.JANUS. '65. 75p. (paperback 47½p.).
    "   "   "   " Weather. '64. 75p. (paperback 47½p.).

GOATS

Goat Husbandry. D.MACKENZIE. '70. £3.75. (the only comprehensive work).
Goats. H.E.JEFFREY. '69. 50p.
Modern Dairy Goats. M.D.GORDON. '50. 30p.

Diseases, Pests and Weeds. (including control)

Biological Control of Insect Pests & Weeds. ed. P.DeBACH.(U.S.A.). '64. £7. (technical).
Biological Methods in Crop Pest Control. G.ORDISH. '67. £1.75.
British Poisonous Plants. MIN.OF AG. '68. 72½p.
Cereal Pests. MIN.OF AG. '65. 60p.
Chemical and Natural Control of Pests. E.R. de ONG. (U.S.A.). '56. £4.65.
Chemicals and Pest Control. G.S.HARTLEY & T.F.WEST. '69. £1.75.(technical).
Chemical Herbicides in Sugar Beet Production. M.EDDOWES. '68. 25p. (H.A.A.C. Report).
Control of Rats & Mice on the Farm. MIN.OF AG. '70. 50p.
Crop Protection. ROSE. '63. £4.75. (comprehensive).

DIRECTORY OF ALTERNATIVE WORK.
10p + 7½p postage from Uncareers,
36, Rookery Road, Birmingham 29.

Excellent guide to who's doing what
alternatively, - organizations, media,
action.

New Barns School

Church Lane, Toddington, Gloucs. Tel. Toddington 200.

A residential school with 12 adults (not called 'staff'), and 32 children from about 8 to 14 who have been classed as 'maladjusted'. They aim to be a living community in which both adults and children are deeply involved - where individuals interact strongly with each other and responsibility is shared. Teaching is fairly informal - in small groups - and not separated too much from other activities. Art and other creative activity play an important part, and there are large grounds where the children can play freely and climb trees.....

Anyone working there should be stable and able to make genuine relationships with the children. There are vacancies from time to time for those with formal qualifications and skills, and also for people less formally qualified.

COUNTRY BIZARRE.
15p quarterly; Annual sub. 70p.
from Bizarre Acres, 19, Danesmoor,
Ruscote, Banbury, Oxfordshire.

A magazine of romantic usefulness.
Detailed recordings of country
culture and practicalities.

corn dollies

For countless number of years, corn dolly weaving has held a high position as one of the loveliest country hand crafts in England; that is until our faithful combine harvester came on the scene. Until that time, these craftsmen would gather the corn stalks and use them to weave many beautiful constructions, but with the advent of mechanical farm equipment all that is virtually gone and in its place are fields upon fields of stubble and brocken stems which prove useless to weave with.
As soon as Leslie Jackaman realized what was happening to his craft, he began to look elsewhere for his material and discovered drinking straws. These he experimented with and after making a fine traditional Suffolk umbrella set about the task of persuading the straw manufacturers of their good fortune; who immediately began producing an unwaxed and somewhat longer version of their paper straws.
These artstraws, as they are generally known, has given the dying craft new life and can be bought from Sweetheart Straws, College Road, Fishponds, Bristol at the price of one pound for 2,000 straws. Weaving instructions are included. **or art shops, or Boots.**

PLANTAIN

The lowly lawn and garden pest known as plantain ranks near the top of the list of nutritional greens. Plantain is said to outrank garden greens in nutrients because it grows more slowly and, thus, has more time to store vitamins and minerals. The early pioneers used plantain extensively in their diets and the plant is still an important food in certain sections of the U.S.

Plantain is available almost everywhere and its appearance is readily discernible: Ribbed, long, broad oval leaves and slender seed stalks growing out of the center of the leaf cluster.

Its bland taste makes plantain a palatable addition to any salad. I much prefer it to dandelion greens. It isn't as tender as head lettuce but plantain can be chopped and made tender enough to suit any taste. As a general rule the young, smaller, rather shiny broad-oval leaves are best. These small plantain leaves are available all summer because new leaves continue to form throughout the season.

DIRECTORY OF COMMUNES (reprinting) (last edition 15p) ➡
COMMUNES MAGAZINE (bimonthly) 20p, 24p by post.
Secretary of Commune Movement - Bob Matthews,
00, Stainmore Ave., Hull, Yorks. HU6 7HN (general
inquiries, news, journal contributions, journal bulk orders).
2nd. Secretary - Patty Dorman, 3, Russell Way, Wooton, Beds.
(publications, subscriptions, membership, accounts).

Communes, dreaming, making, made and unmade. Like they say -
our greatest resources are each other.

Middle Farm: We're a bunch of idiots trying to survive the harsh winters in the far north (Cumberland). There are chickens and an acre of land for food; and pottery and rings to pay the electricity bill. The house is in a bit of a sorry state but we're all working hard to fix it before the snow. At the moment there are nine of us which we hope will be more next year but there is absolutely no more room at the moment 'cos we ain't fixed any more rooms up. The house is way up in the hills with a really bad track. There are nine rooms plus a load of barns and things all built in, flags on the roof, you crap into a stream and stare out the shithouse at beautiful hills and moorland. We're hoping to buy the house sometime 'cos its dead cheap (£1000 approx) and the owner's going bust. At the moment rent is 30/- a week but this is high for the area. In the summer, we're hoping to score a bus (air cheap) so we can travel about and scream even louder
Mail to Middle Farm c/o Commune Movement, 12 Mill Road, Cambridge. (Please send S.A.E.)

MOTHER EARTH NEWS.
monthly, price 60-75p
available from Compen-
dium and Books among
others sometimes

Best known of US
back-to-land mags.,
a lot of it sur-
prising, some of it
downhome corn- but
that's what you
need sometimes if
you want to live
off Mother Earth.

MORE ON "LEATHER BRITCHES"

GRACE V. SCHILLINGER

If you'd like to try preserving beans in an old-time, way-down-south way, here's how to do it:

Pick your green or wax beans when they're tender and "snappy." Wash them and snip off the stem end. The other little sharp pointed tip won't matter, so leave it on. Let the beans drain until fairly dry, or at least till the water has dripped off.

Take a large darning needle and thread it with white store string. Kite string will do fine. Then thread your beans on the cord, sticking the needle through the middle of each bean. I don't mean down the center of the bean, just *through* the center, so both ends of the bean are loose.

Fasten the first bean by wrapping the string around it and making a knot so it won't pull through. Then go on stringing till your string's full. Fasten the last bean the same as the first one.

Dry the beans by hanging on a wire in a clean, dry place. An attic or unused room would be okay. Or hang them in your kitchen. They'll be *gab grabbers,* for sure! In the most high fallutin' magazines you'll see how decorators festoon rooms with the most unusual items. All right—go ahead with your leather britches!

The beans will become dry and wrinkled and you'll wonder what in the world you'll ever do with them, besides just letting them swing there.

In winter, take your dried beans down—several strings for a large kettle—and remove the strings. Rinse well, then put on to cook. When they boil up once, pour off the first water so you know they're clean and to remove any bitter taste. Then pour in fresh water, toss in a ham bone and an onion to keep the beans company and salt and pepper to taste. Cook till tender.

You'll come up with a mighty fine cold weather dish that'll stick to your ribs. These beans will remind you of long-ago years when folks *had* to preserve much of their food by drying.

Happy eating!

C3

KIDS MAKING THEIR OWN TV

There's been a lot of studies made (exclusively in print!) of the effect of television on children, but none have used videotape (*i.e.*, the medium itself) to survey the effects of TV.

Nor is there much information around about how kids can make their own TV. The only guidance available comes from misguided teachers who think it's cute to have their students imitate the behavorial straitjackets of broadcast-TV (*i.e.*, do "news shows" under adult supervision) instead of setting them loose to enhance their own spontaneous behavior.

What follows is experience of our own (Raindance) with a group of a dozen junior high school kids from New York City. They came to our loft one afternoon a week for twenty weeks from the Clinton Project, an experimental school within a public school based on the Parkway Program in Philadelphia.

Essentially each kid gets to choose what he or she wants to do so that if he came to learn about videotape it was because he wanted to.

I have also drawn on the experience of the Media Access Center who, as far as I know, have done the most with kids and videotape. They recommend that you begin with these assumptions:*

1. Videotape is not film. You needn't script what you shoot nor edit the results into a final product. The tape is erasable and its capacity for immediate playback permits uses impossible with film. Record and playback and erase and record again what seems useful and interesting at the time. Shoot first and ask questions later.

2. Videotape is not television. Don't make record sessions into studio exercises or playback sessions into passive engagements with the tube. Arrange the equipment to fit in naturally with what's going on — *i.e.*, have plenty of extension cords around and avoid cumbersome studio accessories like lights — and freely intersperse recording, monitoring, responding,

GUERILLA TV
Michael Shamberg &
Raindance Corp.
pp108; £1.90;
Holt Rinehart Winston (US)
1971.

sequentially or simultaneously. The sooner you break students of standard TV roles (MC, cameraman, audience, etc.) and mindsets about programming, the sooner they'll enthusiastically enter the process of discovering what can be learned via videotape.

3. Videotape is a means of perceptual discovery and interaction; it demands uses more creative than the consumption of instructional knowledge. Students must become active agents in initiating and participating in video projects, with real control over the information generated and its use. The moment kids see themselves as subjects or targets for educational TV, they'll tune out. Teachers must make themselves equally vulnerable to exposure on videotape and be open and honest about the discoveries *they* make.

*Reprinted from **Big Rock Candy Mountain** (an education access and resource catalog), Winter 1970, p. 53. Portola Institute, Menlo Park, California.

Good talking about the magic box, on all aspects of low level TV. It's American, so the badness he attacks is more obvious, but the fact that <u>we</u> have the best broadcasting system in the world (best for who?) doesn't alter the basic few speaking to many situation.

Shamberg gives the lowdown on VTR - systems, methods, crass assumptions to avoid. But watch for the brain police, inside and outside your head - the nature of the medium is towards elitism, technologically, and in its use. Beware.

FELT

If you want felt for covering floors or sound deadening, contact Mr Merkel at J & J Maybank, Maybank Wharf, Herringham Road, SE7 (858 6100). This felt comes off the machines used in paper mills and is obviously not the best, but is remarkably cheap. Ring him before you go down to Herringham Road as he is the only person who deals with the felt and he is not always there. This company usually sells off this felt in big quantities (£3.50 per cwt) but Mr Merkel says he will deal in smaller quantities by weight.

If you want better quality felt for curtains go to the Felt and Hessian Shop, 34 Greville Street, EC1 (405 6215). They sell 72" wide curtaining felt at £1.10p per yd and flooring felt, 54" wide, at £1.47 per yd. Good range of colours.

ALTERNATIVE LONDON
Nicholas Saunders.
pp384; 30p;
or 40p from 65,
Edith Grove,
London SW3.

Not so much use if you aren't lucky enough to be living in the centre of the the universe, but very useful if you do, with all the macro details of ways and means of making life easier in the smoke.

MAKING COMMUNES
Clem Gorman.
pp 132; 75p
Whole Earth Tools
(adress P. C6)

Don't read this book if you're looking for easy ways of communing, because there ain't any, unless your combinations of personal chemistry, hangups, are magically complementary.
Read it because it has some good stuff about the sort of working problems you can expect, but some big gaps as well.

An Ideal Commune

With so many people in Britan sitting around planning communes, it's not surprising that many people come up with various ideas of the ideal commune. In a sense, perhaps they're all true. Probably the ideal commune is one which produces the most love and togetherness while leaving people as free as possible. But that's only my ideal commune. Only one thing seems certain, from experience of British communes; the more flexible a group of people remain in their ideas of what they want and how to go about getting it, the more chance they have of making a successful commune.

Interest

Many communities are set up with the premise that one of the chief things the members want to avoid is reliance upon conventional capitalist notions of the usefulness of money as a store of value or as a means of allocating resources to different uses. This means there will be a variety of attitudes among communities as to whether money should be borrowed at all, and if so whether it should be treated as a loan or as an unspoken gift. It is only those communities who borrow money in the financial market place who have to be concerned with the payment of interest, and usually there is no way around it short of losing the communal house. However, a number of communities accept the notion of interest on loans made by one member to another or to the group.

GRAPHICS HANDBOOK Ken Garland.
pp96; 75p Studio Vista 1966 (right)
PRINT REPRODUCTION POCKET PAL
ed. L. May. Advertising Agency Production
pp136; 50p. Association 1969 ♦

When you're doing a print job,it's
half the battle to speak the same
language as the printer,and to know
what will happen to your lovely artwork
once he's got it.Garland starts from
sratch and gives a good general guide to
graphic processes.Pocket Pal assumes that
you know the basics. Both save money and
temper.

In reproducing halftone originals, it is always necessary to break up the continuous tone into a regular pattern of separate units, which, when printed, will give an appearance of continuous tone. This is done by photographing the original through a glass screen engraved with very fine lines. As the above diagram shows, the lines are placed so that the distance between the lines is equal to the thickness of the lines themselves. It is possible to use a variety of screen patterns ; the simplest is one consisting merely of parallel lines. But in practice the cross-line screen is the most effective for all normal purposes. When the cross-line screen is placed between the image and the negative, the light is split up into pinpoints which vary in size according to the relative tone of the image. The fineness of the screen is denoted by the number of lines to the inch, and usually ranges from 50 to the inch up to about 150.

Diagram of a 100-screen, enlarged 50 times. '100-screen' means that there are 100 lines to the inch.

Type should be set so it can be read with the least effort or eye-strain. Proper spacing can make or break the appearance of an advertisement or printed piece. Each job presents a different problem, depending on the kind of type—whether capital letters or lower case letters are to be used, etc. A good printer will give that little extra service, in the best interests of his customer, to be sure the spacing enhances the typography. In practice, good spacing is usually a matter of common sense.

Letterspacing This is the amount of space between each letter of the word, either for legibility or to fill a certain desired area. This occurs mostly in capital letters used for display.

PRECISION CARTRIDGE

no letterspacing

PRECISION CARTRIDGE

2 point letterspacing

PRECISION CARTRIDGE

4 point letterspacing

Line Spacing The amount of space between each line is known as *leading*. There is no set rule to follow . . . too much leading can sometimes be as bad as not enough. Flush paragraphs require additional line spacing to set off the break.

The most important thing about printing is that it conveys thought, ideas, images from one mind to other minds. This statement is what might be called the front door of the science of typography.

This paragraph set solid

The most important thing about printing is that it conveys thonght, ideas, images from one mind to other minds. This statement is what might be called the front door of the science of typography.

This paragraph set 1 point leaded

The most important thing about printing is that it conveys thought, ideas, images from one mind to other minds. This statement is what might be called the front door of the science of typography.

This paragraph set 2 point leaded

When you're buying printing, important points are
*Find out as much as you can about printing.
*Get as many prices as you can, and chat each
 printer about his gear(size of plate, if he makes
 his own plates,etc.) Fit the job to his equipment
 if you can.
*Half-tones (see extract from Garland, above) ie
 pics with grey tones are relatively expensive,
 because they mean extra work for printer and plate-
 maker. Colour is expensive, because you pay for
 the time it takes to clean all that lovely normal
 black ink out of the press. Two colours on the
 same page...OK if you're printing money.
SILK SCREEN
The low technology print process- knife, paper,
wood, nails, a bit of the right nylon, card
and some paint, and you're in business- just.
If you trot down the local screen printer's with
a big smile and a jam jar, he'll probably sell
you some prper ink, which is much better than
makeshifts like paint or Polycell and powder
paint.
Silk Screen suppliers(all free catalogues)
George Hall(Sales) Ltd.,Beauchamp St., Shaw Heath,
Stockport.//Pronk, Davis & Risby,90-6,Brewery Rd.,
London N7//Selectasine,22 Bulstrode St.,London W1
    Agitprop 248,Bethnal Green Rd.,London E2, supply
a leaflet outlining absolute basics. Send 15p

PRACTICAL SCREEN PRINTING
Stephen Russ.
pp96; £2.10
Studio Vista 1969

All the basic gen to get
get you into screen
printing; good on making
your own equipment.
Get printing.

It is not easy with the bare hands to pull a mesh drum tight. With a pair of canvas stretching pliers, or even a pair of ordinary pliers, the work is somewhat easier. But the easiest, quickest and best way to stretch any kind of mesh is to use a master frame.

This is a separate piece of equipment designed to fit outside the largest screen frame in the workshop. It consists of a strongly built rectangular outer frame and four separate inner pieces connected to the main frame by long bolts and wing nuts. These inner pieces are called floating bars and they can be pulled up tight to the outer frame or set at a distance in from it by adjusting the wing nuts. The apparatus is placed flat on a bench top and the screen frame to be covered is laid in the centre. The wing nuts are slacked off and the floating bars pushed inwards until they meet the sides of the screen frame. The mesh material is now stretched tight across the screen frame and pinned to the floating bars, taking care to align the warp and weft with the sides of the frame. By tightening up the wing nuts, the floating bars will be drawn outwards and the mesh pulled tight. When it is fully stretched a generous coating of adhesive is applied to the mesh where it lies in contact with the screen frame. Use a synthetic resin adhesive and spread it with a scrap of stiff card. As soon as the adhesive is set, the newly covered screen can be cut free by running a sharp knife along the gap between the screen frame and the floating bars. A master frame of this type can be used equally well to cover a number of smaller frames simultaneously. They can be packed in side by side, and cut apart at the end.

Fig 4 Master frame

Over the years a network of 'alternative' presses have been built up.
Below is a list of some we have heard of. They all have different equipment
and facilities and it's best to check around a few to see which best suits
your requirements.

Backyard Press, 75, Roman Road,
   London E12.

Brunswick Press, 12, Brookfield Road,
   London E8 01-980-9845.

Community Press, 11, Hemingford Road,
   London N1. 01-837-3997.

Crest Press, 154, Ladbroke Grove,
   London W10. 01-960-1975.

Falling Wall, 79, Richmond Road,
   Montpelier, Bristol 6.
   0272-422116.

IRAT, Prince of Wales Road,
   London N1.

Liverpool Free Press, 24, Wapping,
   Liverpool

Moss Side Press, Nello James Centre,
   136, Withington Road, Manchester 16
   051-226-3458.

Outsider, 9, Leonard Street, Hull
   0482-20222.

Partisan Press, 45, Gamble Street, Forest
   St West, Nottingham. 0602-74504.

Rank and File Workshop, 30, Primrose Hill,
   St., Coventry. 0203-51723.

Suburban Press, 9, Sidney Road, SE20.
   01-654-0277.

SW Litho, 6, Cotton Gardens, London E2.
   01-739-1704

Whole Earth Tools, The Mill Cottage,
   Swaffham Road, Bottisham, Cambs.
   0223-811071.
   (Interested in publishing practical stuff
   on living independantly of the system.
   Have a press, typesetter, and binding
   equipment.)

Coming soon or in existence by now,

Aberdeen Community Workshop, Neil,
   c/o 6b, Powis Circle, Aberdeen.

Black Flag Bookshop, 1a, Wilne Street,
   Leicester.

Tyneside Press, 14, Netherton Gardens,
   Woodland Park, Wide Open, Newcastle.
   039-426-3693.

Printing It
Clifford Burke
PP 127: £1.45
Ballantine (US)
1972

Just before finishing, we found a very useful book on printing in Compendium.
It's called "Printing It" by Clifford Burke, a San Francisco hip printer. He goes through
the basic techniques of printing from printing processes, through design and
paste up to bindings, and encourages you towards setting up in printing.
Very good, despite being American.

Against police repression in the streets, from its first manifestations.
May 17 **39**; May 18: finished off by workers in a printer's, this poster was printed in
large numbers **40**; Third week in May: to go with the two preceeding posters **41**

CRS SS

ATELIER POPULAIRE — Texts and Posters
from Paris May 1968.
pp95; £1.00; Dobson (Currently
unavailable)

The story and techniques of the
superb fighting designs that came
out of Paris '68.

C6 Page 40   **40**   **41** Page 41

```
EDUCATION AND VISION    pp208.
NATURE AND ART OF MOTION    pp230.
STRUCTURE IN ART AND SCIENCE  pp208.
MODULE, SYMMETRY, PROPORTION  pp233.
SIGN, IMAGE, SYMBOL   pp282.
THE MAN MADE OBJECT   pp230.
Edited by Gyorgy Kepes. Studio Vista (Currently out of
print).
```

Some good people expound their own thing in heavyweight
interdisciplinary blockbusters. Don't be put off- there are
many good things, (some
not so good) in this lot;
Kepes has succeeded in making it all work together.

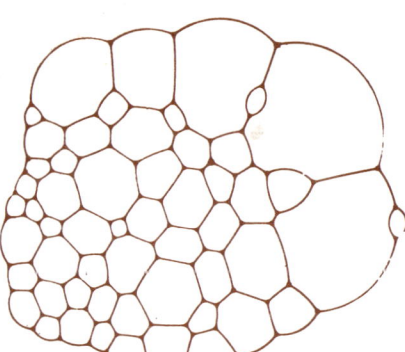

Fig. 9. Crystal grains of a metal (brass) separated from an aggregate, showing the natural shape of crystals when packed randomly into contact with each other. Note the frequency of pentagons and curved surfaces.

Fig. 12 shows a topological mapping—that is, a mapping which preserves neighborhoods—of our body with respect to the sensation of touch into the appropriate cortical regions. This "homunculus" is obtained by registering with microelectrodes those regions in the brain which become active when certain regions of the body are stimulated.[7] Such a "signal representation" must not necessarily conform with original proportions, as seen by the emphasis of organs that convey most of the tactile information.

I ran an experiment with a number of Eskimos. I sketched on paper some twenty figures, each oriented in a different direction. Then I asked each individual to point to the seal, the walrus, the bear. Without hesitation, all located the correct figures. But though I had myself made the drawings I found it necessary to turn the paper each time to ascertain the accuracy of their selections.

Igloo walls are often covered with magazine pictures obtained from the trader. These reduce dripping; perhaps they are enjoyed for their colors as well. Some effort is made at vertical rendering but really very little, and the over-all result is haphazard. When the children wanted to imitate me, a sure way to provoke delighted laughter was to mimic my twisting and turning as I tried to look at the *Life Magazine* pictures.

Walrus tusks are carved into aggregates of connected but unrelated figures; some figures face one way, others another. No particular orientation is involved, nor is there a single "theme." Each figure is simply carved as it reveals itself in the ivory.

In handling these tusks I found myself turning them first this way, then that, orienting each figure *in relation to myself.* Eskimos do not do this. They carve a number of figures, each oriented—by our standards—in a different direction, without moving the tusk. Similarly, when handed a photograph, they examine it as it is handed to them, no matter how it is oriented.

The value we place on verticality (it influences even our perception) stems from the strength of literacy in our lives. Children must be taught it. Natives do not know it. And when the mentally ill in our society withdraw from the burdens of literate values, and return to nonvertical, nonlineal codifications, we call them childlike, and even note parallels with primitives. To the lack of verticality can be added multiple perspective, visual puns, X-ray sculpture, absence of background, and correspondence between symbol and size: all examples of non-optical structuring of space.

```
LOOKING AND SEEING - Kurt Rowland.
Vols. 1,2 & 3. 130pp each 70p.
Vol. 4. pp182; 75p.  Ginn 1965.
```

Hated art at school? All that crap
about composition? Never mind;
educate your vision with these
lovely little books.

If you compared the two parts of the divided line or two sides of the favourite rectangle you would find that the longer is approximately 1·618 times as long as the shorter. In other words the ratio between them is 1·618:1. This ratio may be written as 1·618, a number which has many fascinating qualities first noticed by Euclid, the father of modern geometry, about the year 300 B.C. It has always been considered an important number: mathematicians have given it the name ϕ (pronounced fie); the artists of the Renaissance called it the Divine Proportion; the Greeks used the pentagon, which includes a number of ϕ relationships, as a holy symbol.

This wonderful number, which is also known as the Golden Section, the Golden Ratio, or the Golden Number, has more than mathematical applications; it is also significant in the living world. We can see that natural organisms, including the human body, are really based on the ϕ relationship. In preferring proportions based on ϕ we are therefore following natural laws.

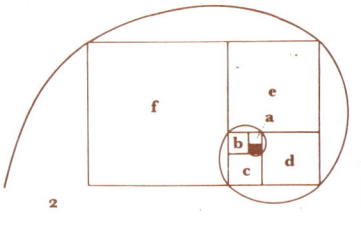

In the ϕ rectangle the ratio between the two sides is 1·618:1. This rectangle has a number of peculiarities. If you construct a square on its longer side, as shown in diagram 1, the square taken together with the rectangle will form a new, larger ϕ rectangle. In diagram 1 the ratio between the long side M and the short side m is the same as the ratio between the long and the short sides of the larger rectangle. We can show that the two ratios are the same by writing M:m = (M + m):M. *This is a mathematical proportion. There are also arithmetical relationships in ϕ. If you divide 1 by ϕ you will get 0·618. If you multiply ϕ by itself the result will be 2·618. Compare these two figures with ϕ and you will notice something strange about their relationship.*

In diagram 2 the square a has been added to the small black ϕ rectangle in the centre, in the same way as in diagram 1. Together they make a larger Golden Section rectangle. If you now add another square, b, on the longer side of the new rectangle another Golden Section rectangle is found. You can go on doing this with squares c, d, e and f. The corners of all the rectangles, when connected, form a spiral, such as we found in natural shapes.

In the pentagon, 4, there is a Golden Section relationship between any diagonal and any side of the pentagon. AC:AB = ϕ. All the diagonals intersect each other according to the Golden Section, so that AD:DE = ϕ and CE:ED = ϕ. The smaller, inner pentagon formed by the diagonals contains similar relationships which can be expressed by ϕ. It is easy to understand why the Greeks thought the pentagon such a perfect shape and used it as a sacred symbol.

```
PHOTOGRAPHY : MATERIALS & METHODS
J.Hedgcoe, M. Langford.
pp 176; £1.50;
OUP 1971.
A good beginning book, with
comprehensive coverage of techniques,
plus practical things like a where-
you-went-wrong table to diagnose
the inevitable ballsups.
```

25. Method of making a series of test exposures on one piece of sheet film. Starting with the sheath fully removed 1 unit (e.g. 1 second) is given. The sheath is then returned, one quarter at a time, doubling the exposure given at each stage.

Print quality. 'Quality' in a black & white print is today highly subjective in that so much depends upon the original aims of the photographer. Generally, however, a good quality print should have really rich blacks in its darkest shadows, and clean highlights closely matching white paper. Between these extremes there is then room for a wide range of well-separated grey tones.

Blacks will not be rich if the print received insufficient development, or was under-exposed on a paper grade too soft in contrast. White will be greyed or stained if the print was greatly over-developed, processed in exhausted developer, or if the enlarging lens was dirty, stray fogging light reached the paper, or the paper was very old. See plate 36.

Photographs for reproduction must have a good range of separable tones; as the blockmaking process itself inevitably reduces tone range. Make the prints on glazed glossy paper—this makes the blacks even richer when the print is suitably lit. Never use stipple surfaced paper as its tiny highlights cause technical difficulties with the blockmaker's screen.

Printing on a hard paper results in well separated but a very restricted number of tones between black and white, culminating in (lith paper) black and white only. This gives stark graphic quality which in itself reproduces well, as the blockmaker can treat it as a line image. All the silhouettes of photographic equipment in this book were produced this way, using extremely soft subject lighting reflected off a white canopy, and printing the negatives on lith paper.

Soft prints have an extremely wide range of barely separable greys which can be helpful for romantic high or low key images—but on the whole it is better to achieve these effects by the original lighting and camera work, allowing printing to emphasize rather than make the total effect.

Line negatives consisting of dense black and clear film would seem very easy to print because no greys are required. In practice take care not to over-expose as this slightly 'spreads' black lettering, making it appear unsharp. A good line negative prints well on any grade because all grades give good blacks and whites—only the range of greys varies.

```
THE CRAFT OF FILM
Ed. David Fisher.
pp 260 (loose leaf binder)
£12.00 including updating material.
Details from Attic Publishing Co.Ltd.
306, Fulham Rd., London SW10.

An introduction to professional
filming equipment and methods.
Lots of useful stuff, but some bits
that seem a bit redundant, (like how
to load an Arriflex - if you're up
to an Arri you ought  to know how
to load the pig.)
```

Tool bag

1 The quality of precision is basic to animation, for through precision we enjoy freedom of almost absolute control. The first element of this is the registration system, which gives accurate location of artwork - both between one drawing and the next, and between separate parts of the same drawing. The system has two components: (a) the peg bar - a flat strip of metal carrying raised pegs of standard dimensions; (b) the cel punch - a device for punching holes in thin materials so they can be located on standard pegs.

2 Ready-made artwork - such as photographs or printed material - can be 'pegged up' by mounting on cel, or by sellotaping to 'peg-strip', which consists of old 35mm film with holes punched along its length.

3 The standard format for peg holes is shown down the side of this sheet, and is known as acme pegs. There are also a few other formats; but acme is greatly predominant.

4 An animation desk has one essential feature - a built-in light box - to enable accurate tracing work to be done. The desk surface contains an area of opal glass, or similar translucent material, with a light underneath it. A more sophisticated desk incorporates a swivel board: the glass is mounted in a circular frame which is free to rotate, and also has removable pegs.

```
MACARTHUR MICROSCOPE
Standard version (mag x80, x200) £15.50 post free.
Triple objective version (x80, x200, x400) £29.90
From Marketing Division, Open University,
Walton Hall, Bletchley, Bucks.

A really handy microscope, that gets you away
from static flat surfaces, can be used in any light,
at any angle, and carried easily in the pocket.
The world doesn't stop at the limits of vision.
```

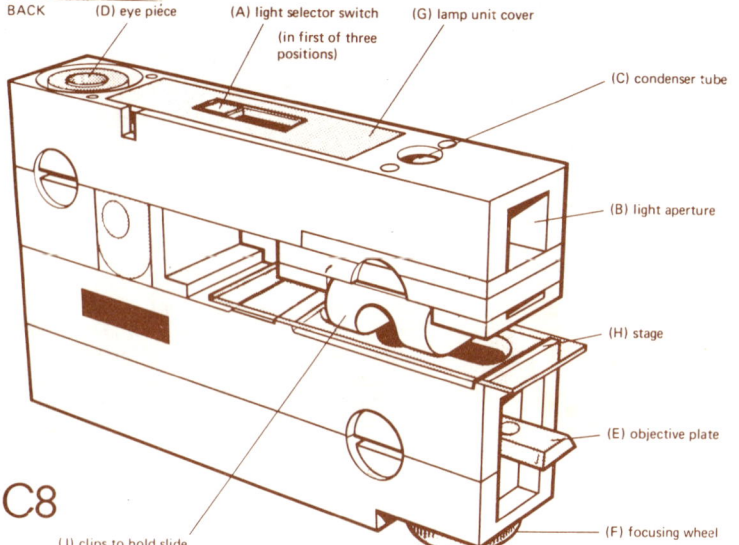

```
FOCAL PRESS
31, Fitzroy Sq., London W1P 6BH
Catalogue free.

Big range of books about audio
visual things, at all levels from
idiot to academic

Suppliers of film, paper, and
 other materials at good prices-

Marston & Heard Photographic L d.
378, Lea Bridge Rd., London E10.
Direct Photographic Supplies,
224, Edgeware Rd., London W2.
A.W.Young Photographic,
159, Chatsworth Rd., London E5.
Harringay Photographic Supplies,
35, Green Lane, London N4.

All free lists (SAE to Young)
```

```
SCIENTIFIC AMERICAN,
Monthly 50p.
Catalogue of books
and offprints free from
W.H.Freeman and Co,
58, Kings Road,
Reading. RG1 3AA.

Scientific American has been demystifying and
disseminating science for years. They publish reams
of offprints from the magazine (see extract from
catalogue lower right) and also reshuffle them into
books about special fields (Plant Agriculture,
Frontiers of Astronomy.)

   In recent years, September's issue has been
devoted to one subject. Sept.'71 on Energy and Power
is a really good introduction to the subject (extract
lower left). Like previous September issues it has
been republished as a book at a somewhat energetic
price but is still available at time of writing as a
back issue for 70p from Freeman's. You can also still
get the two previous September specials, on The Ocean
and The Biosphere at the same price while stocks last.
You also get the pretty eco-ads. from Boeing and Esso
too.
```

It may not be improper to characterize as ecological imperialism the elaboration of a world organization that is centered in industrial societies and degrades the ecosystems of the agrarian societies it absorbs. Ecological imperialism is in some ways similar to economic imperialism. In both there is a flow of energy and material from the less organized system to the more organized one, and both may simply be different aspects of the same relations. Both may also be masked by the same euphemisms, among which "progress" and "development" are prominent.

The anthropocentric trend I have described may have ethical implications, but the issue is ultimately not a matter of morality or even of *Realpolitik*. It is one of biological viability. The increasing scope of world organization and the increasing industrialization and energy consumption on which it depends have been taken by Western man virtually to define social evolution and progress. It must be remembered that man is an animal, that he survives biologically or not at all, and that his biological survival, like that of all animals, requires the survival of the other species on which he depends. The general ecological per-

spective outlined here suggests that some aspects of what we have called progress or social evolution may be maladaptive. We may ask if a worldwide human organization can persist and elaborate itself indefinitely at the expense of decreasing the stability of its own ecological foundations. We cannot and would not want to return to a world of autonomous ecosystems such as the Tsembaga's; in such systems all men and women are and must be farmers. We may ask, however, if the chances for human survival might not be enhanced by reversing the modern trend of successions in order to increase the diversity and stability of local, regional and national ecosystems, even, if need be, at the expense of the complexity and interdependence of worldwide economic organization. It seems to me that the trend toward decreasing ecosystemic complexity and stability, rather than threats of pollution, overpopulation or even energy famine, is the ultimate ecological problem immediately confronting man. It also may be the most difficult to solve, since the solution cannot easily be reconciled with the values, goals, interests and political and economic institutions prevailing in industrialized and industrializing nations.

AMERICAN POLICE WHISTLE sounds when air is blown through the mouthpiece and creates an edge tone in the slot at top. According to one description of how this whistle works, part of the flow from the mouthpiece represented by swirling lines travels around the inner surface of the cavity and returns to the slot, where it reinforces the edge tone. The air could carry the ball with it (*as indicated by arrow*) so that the slot is periodically blocked. This would explain the whistle's rapidly varying tone.

Wind as power source is attractive because it does not impose an extra heat burden on the environment, as is the case with energy extracted from fossil and nuclear fuels. Unlike hydropower and tidal power, which also represent the entrapment of solar energy, the wind is available everywhere. Unfortunately it is also capricious. To harness it effectively one must be able to store the energy captured when the wind blows and release it more or less continuously. One scheme would be to use the electricity generated by the wind to decompose water electrolytically. The stored hydrogen and oxygen could then be fed at a constant rate into a fuel cell, which would produce direct current. This would be converted into alternating current and fed into a power line. Off-peak power generated elsewhere could also be used to run the electrolytic cell whenever the wind was deficient.

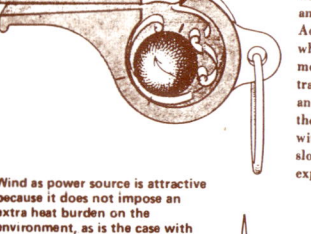

regenerate the thin disks containing visual pigment. Cones renew themselves in another way.
October 1970

1202. F. Herbert Bormann & Gene E. Likens THE NUTRIENT CYCLES OF AN ECOSYSTEM
When all vegetation was cut in a 38-acre watershed in an experimental forest in New Hampshire, the output of water and nutrients increased. The experiment illustrates ecological principles of forest management.
October 1970

1203. Ursula W. Goodenough & R. P. Levine THE GENETIC ACTIVITY OF MITOCHONDRIA AND CHLOROPLASTS
These organelles of cells contain DNA, RNA and their own apparatus for synthesizing proteins. Their resemblance to bacteria suggests that they may be descended from free-living bacteria-like organisms.
November 1970

1204. W. L. N. Tickell THE GREAT ALBATROSSES
The royal albatross and the wandering albatross are the largest birds in terms of wingspan. The species are so much alike that they probably evolved from a common ancestor in the recent past.
November 1970

phenomena that enrich our understanding of the physical world.
June 1949

207. Sergio De Benedetti MESONIC ATOMS
For brief instants mesonic atoms may spin like electrons on orbits around atomic nuclei. The X-rays they emit, as they jump from orbit to orbit, may illuminate the nature of the nuclear binding forces.
October 1956

208. Freeman J. Dyson FIELD THEORY
The physics of the 19th century discovered "classical" fields; modern physics deals with quantum fields. What is the nature of these quantum fields, and what place do they occupy in our present view of reality?
April 1953

209. Albert Einstein ON THE GENERALIZED THEORY OF GRAVITATION
An account of the extension of the general theory of relativity against its historical and philosophical background.
April 1950

210. William A. Fowler THE ORIGIN OF THE ELEMENTS
The relative abundance of the various kinds of atoms is a powerful clue to the history of the uni-

---

The next generation of airships could look like this. A 1200-ft long monocoque hull, with a cargo capacity of 500 tons, would travel at 100 mile/h. The airship would not need to moor at its journey's end, instead both cargo and passengers would be shuttled to and from the ground by helicopter. A diesel-electric powered ship could stay aloft for months and be refuelled by a tanker airship—a nuclear-reactor powered airship could stay in the air for years

```
NEW SCIENTIST
Weekly 15p.
IPC.

More concrete real
world information
every week than a
month of Sundays.
```

Hindu (Brahmi), c. 300 B.C.

Hindu (Gwalior), A.D. 876

Hindu (Devanagari), 11th Century

West Arabic (Ghobar), 11th Century

East Arabic, 1575

European, Most of 15th Century

European, 16th Century

Bank cheque numerals, 20th Century

A written numeral's form is closely related to the writing materials used— slate, pencil and clay tablet of the Babylonians, pen and papyrus of the Egyptians. Today's familiar numerals derive from early Hindu script and Arabic numerals of Moorish Spain, with subsequent European refinements. The round dot at the end of some of the rows represents the symbol for zero, whose importance the Arabs recognized in one of the most trenchant sentences in mathematical history: "When (in subtraction) nothing is left over, then write the little circle so that the place does not remain empty."

MATHEMATICS
David Bergamini.
pp190; 75p; Time Life 1969.

Highly readable history of maths from the beginnings of number to the computer. Down to earth stuff without too much to confuse the number blind.

Square arrays of rods show what happens in the algebraic factoring of $x^2 - y^2$. If the block representing y^2 is put on top of the x^2 block, the area of x^2 left exposed can be rearranged to show its sides are $(x + y)$ and $(x - y)$.

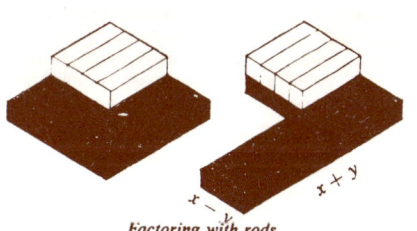

Factoring with rods

THE GENERAL PLAN OF THIS BOOK

In this diagram each block represents a chapter. Chapters 1, 3, and 4 are of a general nature, and are not included in the diagram.

Each block depends upon the blocks below. Thus, it is impossible to understand Chapter 11 without first having read Chapters 6, 9, and 10, and Chapters 9 and 10 in turn cannot be understood without Chapter 8, etc.

In some cases, the upper block depends only on a small part of the lower one. For instance, Chapter 8 can be understood without understanding the whole of Chapter 6. In fact, it is only the part of Chapter 6 explaining the meaning of the signs 4^5, 10^5, etc., that is needed for Chapter 8. It is not possible to show this on the diagram.

Chapter 13 is split into two parts. 13*a* represents the greater part of the chapter, which is quite elementary. 13*b* represents the end of the chapter, which is more advanced.

If a reader finds difficulty, say in Chapter 10, he may find it worth while to leave Chapters 10, 11, and 12, for the time being, and to read the easier part of Chapter 13.

MATHEMATICIAN'S
DELIGHT
W.W.Sawyer
pp238; 20p;
Penguin 1943,69

COMMON SENSE & EVERYDAY EXPERIENCE

This book sits alongside my 85p Boots slide rule as a liberator of my mathematical mind. If maths is a foreign language to you, he gently translates you into it. Once you're into it, it's one of those things that you wonder how you managed without.

MATHEMATICAL MODELS
H.M.Cundy and A.P.Rollet.
pp288; £1.50;
OUP 1961.

This book reminds me of school — it's written and illustrated in that textbooky sort of way. Nonetheless, it's good, particularly for details about modelmaking.

1.2. THE USE OF MODELS

The main use of a model is the pleasure derived from making it. When it is made it can be used to demonstrate the fact which it illustrates. Finally, it may form part of a permanent collection of similar constructions. People have collected many stranger things than polyhedra on occasion. If words must be found, we can describe these uses as the creative, demonstrative, and collective uses of models.

The creative value of a model is there for anybody who will take the trouble to make it. A mathematician who cannot express himself in other ways may be able to make an attractive model, and to make it well. In many cases great technical skill is not required, and some of the most complicated models described in the following pages require nothing beyond care and patience. Further, the materials are not usually expensive, and even scrap can often be used. The keen model-maker is always on the look-out for possible raw material.

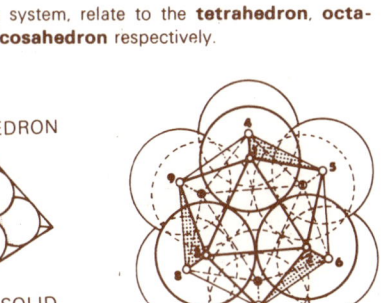

ORDER IN SPACE
Keith Critchlow
pp120; £2.10;
Thames and Hudson 1969.

A sourcebook of spherical geometry. Not exactly lightweight stuff, but pretty useful if you're exploring other ways of building spherically than standard Fuller Geodesic.

Thus far we have established that the tetrahedron is the prime plane solid, it is the minimum definition of solid space, and is also the strongest configuration to resist forces from without. The octahedron and the icosahedron complete the range of the three triangulated and 'structural' regular solids. These three figures are the regular representatives of 2, 3, 3-symmetry, 2, 3, 4-symmetry, and 2, 3, 5-symmetry in the solid. The other two regular solids, the cube and dodecahedron, are the duals of the octahedron and icosahedron respectively. The three proportional systems traditionally used in architecture, the root 3, the root 2 and the Golden Mean system, relate to the **tetrahedron**, **octahedron** and **icosahedron** respectively.

TETRAHEDRON

PRIME SOLID

It's a buyer's market in electronic components at the moment due to over-capacity in the industry following cut-back in the space programme etc.

If you are buying anything more than a couple of resistors, it pays to look at the prices in the current electronics mags.
Prices of all sorts of things dip and turn from month to month.

ELECTROVALUE,
28a, St. Judes Rd.,
Englefield Green,
Egham, Surrey.
Catalogue (pp96)
25p
My favourite electronic catalogue. Loads of info. loads of pics. loads of goodies.

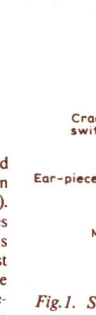

JACK SOCKETS

2.5 m.m. with shorting contact	10p
3.5 m.m. with shorting contact	10p
Standard British .25" 2-circuit with chrome facia nut and black, white, red, blue, green or grey bezel	
Type S5/SS & colour	16p
Type S5/BB & colour (with two break contacts)	19p
Standard British .25" 3-circuit stereo available moulded in three colours, black, white and grey.	
Type S3/SSS & colour	19p
Type S3/BBB & colour (with three break contacts)	23p

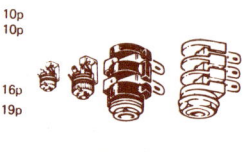

JACK PLUGS

2.5 m.m. unscreened	10p
3.5 m.m. unscreened	10p
3.5 m.m. screened. Type P5	11p
Standard type screened. Type P1	20p
Side entry screened type SEP1	24p
Standard stereo screened type P3	34p
Side entry stereo screened type SEP3	38p

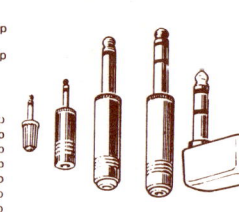

WIRELESS WORLD
20p; monthly IPC.

Not really about wireless, more about fairly advanced electronics, as applied particularly to audio/ radio/TV, but with lots of diversions(build it yourself electronic calculator, private telephone exchange, digital clock etc.)
Not for beginners but always a good read and plenty of useful ads.

Connecting two telephones

The telephones are wired in parallel and supplied with d.c. from a 50V supply in series with a 1kΩ resistor (R, Fig.2.). When both handsets are on their cradles no current is drawn. If one handset is lifted and the dial turned to its fullest extent, the impulses produced will be transmitted to the bell of the other telephone via its built-in capacitor, and cause it to ting. Then, on lifting that handset, both d.c. circuits will be complete and speech modulation produced in the microphone of one telephone will be transmitted to the receiver of the other. The resistor drops the voltage across the telephones to about 5V while talking, but allows the capacitors to charge up to the full battery voltage for ringing. Some telephones may have three or four wires coming out. If this is the case it is necessary to remove the base of the telephone and refer to the circuit diagram and notes within. This will show which two wires to use and which to join together.

I made it myself

The communications division of Motorola have taken a step in the right direction by adding an important commodity to one of their radio paging receivers. Each receiver is assembled, tested and packed by one assembly technician. Gone is the production line where each worker did the same job over and over again with little idea of what the final product looked like. The assembly workers are now completely involved. They are responsible for the quality and reliability of the receivers they have each made and an extra something is added which is called pride in one's work. A signed note with the receiver tells the customer who made it.

The receiver in question, called the Pageboy-2, uses only 80 components (if a hybrid i.c. can be called a component) and makes the one-person production technique possible. Motorola are so pleased with the results of the exercise they are now looking at other areas where the idea could be applied.

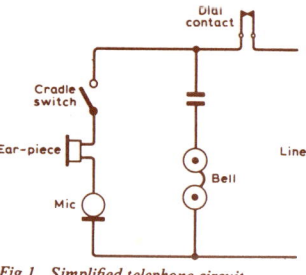

Fig.1. Simplified telephone circuit.

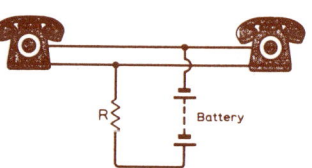

Fig.2. Method of connecting two telephones. R should be selected to suit the battery employed as follows: for 50V use 1kΩ, for 67.5V use 1.5kΩ and for 90V use 1.8kΩ.

HART ELECTRONICS,
Penylan Mill,
Morda, Oswestry,
Shropshire.
Large SAE for lists.
POWERTRAN ELECTRONICS,
22, The Pantiles,
Bexleyheath, Kent
List free.

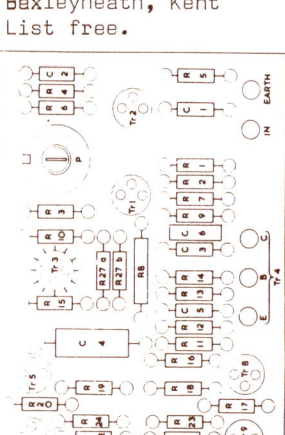

Harts' 30w. Bailey printed circuit.

Building your own amplifier is economical, apart from being interesting. For £20-£50 you can buy kits of parts for amps. which are technically the equal of pricier ready-mades. The Bailey 30 watt amp. and preamp. is one of the best designs around at the moment and costs £30-45 for stereo, depending on what you get.

Powertran have a good range of kits and their board designs avoid some common problems. They are also pretty cheap. Harts' boards are beautifully designed, and they supply top quality components, but they're pricier. Take your pick.

WARNING - Know what you're doing before you start. Expensive pitfalls await you.

If you don't know what you're doing take a look at Heathkit. Catalogue free. Heathkit Ltd., Gloucester.

FOUNDATIONS OF WIRELESS AND ELECTRONICS.
M.G.Scroggie.
pp521; £1.80; Butterworth 1971.

Another multi-edition classic leading you gently by the soldering iron into the electronic jungle.

Fig. 2.11—The rule for resistances in series proves that doubling the length of a uniform conductor doubles its resistance (a). By the rule for resistances in parallel, doubling its cross-section area halves its resistance (b); and doubling its diameter quarters its resistance (c)

So far we have assumed the possibility of almost any value of resistance without considering exactly what determines the resistance of any particular resistor or part of a circuit. We understand that different materials vary widely in the resistance they offer to the flow of electricity, and can guess that with any given material a long piece will offer more resistance than a short piece, and a thin piece than a thick. We have indeed actually proved as much and more; by the rule for resistances in series the resistance of a uniform wire is exactly proportional to its length—doubling the length is equivalent to adding another equal resistance in series, and so on (Fig. 2.11a). Similarly, putting two equal pieces in parallel, which halves the resistance, is equivalent to doubling the thickness; so resistance is proportional to the reciprocal of thickness. Or, in more precise language, to the cross-section area (Fig. 2.11b). Altering the shape of the cross-section has no effect on the resistance—with steady currents, at least. Fig. 2.11c shows how doubling the diameter of a piece of wire divides the resistance by four.

NOISE R.Taylor
pp268; 36p; Penguin 1970.

The nearest that most of us get to acoustics
is complaining about the neighbours/Concorde/
traffic/etc. 'Noise' is about the acoustics
of everyday life - why things make a noise,
ways of stopping them where possible.

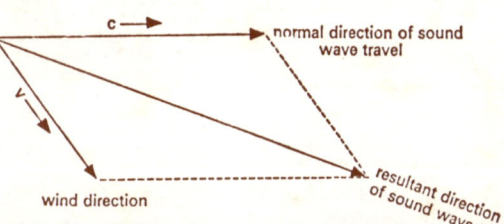

The effect of wind on the direction a sound wave travels

However, sometimes more important is the effect of wind and temperature variations with altitude. The atmosphere is never completely still and of equal temperature at all altitudes. Many people will have noticed that it is difficult to hear upwind, quite apart from the fact that wind noise itself is present to mask the sound one is listening to. Some people put this down to the fact that the wind is 'blowing' the sound back, but this is not quite true unless the wind reaches the speed of sound, in which case you would not be standing there.

Wind has several effects on sound, the first being a simple matter of velocity vectors. Figure 32 shows the case of a sound wave travelling upwind at a slight angle, and the parallelogram law is used to work the resultant direction and velocity. The other effect that wind has on sound propagation is due to the fact that wind speed near to the ground tends to be lower than that higher up. This means that the sound travelling upwind will have a greater overall velocity close to the ground.

TAPE RECORDERS - P.Spring.
pp208; £2.25; Focal Press 1967.

Tape recorders have got more things to
go wrong than most sound equipment; this
is a straight, fairly non-technical run
through their mechanics and electronics.

It is of utmost importance for the pressure roller to be perfectly parallel with the capstan spindle.

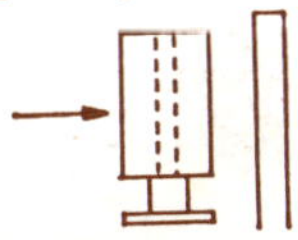

FIGURE 45
The pressure roller must be quite parallel to the drive spindle.

FIGURE 46
When the pressure roller is at an angle to the drive spindle, then the tape moves to the point of maximum pressure.

A good estimation of whether or not the pressure roller is parallel to the capstan can be obtained by moving the pressure roller against the capstan until only a thin hairline is separating the two. Any gross maladjustment of either the pressure roller or the capstan spindle is then quite obvious.

Where the pressure roller is not parallel to the capstan spindle, then a pressure gradient will result from top to bottom and the tape will have the tendency of travelling towards the point of maximum pressure. If the tape rises then the pressure roller is leaning towards the capstan spindle, if the tape falls then the pressure roller is leaning away from it.

The tape moves to the point of maximum pressure.

An incorrect alignment not only leads to the tape travelling up or down, but one edge of the tape also has a tendency to bulge out while passing the capstan spindle.

FIGURE 47
Where the pressure roller is not parallel to the drive spindle, then the tape bulges and twists before or after leaving the drive spindle.

TAPE BELCHES AND TWISTS

Speakers are the easiest part
of a hi-fi system to build
yourself. They're also dead
easy to build badly. If you
want a good simple cheap
design look in the back of the
Mullard book 'Do it Yourself
Stereo', which tells you how
to build a pair of speakers
for £12-14. You'll get better
quality from the Goodmans DIN
20 kit - about £9-10 from
discount dealers. If you want
bigger speakers, the KEF B139
or Goodmans 12" are both OK.
A useful book about the details
of building cabinets is
'Cabinet Handbook' by G.A.Briggs (pub. Rank Wharfedale)
More technical - 'Loudspeakers' by E.J.Jordan (Focal
Press).
Note about stereo radio. If you fancy grooving to
Sounds of the Seventies in staggering stereo, check the
following :-
1)You need a good radio, or more properly a tuner,
   plus some sort of aerial. See 'Practical Aerial
   Handbook' by G.J.King.
2)You need a stereo decoder. Motorola have just
   produced a new, simple good one. (See Wireless
   World July 1972). Motorola MC 1310P plus printed
circuit board and components £3.50 post free from Fi-Comp
Electronics, Burton Road, Derby DE6 6GY.

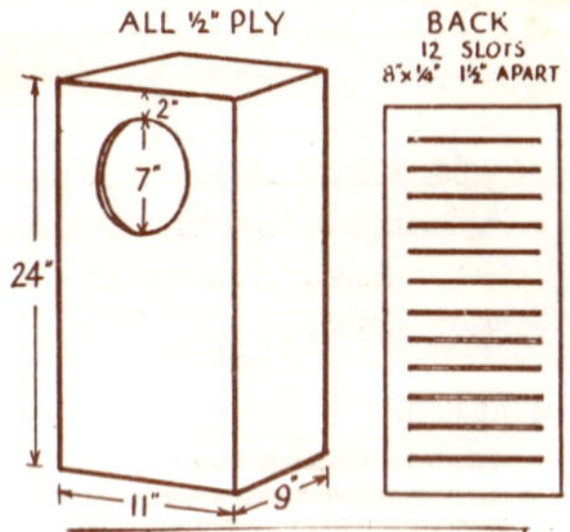

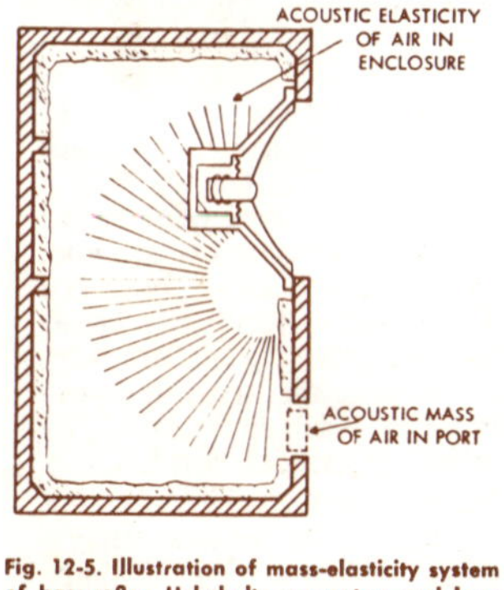

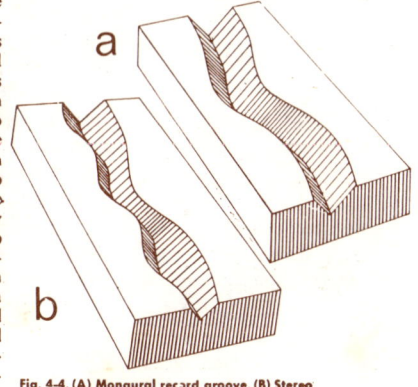

DP Cabinet suitable for all types of 8" unit.
Materials: ½" plywood lined on all four sides with 1" absorbent. Back lined with soft woollen cloth.
Weight: 14 lb. approx.

From 'Cabinet Handbook'

Fig. 12-5. Illustration of mass-elasticity system of bass-reflex Helmholtz resonator, and how it couples the rear of the speaker cone to the outside.

REPRODUCTION OF SOUND.
E.Villchur.
pp92; 50p; Dover 1965.

If you can't tell an
impedance from a
frequency responce -
and you want to be able
to, this is the book.
Sound systems in simple
language.

C12

The simplest way to describe the single-groove stereo disc recording system is to say that the left channel is recorded on one side of the groove and the right channel on the other. In terms of the familiar lateral needle motion this does not make sense, since the two groove walls cannot simultaneously give different directions to the needle with regard to lateral motion. If we take into account, however, the fact that the needle is free to move both laterally and vertically we will see that the two groove walls *can* give different directions to the needle tip. The needle can respond to these dissimilar pushes by a single motion which includes a vertical component—the resultant motion will be diagonal. This complex motion contains both left and right channel information, which can be unscrambled back into separate signals by a stereo pickup.

Fig. 4-4. (A) Monaural record groove. (B) Stereo record groove in which the left and right walls contain different information.

THE LORE AND LANGUAGE OF SCHOOLCHILDREN
I.&P. Opie.
pp483; 62½p; O.U.P. 1959.

Records of child culture based on the records collected
by the Opies from all over Britain.

THE teacher's lot, as every schoolboy knows, is an easy one:

God made the bees,
The bees make honey;
We do the work,
The teacher gets the money.

It is considered only right, if a teacher is uncongenial, to show dis-approval. 'If a master has been beastly we put drawing pins on his chair, then we glue his books to the table, then we swing smelly sock in front of his nose by cotton looped through the window-catch and a boy operates the cotton.' Thus a 14-year-old, and a form-mate has written 'TRUE' beside the contribution; but the usual forms of retribution, pranks long prescribed by custom, tend to be safer for the perpetrators. There is the artful trick of 'filling the waste paper basket and fixing so that master knocks it over. Everybody scrambles to pick it up.' There is the old revenge of wetting the blackboard chalk. There is the room-evacuating stench produced when carbide is added to the ink; and the nice disruption caused by thistledown which mysteriously continues to fill the air after every window in the classroom has been shut. There is the ingenious but not always successful trick of throwing scraps of wet blotting-paper on to the ceiling, above where the teacher is to sit, in the hope that they will descend when class is in progress. There is the perpetual buzzing of a bluebottle which nobody can find because its match-box cage is pocketed when the teacher comes near. And there are the flies, delicately harnessed—in a secret manner handed down from one generation to the next—which circle round the classroom trailing insubstantial lengths of black cotton across the line of vision. Tradition (many teachers may feel) could be more discriminating in the skills it chooses to perpetuate.

---

a Pelican Book

How Children Learn
John Holt

a Pelican Book

How Children Fail
John Holt

HOW CHILDREN LEARN
pp176; 25p; Penguin
1970.
HOW CHILDREN FAIL
pp176; 25p; Penguin
1969.
Both by John Holt.

A microscopic look
at the mechanisms
of learning in child-
ren, and how we can
pressurize them into
failure.

10 May 1958

Children are often quite frank about the strategies they use to get answers out of a teacher. I once observed a class in which the teacher was testing her students on parts of speech. On the blackboard she had three columns, headed Noun, Adjective, and Verb. As she gave each word, she called on a child and asked in which column the word belonged.

Like most teachers, she hadn't thought enough about what she was doing to realize, first, that many of the words given could fit into more than one column; and secondly, that it is often the way a word is used that determines what part of speech it is.

There was a good deal of the tried-and-true strategy of *guess-and-look*, in which you start to say a word, all the while scrutinizing the teacher's face to see whether you are on the right track or not. With most teachers no further strategies are needed. This one was more poker-faced than most, so *guess-and-look* wasn't working very well. Still, the percentage of hits was remarkably high, especially since it was clear to me from the way the children were talking and acting that they hadn't a notion of what Nouns, Adjectives, and Verbs were. Finally one child said, 'Miss —, you shouldn't point to the answer each time.' The teacher was surprised, and asked what she meant. The child said, 'Well, you don't exactly *point*, but you kind of stand next to the answer.' This was no clearer, since the teacher had been standing still. But after a while, as the class went on, I thought I saw what the girl meant. Since the teacher wrote each word down in its proper column, she was, in a way, getting herself ready to write, pointing herself at the place where she would soon be writing. From the angle of her body to the black-board the children picked up a subtle clue to the correct answer.

THE OPEN CLASSROOM - Herbert R.Kohl.
pp116; 70p; Methuen 1970.

When you read this book you realise that Kohl made the same mistakes and had the same problems when he started to teach. A call for humanity and relevance in the classroom.

SCHOOL IS A FIGMENT OF THE IMAGINATION WANDERING PURPOSELESSLY AROUND FROM CLASS ROOM TO CLASS ROOM I REPEAT: SCHOOL IS A FIGMENT OF THE IMAGINATION IT MAKES A LOVELY CHORUS FOR A HORRIBLE HORRIBLE SONG SCHOOL IS A FIGMENT OF THE IMAGINATION AND BESIDES THAT ITS BEGINNING TO BE TRUE.

Michaele Lundberg   HA!

Our schools are crazy. They do not serve the interests of adults, and they do not serve the interests of young people. They teach "objective" knowledge and its corollary, obedience to authority. They teach avoidance of conflict and obeisance to tradition in the guise of history. They teach equality and democracy while castrating students and controlling teachers. Most of all they teach people to be silent about what they think and feel, and worst of all, they teach people to pretend that they are saying what they think and feel. To try to break away from stupid schooling is no easy matter for teacher or student. It is a lonely and long fight to escape from believing that one needs to do what people say one should do and that one ought to be the person one is expected to be. Yet to make such an escape is a step toward beginning again and becoming the teachers we never knew we could be.

There are huge quantities of equipment of all sorts lying around schools, colleges, and universities. Explore possibilities of their use, although give is usually needed as well as take.

An entry into these facilities is available through City and Guilds Day and Evening classes. Check your local tech college, talk to tutors about joining DI class, and thus using all that equipment that just lies around for 90% of the time.

AUTOMOBILE TIRES

FARALLONES SCRAPBOOK.
pp144; £2.20;
Farallones 1971.
(or from Books)

Ask, and ye shall be given. If you're in education at any level and you want materials of any kind, pick up the phone and start asking around. You'll be amazed at what you get.

Farallones, a group in California work in this way, using cheap materials to create new teaching/play environments in and outside the classroom. Plenty of good ideas.

Man has yet to figure out a decent way to rid himself of the over abundance of used automobile tires. Yet, automobile tires are a natural for the playground with their push, pull, stretch, bounce qualities. We have only designed one piece of playground equipment (the Tire Toy) specifically using tires but we have seen them used in quite a variety of ways (swings, mounds, nets, etc.), and all utilize the same basic joining techniques.

Tires can be found in abundance at many local gas stations, recapping factories, and junk yards and are usually given away absolutely free for the asking. Tires come in a variety of rim and tread sizes and joining operations are somewhat easier if rim sizes are kept constant. Care should also be taken to avoid tires which are worn through to the cord as these tires tear quite easily -- conversely, the more tread the better.

There are two basic joining techniques which we have been experimenting with. The first involves encasing lengths of chain in rubber hose, looping the chain around the tires and closing the loop off with a repair link. (We've never tried it without the hose casing, but you might find that you can get by with just the chains.) In most cases 700# test chain will be sufficient. This however, requires that you do a little figuring beforehand so that you can do most of the chain cutting at the hardware store. If you choose to do the chain cutting on site, heavy duty bolt

and rod cutters are advisable. (Rope used in a similar fashion has proven to be a rather nice substitute.)

The other technique uses a hole punched thru the tire wall plus bolts, metal washers, and tire washers as the connector. Holes should be punched with a diameter slightly smaller than that of the bolt as the tire will easily stretch to fit. Be careful to place the hole as close to the edge of the tread surface as this is the thickest part of the tire. Punching operations will go quite easily if the tire is set over a 2X4 stake for support.

The tire washers are made by cutting up an extra tire into two inch squares and punching a hole in the center. The most effective tool we've found for cutting the tire squares is a pair of metal sheers made by Weiss called M-3's.

Start with a 1/4 X 3 1/4 inch bolt; a metal washer; then a rubber washer and put it thru from the inside of the first tire. Push the bolt thru to the other tire; another rubber washer; a metal washer; the nut; and tighten. To keep the nut in place it is best to use lock nuts, epoxy glue, or score the bolt threads after the nut has been tightened down. Drain holes should also be provided so that rain water can escape.

We've experimented with both joining techniques and the first joining method is the quicker of the two. However, it is usually about twice as expensive.

CHAIN OR ROPE CONNECTION

PUNCHED HOLE AND BOLT CONNECTION

BEE (Bulletin of Environmental Education)
Monthly; £2 p.a.
From Education Unit, Town and Country Planning Association, 17, Carlton House Terrace, London. SW1 5AS.

Essential monthly inventory of resources and ideas for those teaching about the environment.

Dear BEE,

My fourth year leavers are planning a playground for infants and juniors. Can you suggest some books which will give them ideas and technical details?

BEE replies :

Best to send them out first to watch the way younger children play and report on the way children use the objects to be found in their environment. There are several very good copiously illustrated books to be found in the public library :

PLANNING FOR PLAY by Lady Allen of Hurtwood (Thames & Hudson 1968 £2.10)

ENVIRONMENTAL PLANNING FOR CHILDREN'S PLAY by Arvid Bengtsson (Crosby Lockwood 1970 £4.50)

CHILDREN'S PLAY : A STUDY OF NEEDS AND OPPORTUNITIES by Anthea Holme & Peter Massie (Michael Joseph £3.25)

NEW PLAYGROUNDS by Lady Allen of Hurtwood (Housing Centre Trust, 13 Suffolk Street, London SW1   37½p plus 3p postage)

DESIGN FOR PLAY by Lady Allen of Hurtwood, now out of print but obtainable in libraries.

PLAYGROUNDS by W D Abernethy (National Playing Fields Association, 57b Catherine Place, London SW1 30p plus 5p postage). This excellent little book is one of a series published by the NPFA.

CARD SLIDE RULE from Tarquin Publications, Stradbroke, Diss, Norfolk.

Slide rules liberate maths. Start early with throwaway 6½p rule from Tarquin.

D2

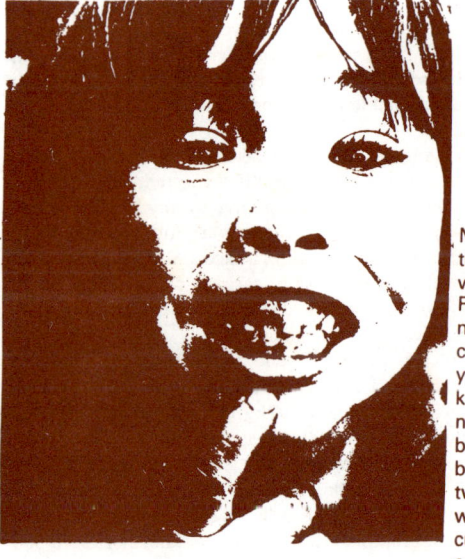

NEILL AND SUMMERHILL-A MAN AND
HIS WORK   A pictorial study by
John Walmsley 35p.
Penguin Education 1969

Pics and words of the old
guru and his kids.

Not so very long ago he said to me, 'The only
thing I regret in my life is that I didn't sin more
when I was young.'   *Willa Muir*
From time to time everybody in the school had
nicknames and diminutives. But Neill was very
conscientious, and always addressed you by
your proper first name. Other staff, if they
knew you well, might call you by your
nickname. But Neill never risked it – not
because he didn't want to be matey, but
because he knew nicknames are very often
two-edged, and can be given you against your
will, something you really hate. He was at once
curiously aware and yet unaware of what went
on in the school.   *David Barton*

What strikes you immediately, coming from
the world outside and talking to the kids at
Summerhill, is that you can't tell the boys
from the girls. This is important. It's not just
hair styles and jeans. The girls are so self-
reliant and the boys so concerned, the girls
so calmly tough and the boys so gentle. No
boy's voice has that conditioned flick of
off-handedness that says, 'I am male.' They
are interested voices, friendly and lightly
generous, and their bodies are not tautly
aggressive but trusting. You are startled
when you hear their names. You begin to
wonder how early children are warped in the
world outside, dumped straight from the
cradle on to one side of the line they must
never step over, separated from one another
and from their complete selves, permanently
angered. Neill once said, at a progressive
school conference, listening to them talk
about how to keep the boys from the girls
and pressed for his opinion, 'Why don't you
put up barbed wire?'   *Leila Berg*

Learning, in its essentials, is not a
distinct and separate process. It is a function of growth. We took
it quite seriously in this light, and found ourselves getting more
and more involved in individual lives. It seems likely to me that
the actual features of this involvement may prove useful to other
people. At the same time, I would like to try to account for the
fact that almost all of our children improved markedly, and
some few spectacularly. We were obviously doing something
right, and I would like to hazard a few guesses at what it might
have been. All instruction was individual, and that was obviously a factor. The improvement I am speaking of, however,
was not simply a matter of learning, but of radical changes in
character. Where Vincente had been withdrawn and destructive,
he became an eager participant in group activities and ceased
destroying everything he touched. Both Eléna and Maxine had
been thieves and were incredibly rebellious. After several months
they could be trusted and had become imaginative and responsible contributors at school meetings. Such changes as these are
not accomplished by instruction. They proceed from broad environmental causes. Here again, details which may seem irrele-
vant to the business of a school will give the reader an idea of
what these causes may have been. A better way of saying this is
that the business of a school is not, or should not be, mere instruction, but the life of the child.

LIVES OF CHILDREN
George Dennison
pp242; 45p Penguin 1972
The story of the
The story of the first
street school in the US.
Its foundation,day-to-
day activities, problems,
failures and successes.

LIVES OF CHILDREN

THE STORY OF THE FIRST STREET SCHOOL

GEORGE DENNISON

PENGUIN EDUCATION SPECIALS

22 December 1964

I wanted to take José and Vicente out to do some reading in the
street – store signs, street signs, etc. Kenzo raised such a fuss
that I took him, too, against my better judgement. He reads
better than they do, and they can't stand the competition. I made
a strict rule that each take his turn, otherwise (I knew) Kenzo
would be answering all the time. Kenzo read a sign – LICENSED
PLUMBER – not without difficulty; and then José failed to read
FOR RENT. Kenzo cried gloatingly, 'I see what you mean!' A
few minutes later he was whispering the 'answers' to José and
Vicente, trying to con everyone. José and Vicente, and I, too,
heartily wished he wasn't there.

Jose spoke today of his lack of knowledge. It was his first
direct admission of the shame he has always felt. He told me –
looking away and almost hanging his head – that he had gone to
school in Puerto Rico and was learning to read. When they first
moved to this country, it had been he who had read his father's
postcards, since his mother cannot read. But he said he had for-
gotten. I told him that when he could read English well, he
would be able to read Spanish, too.

The dodge-ball game was ugly today – endless lying, argu-
ments, and the possibility of fights. The boys asked me to referee.
I have always refused in the past. I consented this time, and it
made matters worse. It occurred to me that if I left the room,
they would become more rational in order to play at all. I left
and listened from the hall, and it worked.

LOST FOR WORDS

LANGUAGE AND EDUCATIONAL FAILURE

LOST FOR WORDS
J.W.Patrick Creber
pp216; 45p Penguin 1972

The importance of language in the
development of thought processes,
and the educational failure which
results from linguistic deprivation.
Argues for a new emphasis to be
placed on spoken and written
language in schools.

Certainly there has been too often an effort to
keep the school somehow inviolate – uncontaminated by the
smut all around. And because it is based upon inadequate sym-
pathy and understanding, this effort is likely to be sterile. It is
hard to protect any child if you disapprove of him. When he
says: 'Well, Miss, 'e pissed off round the corner an' went ass-
avatip in t' sandpit!' – what reaction might one expect from a
teacher to this vivid communication? A glint of appreciative
humour? Such a reaction is rare in schools where teachers
attend, not to the message the child is seeking to convey, but to
the formal or surface characteristics of the language he uses to
convey it.

On the whole our adult's view of children's language has
focused too much upon its surface characteristics. In this connection one may note the valuable distinction that the celebrated
American linguist Chomsky has drawn between *competence*
and *performance*. When a child correctly uses a past tense,
Chomsky suggests, this may be only a matter of simple imita-
tion – we would be unwise to infer that the child understands
the use in question. He 'walked' is an example of a past tense
to be found in the performance level of many children and it is
to be carefully distinguished from, let us say, 'he "goed"' for a
walk'. At a superficial level, 'walked' is correct, 'goed' incorrect, yet it is the latter which we should see as evidence of effective learning. Fundamentally, Chomsky argued, 'goed'
demonstrates real *competence* for the child has not heard anyone say this but has constructed a tense inflection that reveals
his growing understanding of a rule. 'Walk on the other
hand, reflects normal *performance* but whethe   is evidence of
competence – of real understanding – we cannot tell, since we
have no means of measuring it. Chomsky's account may nevertheless afford some reassurance to parents irritated by children
making mistakes which they previously managed to avoid – for
instance the four year old who says 'buyed' when two years
earlier he said 'bought'!

NUFFIELD SCIENCE
Junior Science. pub. Collins.
Secondary Science. pub. Longmans (extracts
                                below,right)
Biology. pub. Longmans/Penguin
Chemistry. pub. Longmans/Penguin
Physics. pub. Longmans/Penguin
Mathematics. pub. Murray and Chambers
Advanced Biology. pub. Penguin
Advanced Chemistry. pub. Penguin
Advanced Physics. pub. Penguin

These books make me realise how crushingly
useless was the science served up at school,
hardly ever out of the lab, never looked
through a microscope, never shown that science
is really only another way of describing and
explaining the real world.
The Nuffield approach is based on observation
and experiment by the kids, with the emphasis
on direct experience right from the Junior
Science on up. It's also science about real
things and everyday life. Really good.
(Suggested by Pauline Storie)

red blood cell model
cut in half

blood cells seen against
a blue sky

white blood cell
model cut in half

The following productivity figures are average figures for Great Britain, and schools will find considerable variations from these in different localities. However, these figures will provide a basis on which work can start and enable useful comparisons to be made with figures obtained locally.

None of the figures quoted should be taken as exact in any way; they are simply rough guides to what might be expected. In particular, these figures should not be taken as applying to any other country where the agricultural productivity might be very much lower.

Beef 4 000 square metres of pasture will produce 180 kg of live-weight beast in a year. This will produce 99 kg of carcase, which will produce 69 kg of saleable beef which contains 14 kg of protein and approximately 240 000 kilocalories (1 000 megajoules).

Bread 4 000 square metres of arable land will produce 1 423 kg of wheat which will produce 1 169 kg of flour which will produce 1 587 kg of bread which will contain 127 kg of protein and approximately 3.8 million kilocalories (16 000 megajoules).

Milk 7 000 square metres of meadow will support a milking cow which will give 3 637 litres of milk a year, so 4 000 square metres of meadow will 'produce' 2 022 litres of milk a year which will contain 76 kg of protein and approximately 1.5 million kilocalories (6 300 megajoules).

Eggs 4 000 square metres of arable land will produce 1 423 kg of grain which will feed 278 laying hens for a month (thirty days). In that month they will lay 4 726 eggs which will contain 32 kg of protein and approximately 361 000 kilocalories (1 700 megajoules).

Potatoes 4 000 square metres of arable land will produce 7 823 kg of potatoes which contain 156 kg of protein and over 5 million kilocalories (21 000 megajoules).

a. A large picture could be made up on a green or brown background with a scale representation of the quantity of each food produced from the same area, together with an indication of the proportion of the product that is edible protein.

b. Similarly, the fuel value in megajoules (or kilocalories) of the produce of a hectare (10 000 square metres) of land can be found.

c. The exercise could be done in the reverse direction to find the area of land required to produce:
   i. 70 g of protein per day.
   ii. 12 MJ (3 000 kilocalories) per day.

SURPLUS BUYING AGENCY
Building A1,
University Park,
Nottingham NG7 2RD.

Another recycling setup,
this time for education-
al resources (although
of course all resources
are educational) Try and
persuade your LEA to join,
if they aren't too thick
to see the point.

J Materials

Araldite (cast)	10p/lb
Cork (sheet)	20p/lb
Paxolin	12p/lb
Perspex	8p/lb
Rubber Sheet	10p/lb
Veroboard Approx. 5'' x 2½''	10p ea.
or 12 for	£1
Formers (Paxolin) for Coil and Transformer Building	3p
Steel Tube 20'' x 1¼'' O.D. 1/16'' Wall ..	2p

Steel Tube M.S. Seamless 20'' x 1'' O.D. x 1/16''	2p
Steel Tube M.S. 30'' x ½'' O.D. x 1/16'' .	3p
Aluminium Offcuts Drilled Panels and sections	8p/lb
Plastic Offcuts	8p/lb
Teflon and polythene	10p/lb
Polythene Tube	1-4p per foot
Nylon Tube	2-4p per foot
Rolls Rubber Tape	5p

SCHOOL NATURE SCIENCE SOCIETY
List (SAE) from Publications
Officer, 44, Claremont Gardens,
Upminster RM14 1DN.

Simple books about living things
for unscientific minds of any age.

We realize, therefore, that a supply of water and a suitable temperature are both needed for germination. A less obvious condition is a supply of oxygen for respiration. Seeds buried very deeply in the soil remain dormant for many years; this is due to an insufficient supply of oxygen in the deeper levels of the soil. Also, in making a seed bed, one aim of the gardener is to have soil sufficiently porous to allow the penetration of the necessary air.

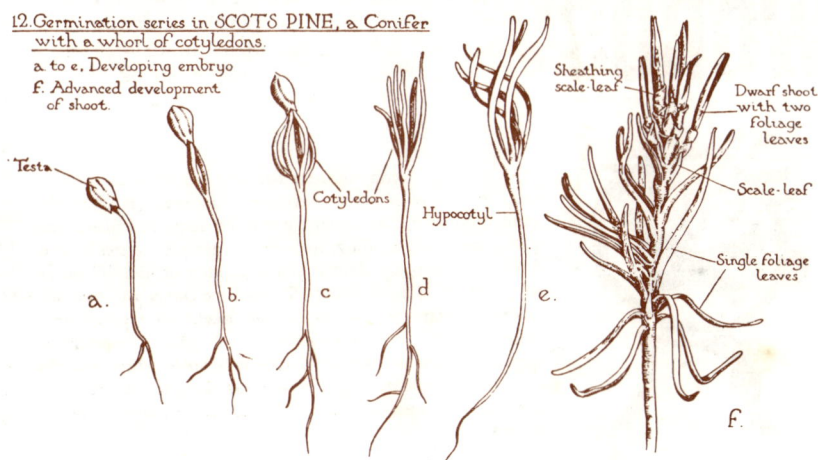

```
THE LAST WHOLE EARTH CATALOG
pp450; £1.75;
Penguin 1972.
```

I've hardly looked at my copies of Whole Earth Catalog
since starting work on this section of Scrapbook. Having
all but finished, and needing to write this, I've been
looking over them, and all that first excitement of
opening up a copy comes back.

It's difficult to pin down the significant things about
the Catalogs. There's obviously the appeal of quantity
and quality, of all that information, all those things you
never heard of, and that you'd never need, but that are
nice to know about anyway. That's a sort of coffee table
way of looking at it - ah, wow, toomuch stuff.

But besides the appeal of the arcane (good word IIC) what
grabbed me was the calm assumption that there were the
tools, there was the information, and that you got on
with it - page after page of an anybody-can-do-anything
philosophy which caught me and a lot of other people too.

Other good things - the feedback, which is an essential
element of any publication like this, and really good,
the fact that it stopped just when it was getting too
big, which is a lesson that could be usefully learned
by 99.94% of the world's socio-economic structures.
Whole Earth Catalog was right for a particular set of
people in a particular situation. The time it takes for
the organization to start dictating the content, instead
of vice versa is not very long, and Stewart Brand had the
sense to know this, and to cut the Catalog before it
started to get big and lumpy and nasty for people
reading it and people producing it.

Even so, the big last one is a bit much - the earlier
editions were about as much of the universe as I
could take in at one go - much more brain sized than
the final monster.

All in all, though, the Last Whole Earth Catalog is
a fantastic achievement and a fantastic tool - a living
proof of the idea that if you want to do it, you can.

Cut Wood Quick

A down-home idea: if you heat with wood and hence have
to cut up logs to size, you usually have 2 people at it, one
holding and feeding the log along a sawhorse while the other
cuts with the chainsaw. Instead try sinking say 12 posts in
the ground like this:

and throw the logs to be cut in between. Then just cut down
in one stroke and they're all done. Saves hours of nasty,
noisy work!

> Elias Velonis
> Glen Rock, N.J.

Cheap Firewood

Most lumber mills will sell slab leftovers--great stove size--in truck
loads for about $20. We get maple, birch and oak. We feel it is
better to buy from them to supplement the standing dead wood we
cut than to cut live trees. Also, Forestry Dept. will "sell" (free) lots
to anyone who wants to clean up, either after there has been
commercial lumbering or in anovercrowded or diseased area.
It is quite cold in Goshen (where we live) and we get a lot of snow.
We insulate the house with polyurethane and pile snow up along
the sides. It acts as insulation. We heat with three fire places and a
cook stove.

In this area, the old timers are very friendly and full of great information. One woman knows the woods intimately and can find
wild leeks, 12 kinds of mushrooms, herbs, berries, and vegetables.
Many have tales to tell and medicinal "secrets" to impart to the
interested.

We have a friend with female goats and the deer bucks are very
interested. We hear they will mate and are interested to find if that
is true. Anyone know what the product would be called? Geer Doat!

> Peace,
> Steve and Boston Gallo
> Geoffrey Byron
> Erik Celeborn   } our babies
> Dawn Galadriel
> Brandon, Vt.

4 Foot Bubbles

*I'd like to recommend for review a publication of the
Franklin Institue titled "True Plastic Bubbles and How to
Blow Them". It's done by the same people who caused such
a stir about a year ago with their giant long-lasting soap
bubbles. The resulting excitement inspired them to greater
heights. This report tells how to blow bubbles up to 4 feet
in diameter! The bubbles are tough, waterproof, and being
made of plastic film, have an indefinite life span. The
report gives brochures and sources for materials. Ask for
"Plastic Bubbles Report" (No. 1) available from the
Franklin Institue, 21st and the Parkway, Philadelphia, Pa.--
$1.00*

> *John Prenis*
> *Utica, NY*

Mercury Seeds?

Could you send me or publish in your (my) next issue of WEC a
list of seed companies who both do and don't coat their seed with
Mercury as a bacteria control agent.
I think this would be of great importance to all those paranoid
about Mercury poisoning and/or organic growing.

> Love,
> William Harrison
> New Hope, Pa.

Dye Kill?

In your July Supplement on p.12 you have a list of "39 Ways to
Save the Earth". The 1st one is to avoid use of colored facial
tissues etc. because the dye forms a residue in water.—On pages 8
and 9 there are several letters printed with advice on dying cloth.
I would like to know about the effects of left-over Tintex-Rit or
Procion dyes which are dumped down the drain when dying is
finished on the water supply. Surely they form residues too.
Or don't they?
What can the home-dyer do about it?

> Carolyn Hendricks
> 199 Dolores No.7
> San Francisco, Ca. 94103

Edlie's Flyer

*Beginners in electronics who don't want to be stuck with
very beautiful but very unusable gadgets (and also experts
who know what's-used-for-what) can get a lot of value from
industrial (civilian) surplus electronics, these days.*

*For the "consumer" uses of electronics—music, p.a.,
TV, repair parts and instruments, experimenting—Edlie
Electronics has the best selection and the lowest prices of
any mail-order dealer I have found.*

*They handle everything from hi-fi components (e.g. an
FM tuner from a discontinued console) to single resistors.
Some of it is new, and some of it is sold "as is" (e.g. small
radios and tape recorders returned to the store under a
warranty).*

*If you don't feel safe about repair work or experiments,
though, better concentrate on getting electronic stuff with
a dependable guarantee, maybe by buying from a repair
shop.*

[Suggested and Reviewed by John Huntley]

Edlie's Flyer Catalog

free

from:
Edlie Electronics, Inc.
2700 Hempstead Turnpike
Levittown, Long Island,
New York 11756

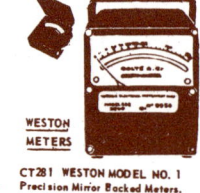

**CT628 CLAIRE STEPPING
RELAYS MODEL 26** (removed
from brand new chassis -- similar
to picture). 26 positions, 10 poles.
24-36 volts.
Price only $8.95

**CT629 CLAIRE STEPPING
RELAYS TYPE 211.** 11 positions,
6 poles. 24-36 volts.
Price $3.95

CT630 TELEPHONE RELAY.
24-36 V. 2500 ohms. No. 37 E.C.
2 sets of contacts: one set 2P, 3T.
second set 2P, 4 T.
Price 65¢

**CT631 WESTERN UNION TEL.
CO. CHASSIS.** Consists of 1 -
No. 26 Relay (as listed above); 3 -
No. 211 Relays (as listed above)
1 - No. 37 E.C. Relay (as listed
above.) Comes mounted on a brand
new chassis.
**Bargain Price for Complete
Chassis (including 5 relays)
only $18.95**

WESTON METERS

**CT281 WESTON MODEL NO. 1
Precision Mirror Backed Meters.**
A) D.C. Voltmeter, dual scale, fan
type 0-75, 0-150 D.C. Volts.
Price $37.50
B) D. C. Voltmeter, Triple Scale,
0-150, 0-300, 0-750 Volts D.C.
Price $41.50

CT548 TRANSDUCER 200 K.C.
Made by Brush. Brand new. For use
with Marine Depth Finder Equipment
or experimental purposes.
Price only $2.95

E1

DOMINATE CONCEPTS

1 Universe
2 Humanity
3 Children
4 Teleology
5 Reform the Environment
6 General Systems Theory
7 Industrialization
8 Design Science
9 World Service Industries
10 Ephemeralization and Invisible Commonwealth
11 Prime Design Initiative
12 Self-Disciplines
13 Comprehensive Coordination
14 World Community and Subcommunities of World Man

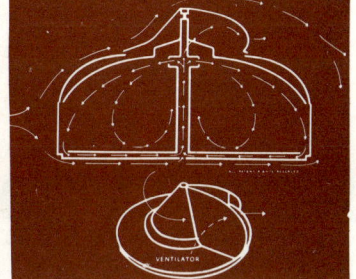
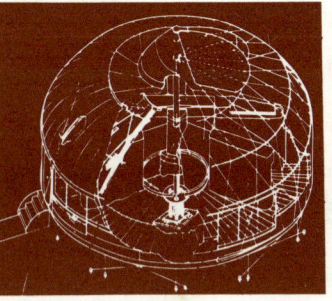

Above – Dymaxion Dwelling Unit by Fuller
BUCKMINSTER FULLER

Bucky, the wizard of us.

Books by Buckminster Fuller. (All US publishers, except where indicated. You can probably get them all from good bookshops if you ask around enough.)
*Education Automation. Southern Illinois UP 1963.
*No More Secondhand God " " "
*Ideas and Integrities Prentice-Hall 1963.
*Nine Chains to the Moon. Doubleday Anchor 1963.
        (1st. pub. 1938)
*Untitled Epic Poem on the History of Industrialization. From Box909, Carbondale, Illinois 62901.
*Operating Manual for Spaceship Earth. SIUP 1969.
*Utopia or Oblivion. (Extracts left) Allen Lane,
        1970, pp416, £3.00.
*Buckminster Fuller Reader. ed. Meller. Penguin 1972
        75p.
*I Seem to be a Verb. Bantam. 1970
*Approaching the Benign Environment. pp128; 45p;
        Collier Macmillan 1971.
Also Dymaxion World of Buckminster Fuller – Robert Marks, a good book about Fuller and his ideas SIUP.
World Design Science Decade Documents Nos. 1-4 Obtainable from World Resources Inventory, Box 909, Carbondale, Illinois 62901. Document 5 is in Utopia or Oblivion, Doc. 6 is published as The Ecological Context, by John McHale, Brazillier NY.

Figure 24   Insideness and outsideness of systems

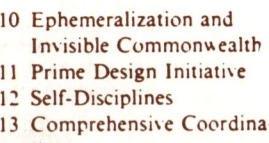

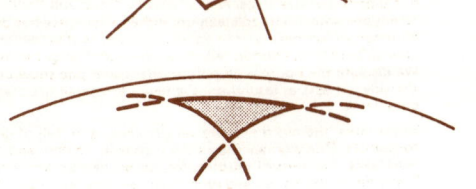

A triangle drawn on the earth's surface is actually a spherical triangle bounded by great circle arcs.

The area apparently 'outside' one triangle is seen 'inside' the other. Because every spherical surface has two aspects – convex if viewed from outside, concave if from within – each of these triangles is, in itself, two triangles.

Concept 12 – Self-disciplines

Working assumptions, cautions, encouragements, and restraints of intuitive formulations and spontaneous actions. My own rule: 'Do not mind if I am not understood as long as I am not misunderstood.'

Personal Self-Discipline. In 1927 I gave up for ever the general economic dictum of society, i.e., that every individual who wants to survive must *earn a living.* I substituted, therefore, the finding made in concept 1, i.e., the *individual's antientropic responsibility* in universe. I sought for the tasks that needed to be done that no one else was doing or attempting to do, which if done would physically and economically advantage society and eliminate pain.

As a consequence, it was necessary for me to discipline my faculties to develop technical and scientific capability to invent the physical innovations and their service industry logistics.

My recommendations for a curriculum of design science:

1 Synergetics
2 General systems theory
3 Theory of games (Von Neumann)
4 Chemistry and physics
5 Topology, projective geometry
6 Cybernetics
7 Communications
8 Meteorology
9 Geology
10 Biology
11 Sciences of energy
12 Political geography
13 Ergonomics
14 Production engineering

*Dymaxion Maps (above) available in various sizes and types - climate, cities etc. from Box 909 (as above).
*World Game Series Document $4.50 inc. post from Box 909.
*Films of the man talking about the World Game; ten in all, available from VPS Film Library, 269, Kingston Road, London SW19 3NR.

Glyn Thompson

63 Another detail from an experiment with vortices. A pair of vortices, the one on the right turning in a clockwise direction and the one on the left in an anticlockwise direction. This experiment is also audible.

CYMATICS
Hans Jenny
pp183; £7.50
Basilius Presse,
Basle,Switzerland,
1967

Words aren't much use when you're describing this one, a real mind-blowing study of oscillations and rythmns in solids and liquids.
    If you're into a D'Arcy Thompson world of growth, form and pattern, this book will really stretch your tesselations.

Wherever we look in Nature, animate or inanimate, we see widespread evidence of periodic systems. These systems show a continuously repeated change from one set of conditions to another opposite set. This repetition of polar phases occurs alike in systematized and patterned elements and in processes and series of events. A few examples may be mentioned in brief. The great systems of the circulation and respiration are virtually controlled by such natural periods or rhythms. Inspiration and expiration of the lungs, systole and diastole of the heart are only these basic rhythmic processes writ large. In the nervous system the impulses occur serially and may therefore be described as frequencies. Much the same applies to the active muscle system which is actually in a state of vibration. The more closely one examines these functions, the more evident do these recurrent sequences become. Events, then, do not take place in a continuous sequence, in a straight line, but are in a continual state of vibration, oscillation, undulation and pulsation. This also holds good of systematized structures. On the largest and smallest scale, we find serial elements, repetitive patterns, and the number of fibre stromata, space lattices, and reticulations is legion. And if we turn our eyes to the great natural domains, periodicity expands to include the ocean itself. The whole vegetable kingdom, for instance, is a gigantic example of recurrent elements, an endless formation of tissues on a macroscopic, microscopic and electron microscopic scale. Indeed, there is something of a periodic nature in the very concept of a tissue.

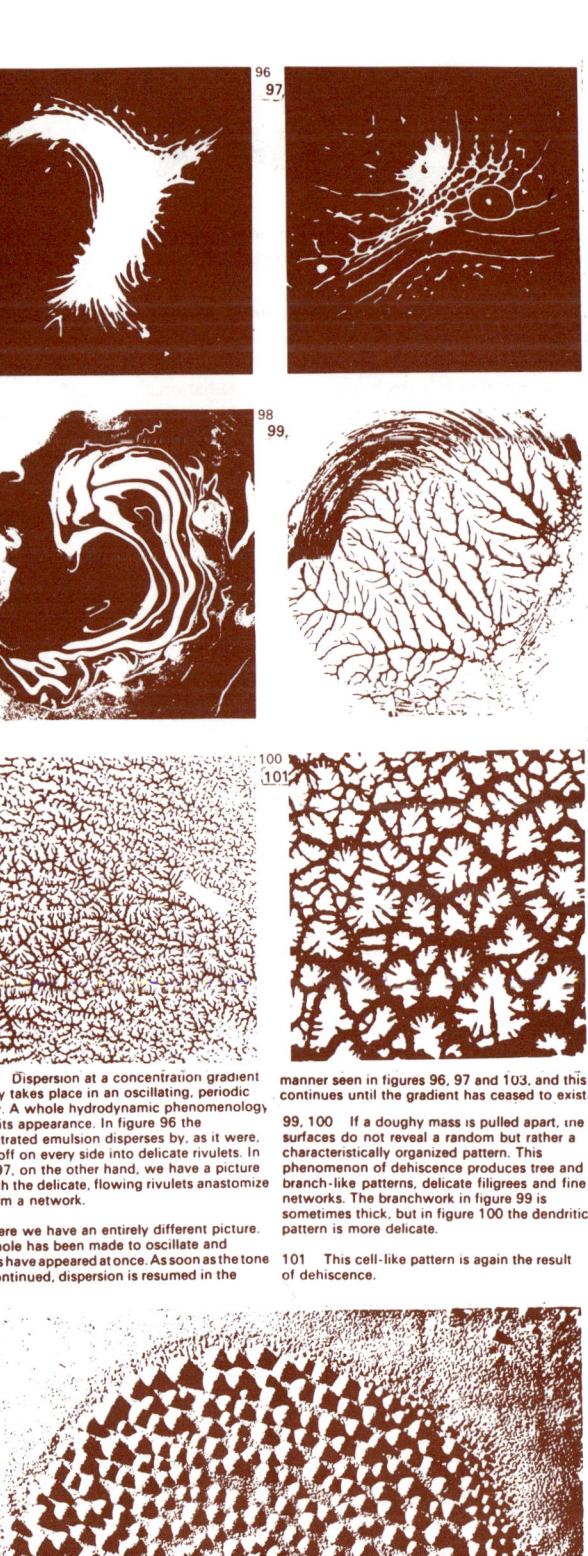

96, 97 Dispersion at a concentration gradient similarly takes place in an oscillating, periodic manner. A whole hydrodynamic phenomenology makes its appearance. In figure 96 the concentrated emulsion disperses by, as it were, tailing off on every side into delicate rivulets. In figure 97, on the other hand, we have a picture in which the delicate, flowing rivulets anastomize and form a network.

98 Here we have an entirely different picture. The whole has been made to oscillate and vortices have appeared at once. As soon as the tone is discontinued, dispersion is resumed in the

manner seen in figures 96, 97 and 103, and this continues until the gradient has ceased to exist.

99, 100 If a doughy mass is pulled apart, the surfaces do not reveal a random but rather a characteristically organized pattern. This phenomenon of dehiscence produces tree and branch-like patterns, delicate filigrees and fine networks. The branchwork in figure 99 is sometimes thick, but in figure 100 the dendritic pattern is more delicate.

101 This cell-like pattern is again the result of dehiscence.

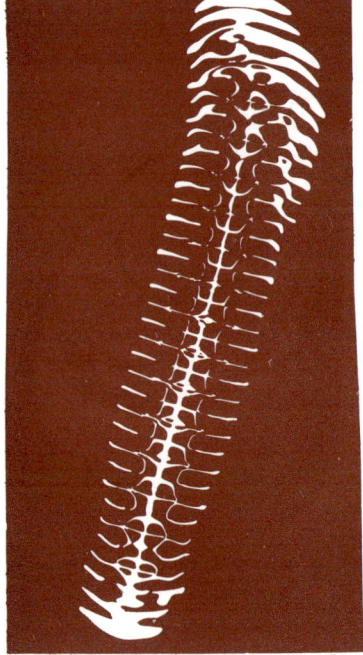

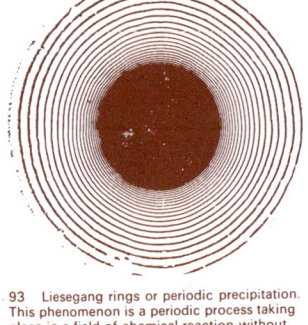

93 Liesegang rings or periodic precipitation. This phenomenon is a periodic process taking place in a field of chemical reaction without vibration. The salt silver chromate is precipitated in regular concentric zones which proceed from the centre to the periphery.

→ Acoustic irradiation transforms the uniform layer of lycopodium powder into a number of round shapes. Each of these rotates on its own axis and at the same time circulates in a constant manner round the whole figure.

← As in figure 44 a layer of glycerine has been made to vibrate by a tone acting upon a diaphragm. The result is a continuous formal pattern.

E3

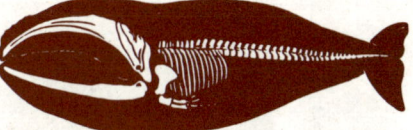

FIG. 37.15 Skeleton of a whale, showing extreme readaptation of the mammalian skeleton to serve an aquatic existence.

It has long been known that nearly all the energy for driving the earth's wind systems is supplied to the air by the sun-warmed tropical oceans which absorb the infrared radiation. Studies of the trade wind clouds in the Caribbean, in relation to heat and moisture, and studies of disturbances of the trade wind currents and the growth of tropical hurricanes in the Pacific, have shown that the energy that powers the atmospheric engine comes mainly from the evaporation, by the sun, of surface water in tropical seas. This water vapor, with its store of latent heat, is carried aloft and borne by trade winds for great distances. The vapor then recondenses as liquid drops to form clouds and finally rain, and the energy is released again as heat. Much of the heat energy is reradiated back into space; some of it drives the winds themselves; and some is carried to cooler regions. As a result the sun's heat in the tropics actually produces a cooling system in equatorial regions and a warming system elsewhere, and also produces the wind transportation system between one region and another. Thus the wind and water cycle work together to reduce regional temperature differences and to produce relatively stable climatic circumstances.

BIOLOGY IN ACTION - N.J.Berril.
pp894; £3.00
Heinemann Education 1967.

A knowledge of living things is basic. If you missed out on it in school, here's the book to catch up with - a good fat general biology book, with plenty of pictures.

FIG. 28.4 Bipedal stance: Goose stepping and standing so that center of gravity is either brought over the foot when only one is on the ground or is in line between the two feet when both are on the ground.

TEETH AND SURVIVAL

The evolution of teeth has played a great role not only in the evolution of horses, and in fact in the evolution of vertebrates as a whole, but because of their hardness and consequent survival as fossils, teeth have often been the main key to deciphering the fossil record (Fig. 38.1).

So far as the animal itself is concerned the teeth have a double significance. An animal can feed and live only until its teeth wear out. Fish and reptiles have no problem in this respect since replacement of old teeth by new continues indefinitely. Birds bypass the issue by having no teeth at all and are able to maintain the horny beak with ease. Mammals have reduced their tooth replacement to a single occasion—the replacement of the milk teeth of the small jaws of the very young by the one and only set of permanent teeth. With the exception of man, when these teeth wear out, the animal dies of starvation no matter how healthy its body may have been until then.

As a general rule larger animals live much longer than small ones. Their teeth must therefore be correspondingly large to serve their immediate function and must also endure for periods corresponding to the potential life span of the animal. With the exception of elephants, even the largest mammals become senescent and die in their third decade, and at the end of twenty years or so of incessant use, most mammalian teeth have had their day. Elephants, which may live four times as long and must continue to eat, have huge complex molars for grinding heavy vegetation.

PARABLE OF THE BEAST - John N.Bleibtreu.
pp283; 60p; Paladin 1968.
(the hardback edition, published by Gollancz, has got a few pictures in it.)

Parables of the animal world that we try to pretend not to belong to. Bleibtreu says '.... the purpose of a parable is to expand the imagination, not to contract it. The book works.

It is true not only of animal populations, but of human populations as well, that when hostile circumstances press upon the community, they seem only to strengthen the communal bonds of co-operation. A large part of that sentimental nostalgia that attaches to the American frontier stems from the sense of communal solidarity that prevails in any frontier settlement. One can even imagine that human societies began to evolve in response to just those frightful kinds of climactic conditions described by Kropotkin, which must have prevailed during the succession of glacial periods of the Pleistocene, during which mankind and its early social institutions were formed.

It is unfortunate that in the recent temperate-zone history of mankind, the mold of crisis, which casts societies into cohesive forms, was not so much provided by the natural environment, as it was by the artifice of human war. Several times in this century we have seen nationalist politicians flay their peoples into communal frenzies by creating war threats for the express purpose of welding the mass of individuals into a cohesive unit.

Strong remnants of neo-Darwinian logic still persist in the doctrines espoused by various military philosophers. Terrorism is still believed (according to political pragmatists) to be an effective device for demoralizing an enemy. Though this experimental situation has been tried again and again during this century, it has not yet succeeded in its hoped-for effects. None of the major population centers, bombed so mercilessly by both sides (with conventional explosives) in World War II, collapsed into demoralization as a result of that bombing. One might call it the "Job Effect"—the more a community is afflicted by suffering, the more it seems sustained by this affliction, the more capable it seems to be of sustaining still more, right up to the point of total physical destruction. It seems that in cases of disaster, either man-made or natural, that the communal nature of communities is reinforced, given a new and viable vitality.

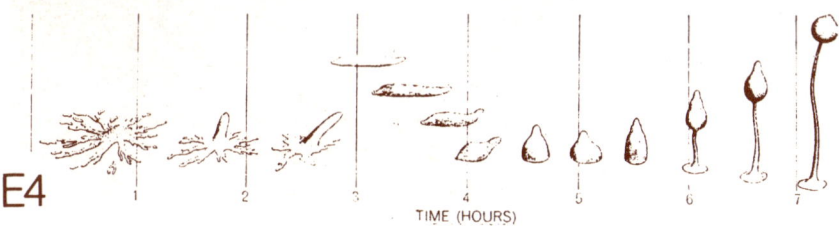

TIME (HOURS)

The life cycle of a colony of slime mould amoeba from aggregation to culmination. (from hardback edition)

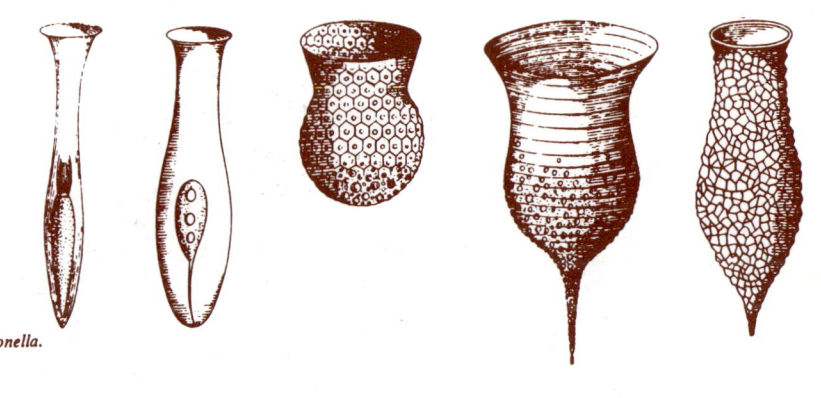

Fig. 21. Various species of *Tintinnus*, *Dinobryon* and *Codonella*. After Saville Kent and others.

```
ON GROWTH AND FORM
Sir D'Arcy Wentworth Thompson
pp 1116(2 vols) £9.00  Cambridge University Press 1942

Abridged version, ed. J.Bonner, pp 346: £1·55 ; CUP 1961

    Good old D'Arcy. Why does a shrew eat so much?
what are the forces affecting the skeleton? Superb
unique book about physics and form in the natural world.

    The two volumes have a lot of stuff that has fallen
by the wayside since 1942, but it's all interesting,
some of it right on. Good old D'Arcy.
```

Tension and Compression

Before we speak of the form of bone, let us say a word about the mechanical properties of the material of which it is built,[1] in relation to the strength it has to manifest or the forces it has to resist: understanding always that we mean thereby the properties of fresh or living bone, with all its organic as well as inorganic constituents, for dead, dry bone is a very different thing. In all the structures raised by the engineer, in beams, pillars and girders of every kind, provision has to be made, somehow or other, for strength of two kinds, strength to resist compression or crushing, and strength to resist tension or pulling asunder. The evenly loaded column is designed with a view to supporting a downward pressure, the wire-rope, like the tendon of a muscle, is adapted only to resist a tensile stress; but in many or most

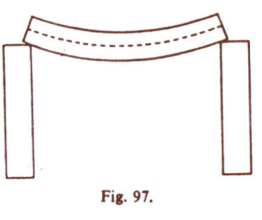

Fig. 97.

cases the two functions are very closely inter-related and combined. The case of a loaded beam is a familiar one; though, by the way, we are now told that it is by no means so simple as it looks, and indeed that 'the stresses and strains in this log of timber are so complex that the problem has not yet been solved in a manner that reasonably accords with the known strength of the beam as found by actual experiment'.[2] However, be that as it may, we know, roughly, that when the beam is loaded in the middle and supported at both ends, it tends to be bent into an arc, in which condition its lower fibres are being stretched, or are undergoing a tensile stress, while its upper fibres are undergoing compression. It follows that in some intermediate layer there is a 'neutral zone', where the fibres of the wood are subject to no stress of either kind.

Fig. 103. Metacarpal bone from a vulture's wing; stiffened after the manner of a Warren's truss. From O. Prochnow, *Formenkunst der Natur*.

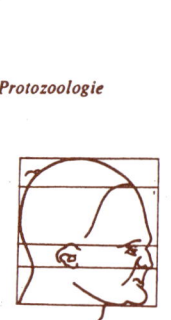

Fig. 67. *Dictyocha stapedia* Hkl. From K. G. Grell, *Protozoologie* (Berlin: Springer-Verlag).

An elementary application of the principle of co-ordinates to the study of proportion, as we have here used it to illustrate the varying proportions of a bone, was in common use in the sixteenth and seventeenth centuries by artists in their study of the human form. The method is probably much more ancient, and may even be classical;[1] it is fully described and put in practice by Albrecht Dürer in his *Geometry*, and especially in his *Treatise on Proportion*.[2] In this latter work, the manner in which the human figure, features, and facial expression are all transformed and modified by slight variations in the relative magnitude of the parts is admirably and copiously illustrated (Fig. 137).

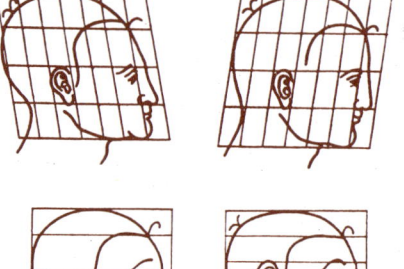

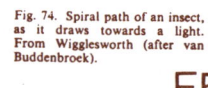

Fig. 74. Spiral path of an insect, as it draws towards a light. From Wigglesworth (after van Buddenbroek).

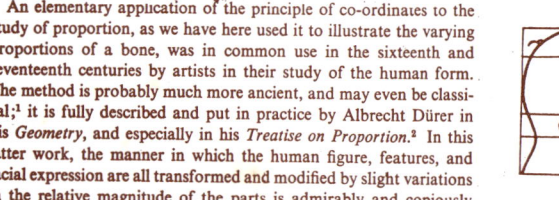

Fig. 137. (After Albrecht Dürer.)

SIGN SYMBOL AND SCRIPT.
Hans Jensen.
pp612; £5.50;
Allen & Unwin 1970.

If the medium is the message,
then here are messages from
languages and societies
across the world, and across
the centuries. Work hard with
this book and you can get
small insights into the
consciousness of other times,
other places.

A curious example of idea-writing is reported from the Yukagirs, a tribe living in the far north of Siberia. It is a matter of a letter-like communication of a girl to her departing sweetheart (Fig. 26b). The detailed explanation of the contents is given by Al'kora[2] as follows: the female figure (*c*) is to be married. The lines (*l–k*) and (*n–m*), which unite it with the male figure (*b*), show whom she is marrying. Similar

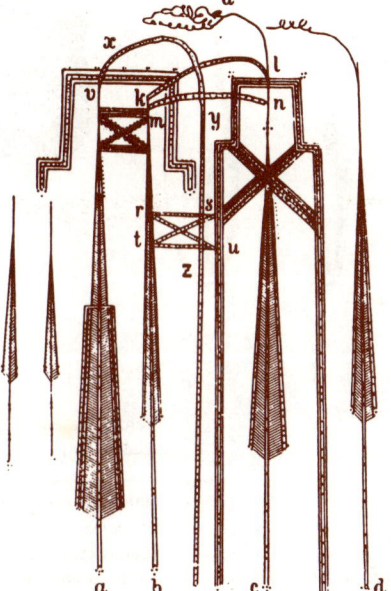

lines are necessary in all cases, whenever other figures of men, apart from this one, are present in the drawing. The lines (*r–s*), (*t–u*), (*r–u*), (*t–s*), which usually serve to convey mutual love, are here crossed through by the line (*v–x–y–z*), which begins at (*v*). It denotes an obstacle that has arisen between (*b*) and (*c*). Next to the female figure (*a*) one can see two little figures, which are the figures of children. The wavy line (*d'–l*), which begins at the upper end of the figure (*c*) indicates that the thoughts of (*c*) remain with (*b*). Such a wavy line always means something to do with the thoughts. The male figure (*d*) sends out a similar line to the female figure (*c*), but receives no response from it. So the whole runs as follows: You are going away. You will fall in love with a Russian girl, who will prevent your return to me. The two of you will have children and you will enjoy a family life. But I, ever sad, will think only of you, although there is a man near here who loves me.

Thus Fig. 564 shows so-called 'tent runes' (*tjaldrūnir*) from the Rök inscription; they are read in a clockwise direction (beginning on the left). Hence, 3–2, 1–4, 2–2, 2–3, 3–5, 3–2 (third group, second rune, reads *u*, etc.)=*ulniru*, to which must be added the rune *þ*, indicated by the bow, and that for *R*, indicated by the short stroke; this piece of the inscription runs, therefore: *ulniruþR=ōl nīrōþr* ='h begat as a ninety-year-old. . . .'

Fig. 564

A further representation in which individual word-signs appear alongside the idea-script is reproduced in Fig. 187, which is taken from the historical *Codex Boturini*.[2] It is a matter here of an episode from the story of the Aztec migration. On the left we see the migrating Aztecs; the black footprints denote the way. At a certain spot (Tamoanchan), by an altar that stands under a tree breaking into pieces, a separation takes place of the true Aztecs from the eight other related tribes on the move with them, whose names are indicated by word-pictures and who, as is shown by the footprints to be found by them, from now on go their own way. Directly below this, the leave-taking is shown: on the left stands an Aztec, on the right a representative of the other eight tribes. The latter is depicted as crying, by the word picture-sign for water to be found below his eye. The image above the fourth tribal sign is supposed to denote the starry sky and to indicate the nocturnal discussion that led to the separation of the tribes. The scene to the right of the altar appears to represent a meal (a sacrificial meal?).

Fig. 187

VOICES OF TIME
J.T.Fraser.
pp710; £4.20;
Allen Lane
1968.

E6

"THE GREATLY ELABORATED INCENSE SEAL" illustrated overleaf was a timepiece featured in the *Hsiang Ch'eng*, a work on aromatics and incense which was popular in Medieval China. It was later included in the *Hsin Tsuan Hsiang-P'u*, or "Newly Compiled Handbook of Aromatics (Incense)," from which the illustration has been reproduced. Incense made from a variety of aromatic powders according to prescribed recipes was placed into the grooves of this incense seal, which was carved in hard wood, and lit at one end of the continuous path. It is probable that the beginning of the path was at the center of the seal, and that the incense burned for a period of approximately 12 hours. Such incense seals were particularly useful during times of drought, when the community water clocks became inoperative. The length of the entire path formed by the grooves is believed to be about 240 inches or 20 feet. According to a writing dated October 1329 A.D. and signed by a "Retired Gentleman of the Central Studio," who cannot be otherwise identified, this seal was presented in the form of a diagram to Tsou Hsiang-hun, a native of Yü-chang Province, an official of the Prefecture of Yü-li. He was a lover of literature, particularly proficient on "The Book of Changes" and held in high esteem by the Court.

Our time system is a product of mechanical
precision. Other systems are sensitive to
other rhythms and cycles, alternative ways
of organizing lives.

Our orientation to the subjective future appears to have the character of a "gradient of tension": we become more and more vigilant as an expected event draws near in time. As the ticking of the clock records the passing of the hours and the fateful moment draws near our hearts beat faster, an experience well described in Adelbert von Chamisso's curious tale *The Shadowless Man*.

Now I remained with my eyes fixed on the hand of the clock, counting the seconds—the minutes—which struck me to the heart like daggers. I started at every sound—at last daylight appeared. The leaden hours passed on—morning—evening—night came. Hope was fast fading away as the hand advanced. It struck eleven—no one appeared—the last minutes—the first and last stroke of the twelfth hour died away. I sank back in my bed in an agony of weeping. In the morning I should, shadowless as I was, claim the hand of my beloved Minna. A heavy sleep towards daylight closed my eyes.[24]

If a sleeper has decided to wake up at a pre-appointed time, he becomes restless as the moment of waking approaches. Every examinee knows this feeling of mounting tension. So does a pregnant woman passively awaiting the birth of her child, a bridegroom the marriage ceremony and a prisoner his execution. The gradient may be demonstrated experimentally (as well as clinically) in animal and man alike. Pavlov's dogs, conditioned to be fed every thirty minutes, betrayed, by changes in breathing and salivation, that they "knew" when the next meal was due. They could fall asleep in the intervening period and awaken, after signs of restiveness, as the food was about to appear. In man we find that the ability to recall or recognize a task which has been started but not completed depends not so much on the amount done as on the amount that remains to be done: the less subjective time needed for completion, the easier the recall of a task regardless of how much time, within limits, has already been spent on it.[25]

THE TEACHINGS OF DON JUAN - A YAQUI WAY OF
KNOWLEDGE Carlos Castenada.
pp 252; 30p; Penguin 1968.

Please do not adjust your brain - there is
a temporary fault in reality. Fantastic,
disturbing book describing faltering steps
into worlds adjacent to our own.
(Also 'A Separate Reality - Further Conver-
sations with Don Juan' pp 317; Bodley Head
1972.

The same day, Friday 5 July, late in the afternoon, don Juan
asked me to narrate the details of my experience. As carefully as
I could, I related the whole episode.

'The second portion of the devil's weed is used to fly,' he said
when I had finished. 'The unguent by itself is not enough. My
benefactor said that it is the root that gives direction and wisdom,
and it is the cause of flying. As you learn more, and take it often
in order to fly, you will begin to see everything with great clarity.
You can soar through the air for hundreds of miles to see what
is happening at any place you want, or to deliver a fatal blow to
your enemies far away. As you become familiar with the devil's
weed, she will teach you how to do such things. For instance, she
has taught you already how to change directions. In the same
manner, she will teach you unimaginable things.'

'Like what, don Juan?'

'That I can't tell you. Every man is different. My benefactor
never told me what he had learned. He told me how to proceed,
but never what he saw. That is only for oneself.'

'But I tell you all I see, don Juan.'

'Now you do. Later you will not. The next time you take the
devil's weed you will do it by yourself, around your own plants,
because that is where you will land, around your plants. Remember that. That is why I came down here to my plants to look for
you.'

He said nothing more, and I fell asleep. When I woke up in the
evening, I felt invigorated. For some reason I exuded a sort of
physical contentment. I was happy, satisfied.

Don Juan asked me, 'Did you like the night? Or was it frightful?'

I told him that the night was truly magnificent.

'How about your headache? Was it very bad?' he asked.

'The headache was as strong as all the other feelings. It was
the worst pain I have ever had,' I said.

'Would that keep you from wanting to taste the power of the
devil's weed again?'

'I don't know. I don't want it now, but later I might. I really
don't know, don Juan.'

There was a question I wanted to ask him. I knew he was
going to evade it, so I waited for him to mention the subject;
I waited all day. Finally, before I left that evening, I had to ask
him, 'Did I really fly, don Juan?'

'That is what you told me. Didn't you?'

'I know, don Juan. I mean, did my body fly? Did I take off
like a bird?'

'You always ask me questions I cannot answer. You flew.
That is what the second portion of the devil's weed is for. As you
take more of it, you will learn how to fly perfectly. It is not a
simple matter. A man *flies* with the help of the second portion of
the devil's weed. That is all I can tell you. What you want to know
makes no sense. Birds fly like birds and a man who has taken the
devil's weed flies as such [*el enyerbado vuela así*].'

'As birds do? [*¿Así como los pájaros?*].'

'No, he flies as a man who has taken the weed [*No, así como
los enyerbados*].'

'Then I didn't really fly, don Juan. I flew in my imagination,
in my mind alone. Where was my body?'

'In the bushes,' he replied cuttingly, but immediately broke
into laughter again. 'The trouble with you is that you understand things in only one way. You don't think a man flies; and
yet a *brujo* can move a thousand miles in one second to see what
is going on. He can deliver a blow to his enemies long distances
away. So, does he or doesn't he fly?'

'You see, don Juan, you and I are differently oriented. Suppose, for the sake of argument, one of my fellow students had
been here with me when I took the devil's weed. Would he have
been able to see me flying?'

'There you go again with your questions about what would
happen if . . . It is useless to talk that way. If your friend, or
anybody else, takes the second portion of the weed all he can do
is fly. Now, if he had simply watched you, he might have seen
you flying, or he might not. That depends on the man.'

'But what I mean, don Juan, is that if you and I look at a bird
and see it fly, we agree that it is flying. But if two of my friends
had seen me flying as I did last night, would they have agreed
that I was flying?'

'Well, they might have. You agree that birds fly because you
have seen them flying. Flying is a common thing with birds. But
you will not agree on other things birds do, because you have
never seen birds doing them. If your friends knew about men
flying with the devil's weed, then they would agree.'

'Let's put it another way, don Juan. What I meant to say is
that if I had tied myself to a rock with a heavy chain I would
have flown just the same, because my body had nothing to do
with my flying.'

Don Juan looked at me incredulously. 'If you tie yourself to
a rock,' he said, 'I'm afraid you will have to fly holding the
rock with its heavy chain.'

EYE AND BRAIN - THE PSYCHOLOGY OF SEEING
R.L.Gregory.
pp251; 70p; Weidenfeld & Nicholson 1966.

What our eyes see and what we percieve aint
always the same. Scientific explanations of
peculiar perceptions.

The people who stand out as living in a non-perspective world
are the Zulus. Their world has been described as a 'circular
culture' – their huts are round, and have round doors; they do not
plough their land in straight furrows but in curves; and few of
their possessions have corners or straight lines. They are thus ideal
subjects for our purpose. It is found that they do experience the
arrow illusion to a small extent, but they are hardly affected at all
by the other illusion figures.

Studies of people living in dense forest have been made. Such
people are interesting, in that they do not experience distant
objects, because there are only small clearances in the forest. When
they are taken out of their forest, and shown distant objects, they
see these not as distant, but as small. People living in Western
cultures experience a similar distortion when looking down from a
height. From a high window objects look too small, though steeple-
jacks and men who work on the scaffolding and girder structure of
skyscrapers are reported to see objects below them without distortion. It seems that actual touch is important in setting the visual
scale of objects.

POPULATION, RESOURCES, ENVIRONMENT. (2nd. edition)
Paul and Anne Ehrlich.
pp 509; £2.60; W.H.Freeman 1972.

Whether you believe the Ehrlichs or not, Population,
Resources, Environment is still the major source
book of the environmental movement, with a relent-
less barrage of facts to prove the general thesis
that population control is the basis of any solution to the eco-crisis.
   When the inevitable conclusions are drawn,
political realities tend to be skated over -
current villains (big companies, government etc.),
it is hoped, will recognise the crisis and abdicate
their power and wealth to save humanity. Mmm.

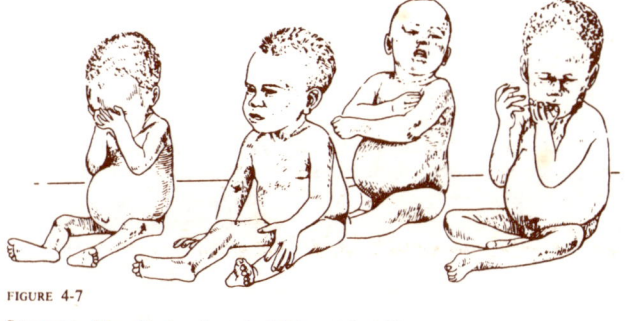

FIGURE 4-7

Symptoms of kwashiorkor (protein deficiency) in African children.
[Drawn from a photograph by Eva D. Wilson.]

Why Have We Let Our Environment Deteriorate?

Historian Lynn White, Jr. of the University of California has suggested that the basic cause of Western man's destructive attitude toward nature lies in Judeo-Christian traditions. He points out, for instance, that before the Christian era men believed trees, springs, hills, streams, and other objects of nature had guardian spirits. These spirits had to be approached and placated before one could safely invade their territories. As White says, "By destroying pagan animism, Christianity made it possible to exploit nature in a mood of indifference to the feelings of natural objects." Christianity fostered the basic ideas of "progress" and of time as something linear, nonseparating, and absolute, flowing from the future into the past. Such ideas were foreign to the Greeks and Romans, who had a cyclical concept of time and did not envision the world as having a beginning. Although a modern physicist's concept of time might be somewhat closer to that of the Greeks than to that of the Christians, the Christian view is nevertheless the prevalent one, in which God designed and started the whole business for our benefit. The world is our oyster, made for man to dominate and exploit. The European ancestors of Americans had held and developed these attitudes long before the opportunity to exploit the Western Hemisphere arrived. The "frontier" or "cowboy" economy which has characterized the United States seems to be a natural extension of the Christian world view.

   Both science and technology can clearly be seen to have their historical roots in natural theology and the Christian dogma of man's rightful mastery over nature. Therefore, as White claims, it may be in vain that so many look to science and technology to solve our present ecological crisis.

It is in the area of international conflict above all else that the old rules must be changed. Most national leaders still view war as an extension of politics, as Clausewitz did in the early Nineteenth Century. They have not yet learned that thermonuclear war itself is a far more deadly enemy than any other nation; they still talk of winning, when in reality only losing is possible. It is to be expected that older people will have more trouble in adjusting to change than the young, and changes in the world military situation over the past 25 years have been so unprecedented as to constitute a serious test of even the adaptability of the most flexible young people. It is lamentable that at the time of its most extreme crisis the world is still largely ruled not just by old men, but by an unfortunate selection of old men.

In the United States, the leadership consists mainly of those people who are most likely to have the ethnocentrism of their society embedded in their characters. Our images of leadership and our political and elective processes seem to require this. Our leaders are unlikely to be familiar with the values and attitudes of other cultures. They are equally unlikely to know anything about the psychology of aggression. They are most likely to have deep emotional investments in patriotic ideals and the glorification of the American way of life, and to have contempt for other cultures. Few have any insight into the psychological tricks which we have built into our world view in order to conceal reality. They do not understand why we talk of military "hardware" instead of weapons, why we say we can "take out" an enemy city instead of "destroy it, killing every man, woman, and child," why we talk of "casualties" in Vietnam instead of "dead and maimed." They do not understand how our preconceptions about the Russians, the Chinese, the Cubans, and other unfamiliar peoples badly distort our perceptions of their behavior. *Moreover, American leaders do not understand that the leaders of the other countries have equally distorted perceptions of our actions and motives.* They have no way of understanding. If the men now leading most nations really had been sensitive to such things as cultural relativity, it is unlikely that they ever would have become political leaders.

THE ENVIRONMENTAL REVOLUTION - Max Nicholson
pp432; 60p; Pelican 1972.

   Conservation in its modern sense is a broader concept, comprehending all of these limited approaches and more. Originating with the work of such scientifically-minded and forest-conscious pioneers as George Perkins Marsh a century ago it became caught up in controversial campaigns of economics, politics and developing technology. Somewhat distorted by these experiences it was redefined sixty years ago by the forester Gifford Pinchot as a *comprehensive and well-planned management of natural resources of every character, based on sound ethical and economic grounds.* His associate W. J. McGee defined it as *the use of the natural resources for the greatest good of the greatest number for the longest time.* The briefest definition runs: *Conservation is wise use,* but this implies acceptance of the sophisticated assumption that non-use may be an acceptable type of use.

   Do such earlier definitions adequately convey what conservation has now come to mean? To meet present needs we might be nearer the mark in using some such formula as this: *Conservation means all that man thinks and does to soften his impact upon his natural environment and to satisfy all his own true needs while enabling that environment to continue in healthy working order.*
While still far from perfect, such wording imports the necessary

You could caricature this
book as being about what
the straights are up to
in in the environmental field.
The angle is conservation,
the perspective change within the system: a detailed
clearly tabulated analysis
of problems seen from a sort
of 'official' viewpoint.

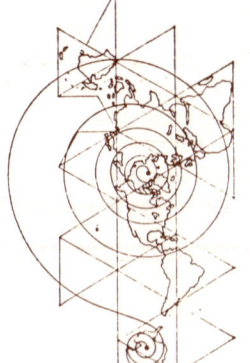

elements of universality and permanence, of conscious collective self-restraint, of the overriding significance, as a limiting factor, of the natural environment and its health, and of the problem of satisfying human needs, both immediate and long term, as one to be solved within this context. All that has gone before can, without straining, be comprehended within such an approach. This is why conservation touches the heart of public affairs, and of ethics, economics and the application of science. It registers the proper limits of human interference with the environment, and shows how to ensure their observance.

OUR SYNTHETIC ENVIRONMENT
Lewis Herbér (Murray Bookchin)
pp 285;   Cape 1963 (Out of print)

My favourite environment book - one of the
earliest assaults on chemicals, pestisides,
food, agriculture, carcinogens, air pollution,-
and for a change, ideas about restructuring
society and technology to create more harmonious
relationships, between people and with nature.
    If you can't get 'Synthetic Environment' from
 the library, Bookchin's book 'Post Scarcity
Anarchism' contains essays which go over the
same ground (i.e. Towards a Liberatory Technology)
pp 288; £1.50- 2.00 from good bookshops.
Ramparts Press 1971. Not yet published over here.

Kotin found that when an efficient automobile engine revolves 500 times per minute for one minute, it produces a gasoline exhaust containing 235 micrograms of benzpyrene. When the engine is accelerated to 3,500 revolutions per minute, the amount of benzpyrene in the exhaust decreases to 10 micrograms. A congested thoroughfare cluttered with idling or slow-moving motor vehicles is a hazard to human lungs. Individuals who spend a large part of their time in such areas, irrespective of the particular metropolis in which they live, are likely to acquire a lifetime dosage of benzpyrene that is thousands of times greater than the amount required to produce cancer in mice.

Nutritionists, in analyzing thirty-one strains of cabbage, found that the ascorbic-acid, or vitamin-C, content varied as much as 350 per cent, while the amount of carotene in different varieties of sweet potatoes has been found to range from zero to 7.2 milligrams per cent. A threefold difference was discovered in the niacin content of forty-six strains of sweet corn. Large variations in nutritive value have been found among different varieties of apples, peas, wheat, onions, and many other crops. The fact that a given variety attains great size does not necessarily mean that it is nutritious. The very opposite may be true. Small cabbages, tomatoes, and onions, for example, contain more vitamin C than those of greater size. Size, appearance, color, and texture are often very poor criteria for judging the nutritive content of a food. Generally, plant breeders are interested in developing varieties of vegetables and fruits that have an attractive appearance, yield more bushels to the acre, are more resistant to disease, and withstand storage and shipment. "It is now realized that in the development of these commercially improved varieties by genetic selection the nutrient content is often decreased," notes Robert S. Harris, of the Massachusetts Institute of Technology. "If the plant breeder were to collaborate with a food analysis laboratory, he could develop commercially improved varieties which are also superior in nutrient content." *

THE COSTS OF ECONOMIC GROWTH
E.J.Mishan; pp 240; 35p Penguin 1969.

The blood flows from this book as sacred
cows are slaughtered right left and centre.
Not bedtime reading by any means, but academic
ammunition against the mindless growth-
merchants.

The piecemeal methods of engineers in the face of traffic problems differ from those of the economist only in being cruder. They turn on the location of 'growing points' in the traffic, and on a variety of formulae, based on traffic growth relative to road capacity, that yield critical ratios purporting to justify increased investment. These formulae are supplemented by *ad hoc* decisions on building bridges, circuses, by-passes, diversions, fly-overs and fly-unders, whenever something 'has to be done'. If the engineers could save us by such methods, or by even more grandiose ones, we should by now have had ample evidence of

their success from the United States where, in many cities, municipalities' engineers have been bending over backwards for years in the endeavour to accommodate the motorist. Yet no relief is in sight. Far from it, cities like New York, Detroit, Los Angeles, lie prostrate beneath traffic that crawls about like armies of locusts devouring the very heart and soul of the city. One might have thought we could, as a nation, save ourselves some bitter experiences by tearing a page from the American diary. Apparently, however, we are determined to subject ourselves to the same experience by using the same piecemeal approach, albeit more cautiously, in response to the growing traffic until we reach the same situation of near chaos. For the overall response of governments since the war has been to do little more than to make stern noises about efficiency while allowing, nay encouraging, the use of the nation's limited resources to install more plant to produce more cars, lorries, and scooters, that show a profit to their makers, and a gain to their users, by steadfastly ignoring the mounting costs of traffic control, of mutual frustration, and of the barely tolerable pressure of noise, stench, dirt and exasperation, to say nothing of the increasing figures for death and mutilation.

THE ENVIRONMENTAL HANDBOOK
Ed. John Barr.
pp 333; 40p;
Ballantine/Friends of the Earth 1971.

Short studies of the British environmental problems
and prospects.

Hedges and trees play a crucial role in the water economy and their removal may affect drainage. They provide shelter for the soil and crops, as well as for animals. Wind speed is reduced to zero on the lea side of a hedge for a distance equal to twice the hedge height; for a distance equal to twelve times the height of the hedge wind speed is halved. In this sheltered area moisture is conserved in the upper layers of the soil and the soil temperature is higher. This may be a

mixed blessing to the farmer since some crops will ripen unevenly, but it can increase yields. Grass yields may increase by 20 per cent.

The removal of windbreaks may lead to erosion on light or sandy soils. In parts of East Anglia and the east Midlands topsoil is lost whenever the wind speed rises above 33 knots. From the 16th to the 20th March, 1968, the wind speed over the fens rose to 20 knots gusting to 40. Dykes were filled to the brim and snow ploughs were called out to clear roads. This was unusually severe, but each year a little more topsoil is lost.

Wind and the removal of windbreaks is not the only cause of erosion, however. In part it is due to a general deterioration in soil structure.

The special case of Iceland:

Iceland, the largest single piece of land which is entirely of volcanic origin, is built of fissure-erupted lava plateaux and large conical volcanoes. Because of its position athwart the actively spreading mid-Atlantic ridge, Iceland is overwhelmingly of basalt close to tholeiite in composition, with lesser volumes of more silica and alkali-enriched fractions, such as rhyolite (Table 1, col. 6). For the same reason Iceland is continually being stretched, its two halves being pulled apart by the spreading sea-floor beneath. The tension causes many cracks to develop in the crust, parallel to the ridge axis, and these become fissures for volcanic eruptions. With subsequent waning of volcanic activity, magma solidifies in the fissures to form swarms of parallel dykes, each dyke representing an increment of crustal extension (Fig. 21.8). The aggregate width of these dykes has been estimated to correspond to a total crustal extension

UNDERSTANDING THE EARTH
I.G.Grass, R.C.L.Wilson, P.J.Smith.
pp383; £2.45; Artemis Press for
Open University 1972.

Up to date meat about the Earth
beneath, and how it's changing.

of some 400 km since the island began to form approximately fifteen million years ago. The oldest rocks in Iceland are therefore in the extreme east and west, and present-day active volcanism is almost entirely confined to the central zone directly over the mid-Atlantic ridge (Fig. 21.10). This model of crustal spreading for Iceland may well apply also to the ocean floors, in which case Iceland offers us a unique laboratory for the study of physical mechanisms at growing lithosphere plate margins.

active volcanic zones
Pleistocene volcanics (approx. extent)
Tertiary volcanics

21.10 Outline geological map of Iceland, showing how the age of volcanism decreases inwards towards the central belt.

INTO THE HIDDEN ENVIRONMENT
Keith Critchlow.
pp125; £2.95;
George Philip 1972.

The sea remains a sort of
fond last hope for many of us –
an eternal answer to what we
do to the land. That in
itself shows how little we
know about it. Find out more
from this book.

The Tonga Trench is shown in cross-section, though with the vertical scale exaggerated. Although its sides do not drop with the same dramatic force, it far surpasses in magnitude the Grand Canyon of Arizona. The Tonga Trench is nearly 800 miles long, and plunges more than 20,000 feet below the general level of the ocean bed around it, reaching a depth of 35,700 feet below sea level. In contrast, the Grand Canyon is 200 miles long and has a maximum depth of 5,000 feet.

Deep trenches

The deep trenches are currently believed to be the planetary incinerators – but on a time-scale that almost outlives the whole of human history. Here the plates that are created under tension along the mid-ocean ridges meet their useful end as oceanic bottom and are apparently forced under the lighter basaltic rocks of the continental mass that confronts them. As they go down – with the accompaniment of quakes and volcanic outbursts – they are believed to take sediment and refuse down with them for recycling within the molten circulations of the mantle's convection currents.

It is an amazing picture: Billions of tons of what man has always experienced as rock-steady solid earth are actually, on another time-scale, as much in circulation as the waters and atmosphere. Maybe it serves to emphasize the realization that the law of being on Earth is the law of circulation, of cycle and recycle, of birth, growth, maturity, decay and death.

The depths of the great trenches reflect the relative sizes of the oceans. Of the 20 greatest both in length and in depth, 15 are in the Pacific Ocean, and the first seven in order of magnitude are also Pacific. Only in eighth position comes the first and deepest Atlantic trench.

FIELDS, FACTORIES
AND WORKSHOPS.
Peter Kropotkin
Nelson 1913
(probably going to
be republished soon)

Alternative ways for
things to have moved,
written at a time whe
when the chance was
more there.

(Recommended by Bill
Challis, John Quail)

Have the factory and the workshop at the gates of your fields and gardens, and work in them. Not those large establishments, of course, in which huge masses of metals have to be dealt with and which are better placed at certain spots indicated by Nature, but the countless variety of workshops and factories which are required to satisfy the infinite diversity of tastes among civilised men. Not those factories in which children lose all the appearance of children in the atmosphere of an industrial hell, but those airy and hygienic, and consequently economical, factories in which human life is of more account than machinery and the making of extra profits, of which we already find a few samples here and there; factories and workshops into which men, women and children will not be driven by hunger, but will be attracted by the desire of finding an activity suited to their tastes, and where, aided by the motor and the machine, they will choose the branch of activity which best suits their inclinations.

Let those factories and workshops be erected, not for making profits by selling shoddy or useless and noxious things to enslaved Africans, but to satisfy the unsatisfied needs of millions of Europeans. And again, you will be struck to see with what facility and in how short a time your needs of dress and of thousands of articles of luxury can be satisfied, when production is carried on for satisfying real needs rather than for satisfying shareholders by high profits or for pouring gold into the pockets of promoters and bogus directors. Very soon you will yourselves feel interested in that work, and you will have occasion to admire in your children their eager desire to become acquainted with Nature and its forces, their inquisitive inquiries as to the powers of machinery, and their rapidly developing inventive genius.

Such is the future—already possible, already realisable; such is the present—already condemned and about to disappear.

TECHNICS AND CIVILIZATION Lewis Mumford.
pp508; £2.00; Routledge 1934.

Technology is inseperable from the
social and financial forces that
support and direct it. Technics and
Civilization is a classic statement of
the relationship as seen just before
the beginning of the electronic village.

1: Wood was the main foundation of
eotechnic industry; not the least important use of it was in mining. Hollow
logs were used in pumps and as pipes to
convey water, as well as in the troughs
shown here: heavy beams were used for
shoring, and planks were used in the
earliest form of the railroad. The use of
wood for smelting, forging, and casting
—as well as in glass-making—caused a
great drain on the forest. Dr. Bauer's
illustrator faithfully depicts this defor-
estation.

(From Agricola: De Re Metallica)

6: Glass and the Ego

If the outward world was changed by glass, the inner world was
likewise modified. Glass had a profound effect upon the development
of the personality: indeed, it helped to alter the very concept of the
self.

In a small way, glass had been used for mirrors by the Romans;
but the background was a dark one, and the image was no more plain
than it had been on the polished metal surface. By the sixteenth
century, even before the invention of plate glass that followed a
hundred years later, the mechanical surface of the glass had been
improved to such an extent that, by coating it with a silver amalgam,
an excellent mirror could be created. Technically this was, according
to Schulz, perhaps the highest point in Venetian glass-making. Large
mirrors, accordingly, became relatively cheap and the hand-mirror
became a common possession.

For perhaps the first time, except for reflections in the water and
in the dull surfaces of metal mirrors, it was possible to find an image
that corresponded accurately to what others saw. Not merely in the
privacy of the boudoir: in another's home, in a public gathering, the
image of the ego in new and unexpected attitudes accompanied one.
The most powerful prince of the seventeenth century created a vast
hall of mirrors, and the mirror spread from one room to another in
the bourgeois household. Self-consciousness, introspection, mirror-
conversation developed with the new object itself: this preoccupation
with one's image comes at the threshold of the mature personality
when young Narcissus gazes long and deep into the face of the pool—
and the sense of the separate personality, a perception of the objective
attributes of one's identity, grows out of this communion.

The use of the mirror signalled the beginning of introspective
biography in the modern style: that is, not as a means of edification
but as a picture of the self, its depths, its mysteries, its inner dimensions. The self in the mirror corresponds to the physical world that
was brought to light by natural science in the same epoch: it was the
self *in abstracto*, only part of the real self, the part that one can
divorce from the background of nature and the influential presence
of other men. But there is a value in this mirror personality that
more naïve cultures did not possess. If the image one sees in the
mirror is abstract, it is not ideal or mythical: the more accurate the
physical instrument, the more sufficient the light on it, the more
relentlessly does it show the effects of age, disease, disappointment,
frustration, slyness, covetousness, weakness—these come out quite
as clearly as health and joy and confidence. Indeed, when one is
completely whole and at one with the world one does not need the
mirror: it is in the period of psychic disintegration that the individual
personality turns to the lonely image to see what in fact is there
and what he can hold on to; and it was in the period of cultural
disintegration that men began to hold the mirror up to outer nature.

THE TECHNOLOGICAL SOCIETY Jacques Ellul.
pp 496; £3.15; Cape 1965.
Technology is not just hardware, but
provides systems of thought and action that
are apparent all around us. This is a resigned
French statement of how we use and think
technology.

The nonintellectual classes of the *bourgeoisie* are perhaps less
caught up in this worship of technique. But the technicians of the
bourgeoisie are without doubt the ones most powerfully taken with
it. For them, technique *is* sacred, since they have no reason to
feel a passion for it. Technical men are always disconcerted when
one asks them the motives for their faith. No, they do not expect to
be liberated; they expect nothing, yet they sacrifice themselves
and devote their lives with frenzy to the development of industrial
plants and the organization of banks. The happiness of the human
race and suchlike nonsense are the commonplaces they allege. But
these are no longer of any service even as justifications, and they
certainly have nothing at all to do with man's passion for technique.

The technician uses technique perhaps because it is his profes-
sion, but he does so with adoration because for him technique is
the locus of the sacred. There is neither reason nor explanation in
his attitude. The power of technique, mysterious though scientific,
which covers the whole earth with its networks of waves, wires,
and paper, is to the technician an abstract idol which gives him a
reason for living and even for joy. One sign, among many, of the
feeling of the sacred that man experiences in the face of technique
is the care he takes to treat it with familiarity. Laughter and humor
are common human reactions in the presence of the sacred. This is
true for primitive peoples; and for the same reason the first atomic
bomb was called "Gilda," the giant cyclotron of Los Alamos
"Clementine," the atomic piles "water pots," and radioactive con-
tamination "scalding." The technicians of Los Alamos have banned
the word *atom* from their vocabulary. These things are significant.

In view of the very different forms of technique, there is no
question of a technical religion. But there is associated with it the
feeling of the sacred, which expresses itself in different ways. The
way differs from man to man, but for all men the feeling of the
sacred is expressed in this marvelous instrument of the power instinct which is always joined to mystery and magic. The worker
brags about his job because it offers him joyous confirmation of his
superiority. The young snob speeds along at 100 m.p.h. in his
Porsche. The technician contemplates with satisfaction the gradi-
ents of his charts, no matter what their reference is. For these men,
technique is in every way sacred: it is the common expression of
human power without which they would find themselves poor,
alone, naked, and stripped of all pretentions. They would no longer
be the heroes, geniuses, or archangels which a motor permits them
to be at little expense.

What shall we say of the outburst of frenzy when the Sputnik
went into orbit? What of the poems of the Soviets, the metaphysical
affirmations of the French, the speculations on the conquest of the
universe? What of the identification of this artificial satellite with
the sun, or of its invention with the creation of the earth? And, on
the other side of the Atlantic, what was the real meaning of the excessive consternation of the Americans? All these bore witness to a
marked social attitude with regard to a simple technical fact. EII

CULTURE AGAINST MAN - Jules Henry.
pp 398; £1.00. Penguin 1972

Jules Henry was an anthropologist.
'Culture Against Man' is an anthropological
study of present day America, with close
observations of people as they bend under
the strain of the culture, with great insight
and love for the victims. This is a little
mentioned book, maybe because it doesn't
fit easily into textbook categories. It
should be read.

Boris had trouble reducing "12/16" to the lowest terms, and could only get as far as "6/8". The teacher asked him quietly if that was as far as he could reduce it. She suggested he "think." Much heaving up and down and waving of hands by the other children, all frantic to correct him. Boris pretty unhappy, probably mentally paralyzed. The teacher, quiet, patient, ignores the others and concentrates with look and voice on Boris. She says, "Is there a bigger number than two you can divide into the two parts of the fraction?" After a minute or two, she becomes more urgent, but there is no response from Boris. She then turns to the class and says, "Well, who can tell Boris what the number is?" A forest of hands appears, and the teacher calls Peggy. Peggy says that four may be divided into the numerator and the denominator.

Thus Boris' failure has made it possible for Peggy to succeed; his depression is the price of her exhilaration; his misery the occasion for her rejoicing. This is the standard condition of the American elementary school, and is why so many of us feel a contraction of the heart even if someone we never knew succeeds merely at garnering plankton in the Thames: because so often somebody's success has been bought at the cost of our failure. To a Zuñi, Hopi, or Dakota Indian, Peggy's performance would seem cruel beyond belief, for competition, the wringing of success from somebody's failure, is a form of torture foreign to those noncompetitive redskins. Yet Peggy's action seems natural to us; and so it is. How else would you run our world? And since all but the brightest children have the constant experience that others succeed at their expense they cannot but

develop an inherent tendency to hate—to hate the success of others, to hate others who are successful, and to be determined to prevent it. Along with this, naturally, goes the hope that others will fail. This hatred masquerades under the euphemistic name of "envy."

Looked at from Boris' point of view, the nightmare at the blackboard was, perhaps, a lesson in controlling himself so that he would not fly shrieking from the room under the enormous public pressure. Such experiences imprint on the mind of every man in our culture the *Dream of Failure*, so that over and over again, night in, night out, even at the pinnacle of success, a man will dream not of success, but of failure. *The external nightmare is internalized for life*. It is this dream that, above all other things, provides the fierce human energy required by technological drivenness. It was not so much that Boris was learning arithmetic, but that he was learning the *essential nightmare. To be successful in our culture one must learn to dream of failure*.

Creative intellect is mysterious, devious, and irritating. An intellectually creative child may fail, for example, in social studies, simply because he cannot understand the stupidities he is taught to believe as "fact." He may even end up agreeing with his teachers that he is "stupid" in social studies. Learning social studies is, to no small extent, whether in elementary school or the university, learning to be stupid. Most of us accomplish this task before we enter high school. But the child with a socially creative imagination will not be encouraged to play among new social systems, values, and relationships; nor is there much likelihood of it, if for no other reason than that the social studies teachers will perceive such a child as a poor student. Furthermore, such a child will simply be unable to fathom the absurdities that seem transparent *truth* to the teacher. What idiot believes in the "law of supply and demand," for example? But the children who do tend to *become* idiots, and learning to be an idiot is part of growing up! Or, as Camus put it, learning to be *absurd*. Thus the child who finds it impossible to learn to think the absurd the truth, who finds it difficult to accept absurdity as a way of life, the intellectually creative child whose mind makes him flounder like a poor fish in the net of absurdities flung around him in school, usually comes to think himself stupid.

LIFE AGAINST DEATH - Norman O.Brown.
pp315; 40p; Sphere 1959.

A very difficult book, but worth reading if you want a Freudian view of civilization, and to understand what he's about.

Until the advent of psychoanalysis and its doctrine of the anal character of money, the profoundest insights into the nature of the money complex had to be expressed through the medium of myth—in modern times, the myth of the Devil. The Devil, we said in our chapter on Luther, is the lineal descendant of the Trickster in primitive mythologies; the evolution of the Trickster, through such intermediary figures as the classical Hermes, into the Christian Devil reflects the history of anality. The Trickster of primitive mythologies is surrounded by unsublimated and undisguised anality. For example, of the Winnebago Trickster Paul Radin writes: [220]

He comes upon a bulb which tells him that whoever chews it will defecate. . . . So he takes the bulb and chews it to find that he does not defecate but only breaks wind. This expulsion of gas increases in intensity progressively. He sits on a log, but is propelled into the air with the log on top of him; he pulls up trees to which he clings, by their roots. In his helplessness he has the inhabitants of a village pile all their possessions upon him, their lodges, their dogs, and then

they themselves climb upon him. . . . And so the whole world of man is now on Wakdjunkaga's back. With a terrific expulsion of gas he scatters the people and all their possessions to the four quarters of the earth. . . . He now begins to defecate. The earth is covered with excrement. To escape it he takes refuge in a tree, but to no avail, and he falls into mountains of his own excrement. . . .

At the same time, as all students of comparative mythology know, this Trickster, with his 'filthy' tricks, is a great Culture-hero, the source of man's material culture. Indeed the Trickster can create the world by a filthy trick, out of excrement or that thinly disguised substitute for excrement, mud or clay, reflecting, in Abraham's words, the idea of the omnipotence of the products of the bowel.[221] In classical antiquity, the period of the most perfect sublimation, the figure of Hermes is produced by sublimation–negation of anality. Though vestiges of unsublimated anality remain, simple excrement is replaced first by the symbolic heap of stones and then by the symbolic bag of money (compare the bag in which, according to Margaret Mead, the Arapesh carefully collect their magic dirt).[222] Luther's Devil is a negation of the classical sublimation; sublimation is repudiated because the body is perceived as fallen and filthy; the Devil regains, by a return of the repressed, his excremental character, but his anality is not cathected with libido or magic life, as in the magic–dirt complex, but is seen as death. The whole evolution from Trickster to Devil and on into the pseudo-secular demonic of capitalism shows the progressive triumph of the death instinct.

FURTHER TO THE BIBLIOGRAPHY (BELOW) :-
THE BODY POLITIC - Compiled by Michelene Wandor.
pp262; 60p; Stage 1 1972.
The basic book about the Movement in Britain. Texts
cover everything from feminism, sexuality and the
family to campaigns, the small group etc. Contains
address lists of regional groups.
* Two apolitical books which are useful starters to
understanding the oppression of women.

WOMEN, SOCIETY & CHANGE. Evelyn Sullerot.
pp254; &1.75; Wiedenfield & Nicolson 1971.
Historical and sociological account of women's inferior role in European society, describing legal
discrimination, low pay, inferior education etc.
SEX, GENDER & SOCIETY. Ann Oakley.
pp221; 95p; Maurice Temple Smith 1972.
Shows how sex differences in behaviour, attitudes and
roles are culturally and not biologically determined.

1. Some general books on women's liberation

BEAUVOIR, Simone de, **The Second Sex**, London, Cape, 1968, Four Square (p), 1969,
& The Nature of the Second Sex, London, Four Square (p), 1968.
Essential study of the nature of female oppression and consciousness.
FIGES, Eva, **Patriarchal Attitudes**, London, Faber, 1970.
*Description of attitudes to women of famous literary, political and psychological
figures in the past.*
FIRESTONE, Shulamith, **The Dialectic of Sex: The Case for Feminist Revolution**,
London, Cape, 1971.
Radical feminist perspective on women's liberation.
FRIEDAN, Betty, **The Feminine Mystique**, London, Penguin (p), 1968.
Description of the pre-liberation movement period in the U.S.
GREER, Germaine, **The Female Eunuch**, London, MacGibbon & Kee, 1970, Paladin (p)
1971.
*Witty attack on the absurdities of the female condition from an individualistic
outsider liberationist. No good, though, on the movement itself.*
MILLETT, Kate, **Sexual Politics**, London, Hart-Davis, 1971.
Images of women in literature, sociology, psychology.
MITCHELL, Juliet, **Woman's Estate**, London, Penguin (p), 1971.
*Short account of various strains in women's liberation thinking. Very useful for
group discussions. Connects feminism and socialism.*
MORGAN, Robin (ed.), **Sisterhood is Powerful: An Anthology of Writings from the
Women's Liberation Movement**, New York, Vintage Trade Books (p), Random
House, 1970.
*Very good. Includes writing on jobs, schools, sexuality, black women, chicana
women, gay liberation, China. Poetry; excerpts from SCUM manifesto.*
ROWBOTHAM, Sheila, **Women: Resistance and Revolution**, London, Allen Lane,
due 1972.
Relationship between feminism and social revolution, in ideas and actuality.
TANNER, Leslie B. (ed.), **Voices from Women's Liberation**, New York, Signet (p), 1971
Anthology of modern American material, plus historical texts. (See section 2.)
*A mystery book, no name yet, is going to appear soon. It is a collection of women's
liberation writing on a wide variety of subjects, ranging from primary school readers to
the law, sexuality to claimants' unions, women in T.V. and trade unions. It is being
written by women from groups in various parts of Britain.*
See Leonora Lloyd, **A Booklist for Women's Liberation**, published by London Socialist
Women, *for a longer list of general books on women's liberation.*

16. General

Some British Periodicals

Enough, Bristol Women's Liberation Group.
General.
IS Women's Newsletter, IS Women.
*Claimants' union, unsupported mothers, work, women and revolutionary
movement.*
Shrew, London Workshop.
*Done by each London group in turn. Personal descriptions, of childbirth, sexuality
upbringing of children, abortion. Discussion of sisterhood, small group, the
family etc.*
Socialist Woman, Socialist Women's Groups.
*Main emphasis on work and economic oppression But also general articles, on
China, Vietnam, Palestine, suffragettes.*
Women's Liberation, Women's Liberation Front.
*Mainly exploitation of women at work, anti-Industrial Relations Bill, anti-
imperialism.*
Women Now, Nottingham Women's Liberation Group.
Mainly directed at women outside the Movement.

WOMEN'S LIBERATION -
A BIBLIOGRAPHY(above)
Sheila Rowbottom.
15p. Falling Wall
Press 1972.
Indispensable work of
reference with useful
address list.

THE DIALECTIC OF SEX.
Shulamith Firestone.
pp224; 50p; Paladin
1972.
Powerful and contra-
versial statement of
the radical feminist
perspective.

SISTERHOOD IS POWERFUL. ED. Robin Morgan.
pp602; £1.25; Vintage (US) 1970.

KNOW YOUR ENEMY: A SAMPLING OF SEXIST
QUOTES

The only position for women in SNCC is prone.
—Stokeley Carmichael, 1966

It would be preposterously naive to suggest that a B.A. can
be made as attractive to girls as a marriage license.
—Dr. Grayson Kirk (former President, Columbia
University)

Women, in general, want to be loved for what they are and
men for what they accomplish. The first for their looks and
charm, the latter for their actions.   —Theodor Reik

My secretary is a lovable slave.
—Morris Ernst, attorney, on the 50th Anniversary
of his having hired Paula Gross, secretary.

The only alliance I would make with the Women's Liberation Movement is in bed.—Abbie Hoffman

The woman's fundamental status is that of her husband's
wife, the mother of his children.   —Talcott Parsons

Man's superiority will be shown, not in the fact that he has
enslaved his wife, but that *he* has made her free.
—Eugene V. Debs

Women should receive a higher education, not in order to
become doctors, lawyers, or professors, but to rear their
offspring to be valuable human beings.
—Alexis Carrel, *Man, the Unknown*

Woman as a person enjoys a dignity equal with men, but she
was given different tasks by God and by Nature which
perfect and complete the work entrusted to men.
—Pope John XXIII

It would be a mistake to attempt to explain the oppression of
women according to this strictly economic interpretation. The
class analysis is a beautiful piece of work, but limited: although
correct in a linear sense, it does not go deep enough. There is a
whole sexual substratum of the historical dialectic that Engels
at times dimly perceives, but because he can see sexuality only
through an economic filter, reducing everything to that, he is
unable to evaluate in its own right.

Engels did observe that the original division of labour was
between man and woman for the purposes of child-breeding;
that within the family the husband was the owner, the wife the
means of production, the children the labour; and that reproduction of the human species was an important economic system
distinct from the means of production.[1]

1. His correlation of the interdevelopment of these two systems in *Origin of
the Family, Private Property and the State* on a time scale might read as
follows:

	recorded history	Greece		Renaissance		Modern Revolution	
Matriarchy							
	Patriarchy						
	Group Marriage	Pair Marriage		Double Standard Monogamy/Hetairism			
1. Savagery (Nomads)	**2.Barbarism** (Tillers of soil)	**3. Civilization**					
adaptation to nature	increasing productivity of nature through human intervention, notably cultivation of land and domestication of animals	Aristocracy ancient... feudal		Aristocracy			
				Bourgeoisie			
	slaves... serfs	mediaeval→capitalists→corporate burghers of the capitalism Industrial revolution					
	Lower class (themselves com- modities)	wage labour					
		Proletariat (production of commodities)					

E13

Virabhadrāsana—I (12, 13, 14)

LIGHT ON YOGA

Over 200 postures and 14 breathing exercises described in detail

Over 600 illustrations

Virabhadrāsana—III (16, 17)

B.K.S. IYENGAR
Foreword by
Yehudi Menuhin

```
LIGHT ON YOGA     B.K.S. Iyengar
pp 342; £2.50  Allen & Unwin 1968
```
The book on Yoga for those already well into it- complete with meanings of all those weird Yoga terms, and planned schemes of asanas.(If you don't know what that means, this book isn't for you.)

Asana

The third limb of yoga is āsana or posture. Āsana brings steadiness, health and lightness of limb. A steady and pleasant posture produces mental equilibrium and prevents fickleness of mind. Āsanas are not merely gymnastic exercises; they are postures. To perform them one needs a clean airy place, a blanket and determination, while for other systems of physical training one needs large playing fields and costly equipment. Āsanas can be done alone, as the limbs of the body provide the necessary weights and counter-weights. By practising them one develops agility, balance, endurance and great vitality.

Āsanas have been evolved over the centuries so as to exercise every muscle, nerve and gland in the body. They secure a fine physique, which is strong and elastic without being muscle bound and they keep the body free from disease. They reduce fatigue and soothe the nerves. But their real importance lies in the way they train and discipline the mind.

Effects

The importance of Sarvāngāsana cannot be over-emphasised. It is one of the greatest boons conferred on humanity by our ancient sages. Sarvāngāsana is the Mother of āsanas. As a mother strives for harmony and happiness in the home, so this āsana strives for the harmony and happiness of the human system. It is a panacea for most common ailments. There are several endocrine organs or duct-less glands in the human system which bathe in blood, absorb the nutriments from the blood and secrete hormones for the proper func-

tioning of a balanced and well developed body and brain. If the glands fail to function properly, the hormones are not produced as they should be and the body starts to deteriorate. Amazingly enough many of the āsanas have a direct effect on the glands and help them to function properly. Sarvāngāsana does this for the thyroid and parathyroid glands which are situated in the neck region, since due to the firm chinlock their blood supply is increased. Further since the body is inverted the venous blood flows to the heart without any strain by force of gravity. Healthy blood is allowed to circulate around the neck and chest. As a result, persons suffering from breathlessness, palpitation, asthma, bronchitis and throat ailments get relief. As the head remains firm in this inverted position, and the supply of the blood to it is regulated by the firm chinlock, the nerves are soothed and headaches—even chronic ones—disappear. Continued practice of this āsana eradicates common colds and other nasal disturbances. Due to the soothing effect of the pose on the nerves, those suffering from hypertension, irritation, shortness of temper, nervous breakdown and insomnia are relieved. The change in bodily gravity also affects the abdominal organs so that the bowels move freely and constipation vanishes. As a result the system is freed from toxins and one feels full of energy. The āsana is recommended for urinary disorders and uterine displacement, menstrual trouble, piles and hernia. It also helps to relieve epilepsy, low vitality and anaemia. It is no over-statement to say that if a person regularly practises Sarvāngāsana he will feel new vigour and strength, and will be happy and confident. New life will flow into him, his mind will be at peace and he will feel the joy of life. After a long illness, the practice of this āsana regularly twice a day brings back lost vitality. The Sarvāngāsana cycle activates the abdominal organs and relieves people suffering from stomach and intestinal ulcers, severe pains in the abdomen and colitis.

```
YOGA FOR HEALTH
Richard Hittelman
pp96; 50p
Hamlyn 1971

   A good beginner's book-
faceless zombies illustrate
postures, next to clear
accounts of the value of each,
and the length of time to hold
hold it. Good section on Yoga
food, and beginner's schemes.

(Both books suggested and
reviewed by Jano Williams)
```

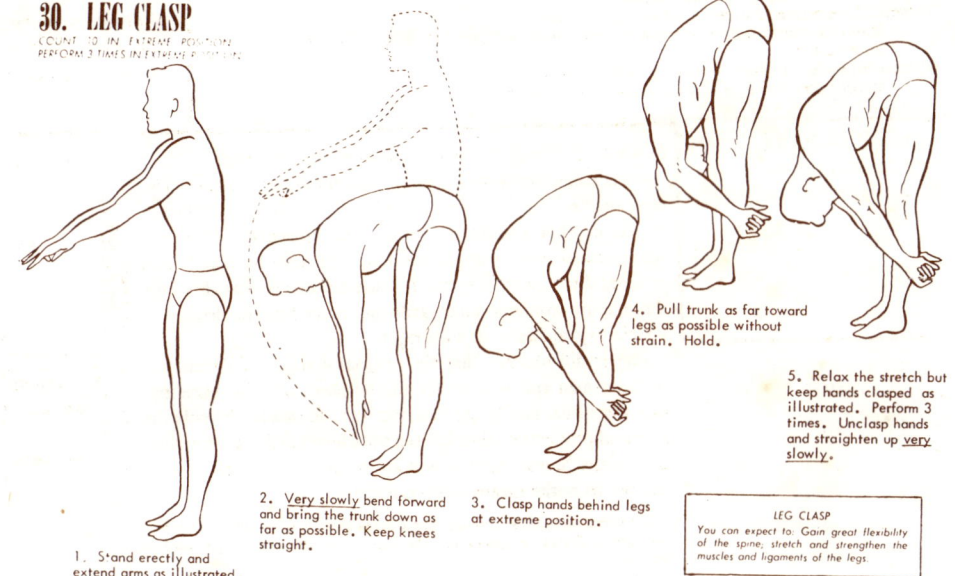

30. LEG CLASP
COUNT 10 IN EXTREME POSITIONS
PERFORM 3 TIMES IN EXTREME POSITIONS

4. Pull trunk as far toward legs as possible without strain. Hold.

5. Relax the stretch but keep hands clasped as illustrated. Perform 3 times. Unclasp hands and straighten up <u>very slowly.</u>

1. Stand erectly and extend arms as illustrated.

2. <u>Very slowly</u> bend forward and bring the trunk down as far as possible. Keep knees straight.

3. Clasp hands behind legs at extreme position.

LEG CLASP
You can expect to: Gain great flexibility of the spine, stretch and strengthen the muscles and ligaments of the legs.

A DICTIONARY OF SYMPTOMS.
Dr. Joan Gomez.
pp490; 60p; Paladin 1970.

Meat and drink for the hypochondriac, but plenty of common sense for the rest in diagnosing everything from acne to xanthelasma.

Front: sites of pain in acute trouble in the abdomen

(a) Gall bladder	(e) Kidney
(b) Stomach; duodenum; pancreas	(f) Appendix; pregnancy in a tube or inflammation in a tube
(c) Gall bladder	(g) Colon; bladder
(d) Small intestine; appendix	(h) Hernia; kidney trouble

HOW TO IDENTIFY YOUR COUGH

Unproductive cough : i.e. nothing is coughed up

1. Short, dry cough brought on by going into the cold. Due to congestion of the back of the throat, as in colds and simple sore throat, Tonsillitis, or smoker's cough.
2. Similar but coming on after talking, inflammation of the larynx.
3. Night cough, often due to chronic congestion of the back of the throat, or to an extra long uvula – the little fleshy part dangling from the arch between the tonsils.
4. Repeated nervous cough: a form of habit spasm.
5. Long, barking, showy cough: a symptom of hysteria.
6. Short suppressed cough, with pain in the side, is likely to be due to pleurisy.
7. Brassy cough, also likened to the sound of a gander, may mean pressure on the bronchi from some swelling in the chest, such as an aneurism, tumour or enlarged glands.
8. Coughs that come by stimulation of the other branches of that nerve, the vagus, which also carries messages from the respiratory tract. In this way cough may be due to:

Digestive disorders, as gastritis, diarrhoea, constipation, worms: a 'stomach cough'. Heart troubles: 'heart cough', one type. Dental troubles, car troubles, possibly.

9. Silent ineffectual cough: paralysis of the vocal cord, a matter for the doctor.

BIRTH CONTROL HANDBOOK.
McGill Students' Society.
pp48; 10p; 1968,70.
Currently not available but must be due for another printing soon. Very good, humane book about vital human concern.

How the IUD works

Many conflicting theories have been suggested in attempts to explain the contraceptive action of the IUD. The exact mode of action is still not understood.

One widely accepted theory suggests that the IUD interferes with the dynamic muscular balance of the cervix, uterus and Fallopian tubes. It is suggested that sperm transport up into the tubes and ovum transport down toward the uterus are disrupted by the IUD's effects on uterine and tubal muscles.

Another group of explanatory theories concentrates on cellular changes in the uterine lining, the endometrium. If the cyclic development of endometrial cells is disrupted, implantation of a fertilized egg is impossible.

One group of theories is primarily biochemical, and suggests that when an IUD is present, the uterine environment is chemically hostile to a fertilized egg.

A recently presented theory suggests that abnormally high concentrations of **macrophages** develop within the uterus when an IUD is present. Macrophages are normal body cells which attack "invading" cells such as bacteria, by **phagocytosis**. (A phagocyte is a cell, such as a white blood cell, that can "swallow" another cell, and thus destroy it). Macrophages normally do not exist within the uterine cavity, and their presence might destroy a fertilized egg.

IUDs do not cause early abortion nor do they prevent pregnancy by creating a low-grade infection in the uterus.

Effectiveness

The efficiency of the IUD is considerably less than the oral contraceptive pill. At best, only 1.5 to 3 women out of 100 become pregnant during the first year after insertion of the IUD. Failure rates tend to decline with further years of use. Many doctors report a contraceptive failure rate of much higher than 3.0. With some devices, up to 8 or 9 women out of 100 become pregnant during the first year after the IUD is inserted.

IUDs are most effective for women who have had several children, and are older than 30 years of age. Age is the more important factor. For example, in one study on the Lippes loop, 5.7% of women 15-24 years old at time of insertion became pregnant within the first year. In the same study, only 4.7% of the women 25-29 years old, and 2.9% of women 30-34 years old became pregnant in the same time period.

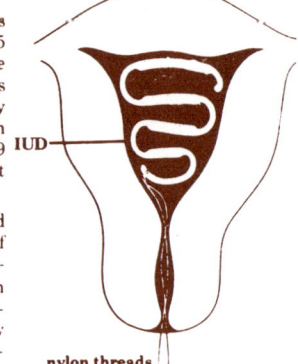

NEW ESSENTIAL FIRST-
AID. A.W.Gardener &
P.J.Roylance.
pp189; 30p; Pan 1972.

A very readable, well illustrated book on first-aid. Seems to have been well recieved by the quacks.

A SYNOPSIS OF PRIORITIES

1. If danger exists, do not become the next casualty yourself.
2. Remove the casualty if necessary from a position of immediate danger.
3. Check that the casualty is *breathing*.

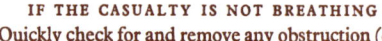

The unconscious position

IF THE CASUALTY IS NOT BREATHING

(i) Quickly check for and remove any obstruction (dentures, debris, loose natural teeth, blood or vomit), then tilt the head *fully* back.

(ii) If breathing does not begin at once, start *artificial respiration* (see page 41).

4. Stop any severe *bleeding* (see page 55).

5. If the casualty is breathing but *unconscious*, turn him into the unconscious (semi-prone) position, check for any possible cause of obstructed breathing (dentures, debris, loose natural teeth, blood or vomit) and apply a slight head-down tip if possible.

The order of doing 2, 3, 4 and 5 will be determined by the nature of the incident, but the correct order should be obvious in any particular case.

6. Cover all *serious wounds and burns*.

7. Immobilize *broken or dislocated limbs* or *suspected fractures*.

8. *Do not delay* by treating minor injuries or trivialities if serious injuries are present – get the casualty *to hospital* quickly. There are always doctors in hospital.

9. At some stage in above, send for help, giving a clear message. If there are many casualties, sending for help should have a very high priority.

Touch
is one of the basic languages
of muscles, nerves, love.
Mothers instinctively
touch their children
to comfort;
hold them close to relax
and reassure.
To be held is support;
to be touched is contact;
to be touched sensitively
is to be cared for.

Some people are touchy,
over sensitive,
don't like to be touched;
others are dying to be touched.
Being touched
is difficult for so many
because of the way
they were handled as children;
not really cared for.

Babies are easily touched,
love to touch.
To be touched is to be reached,
to feel and to be felt.
Touching and being touched
is a pleasure our culture
teaches us to keep away from.
Children and adults
from other societies
show more affection, animation;
touch much of the time.
Men walk down the street
holding hands, arm in arm
because they feel close
to one another.
In American culture
this is sometimes viewed
as a homosexual act.

In early civilizations
people clasped forearms
or embraced
in unselfconscious contact,
exchanging the life energy,
creating a bond.
Today we shake hands
at arms length or embrace
with our shoulders and face,
avoiding real contact.

Touch and pleasure
can be sensuous
without being sexual.
There is a great amount
of communication, caring,
close openness
which can come
in mutual sensory interaction;
satisfaction.

SENSE RELAXATION - BELOW YOUR MIND.
Bernard Gunther. photos by Paul Fusco.
pp190; £1.25; Macdonald 1969.

Somehow more serious and earnest than the
Massage Book, as if trying to prove the
benefits of tactile communication;
nonetheless valuable experiences and
techniques for good interactions.

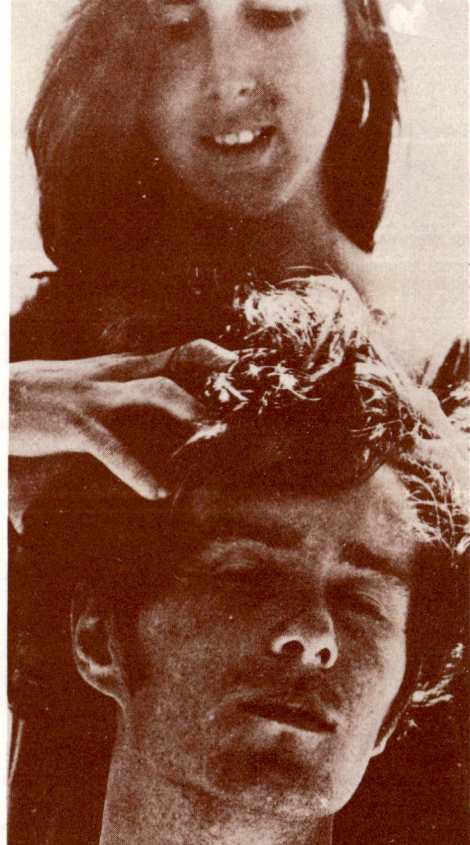

THE MASSAGE BOOK
George Downing, illustrated by Anne Kent Rush
pp184; £1.95;
Random House (US) Jan. 1972.

A working manual of techniques of massage for every part of
the body. There's something so incredible about being touched,
even ever so lightly, when the touching is a deliberate act.
Here are roads into dense tactile experience, written by
people who are beautifully into it, and share it with you.

8 For a last goodby to the arm here is an especially nice stroke made
popular by Molly Day Schackman.

Toss the right arm one more time (see the previous stroke, in
case you have been following a different sequence) to the
left, catch it, and then let it rest in place, the upper arm
on the table beside the head and the forearm partially
resting in the air. Meanwhile place both your palms
lightly against your friend's armpit area, with the fingers
of either hand pointing towards the other.

Now begin spreading your hands to the sides, leading
with the heels of the hands. Start with a light pressure. Send
the right hand down the side of the torso
and the left along the upper arm.

As soon as they have passed the armpit itself turn both hands so
that they are vertical with respect to the table; while
turning them keep them moving apart at the same pace.
At the same time lightly grasp the arm
with your left hand, fingers on top of the arm and
thumb below, and curve your right hand a little so
that the full palm presses against the side of the torso
as it passes.

Keep both hands in this position as you continue moving
them apart. Increase the pressure slightly. Stop when your right hand
reaches your friend's hip and your left reaches his wrist.

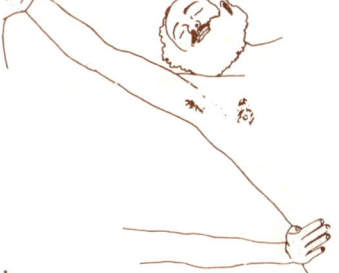

Now, keeping your hands in place, hold more tightly and stretch the arm and the hip
away from each other. Hold this stretch for
about one full second, and then release,
breaking contact just long enough to bring
your hands back to your friend's armpit.

Repeat the entire stroke one more
time. A moment or so after breaking contact
the second time, return both hands to the arm
itself and gently put it back into place at your
friend's side.

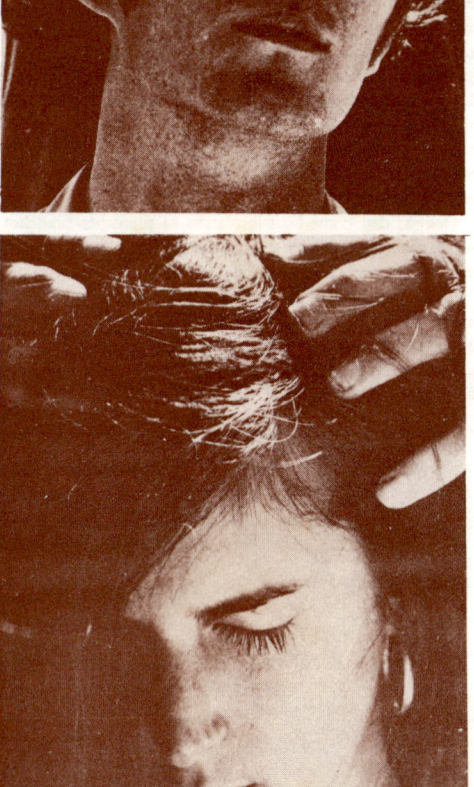

E16 I prefer to massage both the right arm and
hand before going on to the left arm and hand. If you have
just finished your friend's right arm, you may wish to go on to the
following section on the hand before moving over to his or her left arm and hand.

Techniques, equipment and advice for every type of upland activity, from an afternoon strolling up the local landmark, to a stiff climb up the North Face of the Eiger - well, almost. There isn't a better general book about it than this.

(Suggested by Paul Exley)

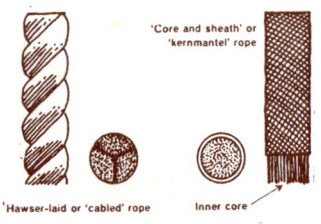

72. *The two main methods of rope construction.*

MOUNTAINEERING - FROM HILL WALKING TO MOUNTAIN CLIMBING
Alan Blackshaw.
pp552; £1.25; Penguin 1970.

78. *Karabiners.* A. ASMU D. B. Simond 10 mm. oval. c. Cassin 1,800 kg. D. D. Hiatt D. E. Marwa kidney F. Allain D. G. Stubai large D. H. Cassin : for rucksacks and *étriers*. I. Russian karabiner : note the large gate opening. See also 101c for the American Bedayn karabiner, particularly good for artificial work.

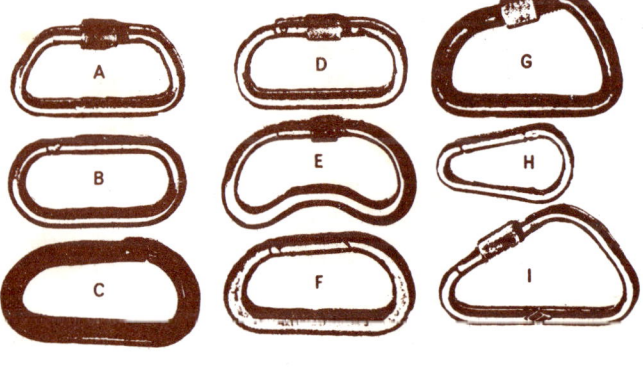

2. *Climbing technique.* The two essential principles are:

- planning ahead, so that you can anticipate the difficulties and work out the best way of solving them;
- conservation of energy, so that you can deploy your full strength when it is necessary to do so. It is best to stand upright, well away from the rock, and to take most of your weight on your feet, and not your hands (§ 39).

In tackling each pitch:

- work out the general line, and note where it is possible to rest. When you reach each resting place calculate exactly how to do the next bit. Get the right sequence of holds – often a move will seem difficult because you are using your right foot where your left foot should be and vice versa (as second man, watch the way the leader does the pitch);
- try not to get held up for too long on any one move; but do not press on until you are sure you can do it. Slowness in working out the right combination of holds may be a sign that you are off form – recognize this;
- take care in finishing off the pitch; do it quickly but neatly and remember the footholds as you go over the top in case it is necessary for some reason to reverse it;
- if you decide to retreat, climb down with determination so that you reach safety before your strength gives out; wavering and lack of determination can lead to delay and exhaustion.

Braking with the axe

19 Braking with the axe is illustrated in Fig 43. A slip on steep snow may sometimes be difficult to check, and the walker may find himself sliding downwards out of control, heading for rocks or a precipice below. If action is taken quickly but calmly it is quite easy to stop. Roll over on to the axe and slowly apply the pick to the surface. One hand must be firmly over the axe head and the other low on the shaft; if both hands are holding the shaft the axe will be torn from them. Fatal accidents continually occur in the mountains because someone slips on snow or ice and slides down slopes, unable to brake because he has no ice-axe or is unable to control one properly. The axe must be in the correct position to start with; the little finger should be towards the pick as the head is gripped by the hand.

Figure 43: Braking with the axe.
The axe is held very firmly with both (gloved) hands, and the pick is applied to the surface with gradually increasing force. The whole weight of the body must remain on top of the head of the axe, otherwise it will be impossible to use enough force.

MOUNTAIN RESCUE
Training manual for RAF teams.
pp178; 62½p
HMSO 1968

QU. "What do experienced climbers do in bad weather?"
ANS. (Whillans) "They stay in the pub."
If you're too daft to stay in the pub, have this book in mind when you go out. It's a training manual for mountain rescue teams, about surviving the sort of conditions that seem to catch too many people every year.

EXPOSURE

6 It is not always easy to decide early enough that you have a mild case of exposure on your hands. It is very important to do so, since it may be possible to avoid a crisis if at the outset you are aware of the symptoms and can begin to treat them. The following are among the most usual symptoms :

(a) Unexpected and apparently unreasonable behaviour, often accompanied by complaints of coldness and tiredness.

(b) Physical and mental lethargy, including failure to respond to or to understand questions and directions.

(c) Failure of, or abnormality in, vision. It should be noted that some failure of vision is a very usual symptom, and when this does occur, the condition should be regarded with extreme seriousness.

(d) Some slurring of speech. There is not necessarily early failure of speech, and the victim may speak quite strongly until

shortly before collapse.

(e) Sudden shivering fits.

(f) Violent outburst of unexpected energy – possibly physical resistance to succour – violent language.

(g) Falling.

Note: It should be stressed that not all of these symptoms may be noticed, nor necessarily in this order. Other symptoms which may sometimes be observed are muscle cramp, extreme ashen pallor, lightheadedness, occasionally a fainting fit.

General

7 In normal conditions the inner 'core' (trunk and brain) of the body remains constant at 37 C (98·4°F); the temperature of the outer shell is always below this. This outer shell consists of the skin, underlying fat and muscle, and extremities (arms and legs, ears, nose), and comprises almost half of the body.

8 What is vital is the preservation of the deep core temperature. A shift in this leads directly to mental deterioration and loss of muscular co-ordination, and eventually to unconsciousness, heart and respiratory failure and death.

9 The body itself acts to maintain core circulation and temperature by restricting the flow to the exposed periphery so that core blood is not cooled at the surface.

10 In any treatment, therefore, the importance must be realized of not increasing peripheral circulation unless there is minimal loss of heat at the skin surface. Further heat loss from the core must at all costs be avoided. Sudden surface warming therefore is wrong.

11 When once the symptoms are clearly established, any further exertion, such as forcing the victim to go on walking, even downhill, must be avoided. The party must stop, and proceed to treatment. It is impossible to overstress the importance of this.

Figure 8: Sample contents of the day sack

HANDBOOK FOR EXPEDITIONS
Brathay Exploration Group   pp138; 63p inc post
from Geographical Magazine, 128, Long Acre,
London WC2E 9XA

Brathay are an educational expedition outfit,
mainly for schools and youth groups, but the book
will be useful for problems and planning details
when you get that trip to India together.

A general purpose ration for temperate conditions should provide a little more than 4000 calories a day with a proper balance between protein (meat, cheese, etc.—thirteen per cent of calories), fat (butter, milk, etc.—thirty-three per cent of calories), and carbohydrate (sugar, biscuits, etc.—fifty-four per cent of calories). For arduous activity in cold conditions the calories should be raised to above 4500 and the proportion of fat increase to about forty-five per cent. In desert conditions or at high altitudes, fewer calories are required, appetite is diminished, and the proportion of carbohydrates, which spare body water best, should be increased to about sixty-five per cent. High calorific

foods, such as chocolate, sugar or butter satisfy hunger quickest, but biscuits and vegetables provide the necessary roughage. If conditions are chilly and damp, Vitamin C tablets may help to ward off colds. More detailed information on the nutritional values of various foods is given in EDHOLM and BACHARACH, Chapter XV.

With the new techniques of 'accelerated freeze drying', AFD, a much wider variety of meats, vegetables and fruit is available in light-weight packs. A conventional one pound tin of meat feeds four, but one pound of AFD meat caters for twelve and the dry granules can easily be sub-divided, and carried in polythene bags. Dried milk is similarly very much handier than tins of condensed. Details of reconstitution are given below, but it may be advisable to take fewer AFD products if water is likely to be scarce.

Weather conditions and expedition tasks seldom make it possible to stick rigidly to a menu plan, but standardised pre-packed man day boxes are a tremendous help towards simplifying administration in the field, and safeguard against particular items being deficient if bulk orders should go astray. When it is fine the use of dry rations and lemonade crystals at lunch time allows maximum time to be spent on field work, but during bad weather 'hooshes' cooked at mid-day go down well, and soups should be saved for this purpose. The inclination to exceed the standard ration when tent-bound must be curbed. In such cases food and fuel consumption should be cut down after a day or so in case the re-supply from base becomes difficult.

EQUIPMENT SUPPLIERS.
*Blacks of Greenock, the major suppliers of general
outdoor equipment, with branches all over. Catalogue
free from branches, or Black & Edgington, Port
Glasgow, Scotland. PA14 5XN.
*Youth Hostel Association Services, 29, John Adam St.
London WC2 N6JE. Catalogue free. YHA supply major
makes, plus their own lines in things like tents and
sleeping bags. We've been using a YHA Venture tent
for a while, and it's fairly light, well designed,
and not expensive. (£26 with A poles)
*Scout Shop, Churchill Industrial Estate, Lancing, Sussex.
Catalogue free.

If you're after the more specialised lightweight gear
two good free catalogues describing and illustrating a
wide range from-
*Mountain Centre, 34, Dean St., Newcastle-on-Tyne, NE1 1PG
*Bryan Stokes, 2, High Court, Sheffield.

CAMPING AND WOODCRAFT
Horace Kephart   £3.15
Collier-Macmillan 1942

Get a whiff of the Great American Outdoors, shootin' them
bars, an' rippin' off the wild bees for their honey. How
to live when you're lost in the woods, which is much easier
over there- how many woods have we got to get lost in?

-Shear Frame
for Lean-to

Fig. 55.—Lopped Tree Den

In walking through a primitive forest, an Indian or a white woodsman can wear out a town-bred athlete, although the latter may be the stronger man. This is because a man who is used to the woods has a knack of walking over uneven and slippery ground, edging through thickets, and worming his way amid fallen timber, with less fret and exertion than one who is accustomed to smooth, unobstructed paths.

How to Walk.—There is somewhat the same difference between a townsman's and a woodsman's gait as there is between a soldier's and a sailor's. It it chiefly a difference of hip action, looseness of joints, and the manner of planting one's feet. The townsman's stride is an up-and-down knee action, with rather rigid hips, the toes pointing outward, and heels striking first. The carriage is erect, the movement springy and graceful, so long as one is walking over firm, level footing—but beware the banana-peel and the small boy's sliding-place! This is an ill-poised gait, because one's weight falls first upon the heel alone, and at that instant the walker has little command of his balance. It is an exhausting gait as soon as its normally short pace is lengthened by so much as an inch.

80.— D. T. Abercrombie Sleeping Bag

WILDERNESS CAMPING IN BRITAIN
Eric Hemery   pp192; £1.75
Robert Hale 1970

About heavy family camping, but
full of places to go to get away from
everyone. Very practical- plenty of
hows and whys of living in comfort when
it's very cold and very lonely.

3. TENT PEGS
Pegs should not be chosen for cheapness, but for suitability to their purpose. A wooden peg is cheap and light and serves well in lowland field or meadow, but a metal one wins every time on stony ground.

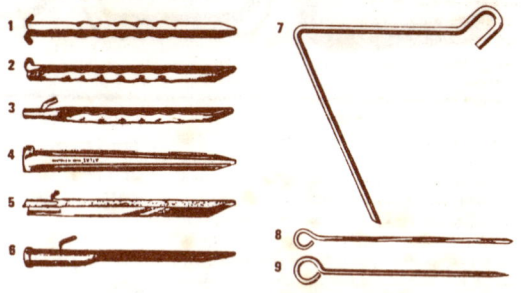
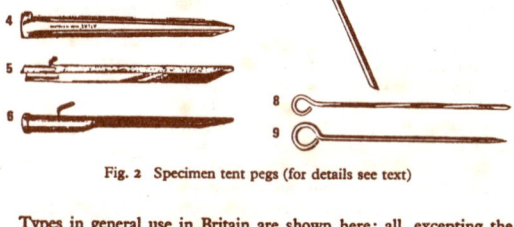

Fig. 2 Specimen tent pegs (for details see text)

Types in general use in Britain are shown here; all, excepting the wooden peg, are manufactured by The Hampton Works (Stampings) Ltd. The note about each peg begins with its trade name, then gives the extremes of length in which it is made (there being in most cases several intermediate lengths) and the weight of the 9 in size as a representative medium.

1. Bulldog. 3½–15-in, 1⅓-oz. Has a good grip, but both head and shank are apt to bend if driven against stone. Once bent, permanently weakened, even if straightened.
2. Bulldog Continental. 7–12-in, 1⅓-oz. Remarks as above except that head is somewhat stronger.
3. Bulldog Thor. 7–12-in, 2-oz. Similar to 1 and 2, but head and tip are reinforced against distortion.
4. Atlas. 7-in and 9-in, 3-oz. Rigid – will not bend. Head inclined to fray guy rope.
5. Fort. 9-in only, 3-oz. Very strong head – which is as well, for it needs considerable driving.
6. Samson. 5½–12-in, 3½-oz. An outstandingly good peg. Head-cap and cut away shank make it easy to drive. Well-shaped hook causes no fraying. Will hold a big tent in mountain weather.
7. Anker. 5-in and 8-in, 4½-oz. High-tensile galvanised steel rod, specially designed for holding in mud and sand. Unique for this purpose; less satisfactory for mountain and moorland use.
8. Skewer. 5–9-in, ¾-oz. Ideal for securing mudflaps.
9. Round Wire. 5–10-in, 1½-oz. Available in steel or alloy (the latter being slightly lighter) with needle tip, blunt tip, or 60 deg point. Good for light pegging duties; far stronger than Skewer, lighter than Bulldog – but without its grip.
10. Hardwood Cleft. 6–18-in, 1⅓-oz. Amazingly strong and will certainly not bend! Clumsy to use and unnecessarily bulky (in numbers) for lightweight tentage. Traditional; and some campers loyally rely upon it, until they have met up with slaty mountain terrain where topsoil is rarely more than an inch or two deep, when they become metal-peg converts in a flash.

MOUNTAIN AND MOORLAND
W.H.Pearsall.
pp415; 60p;
Fontana New Naturalist 1968.

The uplands are harsh on life.
The whole ecology operates
near the limits of survival,
because of climate, geology
and man. The interelationships
are described here, explaining
things that you have noticed,
but not understood. A bit lumpy
in places, but valuable.

Wind Exposure. Before we go on to consider these changes, however, it may be of interest to refer to other features of plant colonisation in this habitat. Every naturalist knows how profoundly shelter and

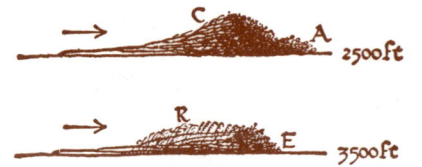

FIG. 18.—Wavelike plant development on high wind-exposed slopes: A, Bearberry; C, Heather; E, Crowberry; R, Hair-moss

exposure affect plant and animal distribution in mountain areas. Nowhere is this more clearly shown than on the mountain-top detritus, where exposure and insolation may be extreme. The Rhacomitrium-carpet is especially liable to be torn up by strong winds, and probably for this reason it is often absent on exposed westerly or north-westerly slopes. It is also almost always absent from areas showing marked solifluction effects of the polygon or stone-stripe type.

It was remarked by C. B. Crampton in Caithness and Sutherland, where exposure to north-westerly winds is especially severe, that heathy vegetation often gradually establishes itself in a wave-like form, and Dr. A. S. Watt has recently described the development of these waves in detail as it occurs in the Cairngorms (see Fig. 18). The essential feature is the presence of small shrubs like heather (*Calluna*)[1], bearberry (*Arctostaphylos*) and crowberry (*Empetrum*), which, once established, grow horizontally with their leaves and branches towards the more sheltered direction. Thus there is gradually built up a sheltered zone in which the mosses and lichens can develop and in which new individuals of the shrubby plants can start. At lower altitudes (say 2,500 ft.) this often gives a "wave" of bearberry and heather, the former growing in the shelter of heather but being suppressed by the heather growing over it. At levels above 3,000 ft. crowberry is more usually the "holdfast," with Rhacomitrium and lichens growing among its older and leafless branches, often with such species as bilberry and three-leaved rush (*Juncus trifidus*).

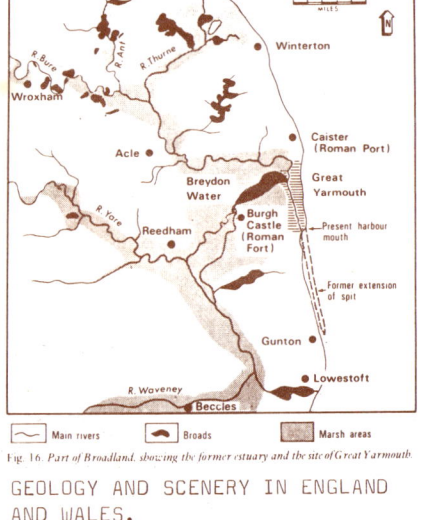

Fig. 16. Part of Broadland, showing the former estuary and the site of Great Yarmouth.

GEOLOGY AND SCENERY IN ENGLAND
AND WALES.
A.E.Truman.
pp400; £1.25;
Penguin 1971.

A straightforward book about the
geology and scenery of England and
Wales. What more could you ask.

Certainly the Broadland area must have been, probably as late as Roman and Anglo-Saxon times, a wide open estuary, with exits to the sea near Horsey, about twelve miles north of Yarmouth, at Yarmouth itself and at Lowestoft (Fig. 16). Silt deposition must have taken place in the quieter waters inside the estuary, more particularly at the seaward end, with Breydon Water as a present reminder of these conditions. This would have given rise to brackish, swampy conditions at the upstream end, where the Broads are found today. Here there would have been dense vegetation, perhaps alder thicket and sedge fen in the main. Death and regeneration of this vegetation led to the formation of thick layers of peat.

It is now thought that the Broads themselves are vast, flooded, medieval peat diggings, the peat having accumulated during swampy conditions, and been dug subsequently for fuel. The digging was made possible by a relative rise of the land during medieval times. The main evidence for this conclusion came from a painstaking investigation by boring of the nature of the beds of the Broads. It is well known that the Broads are not widenings of the main channel of the rivers, but are connected with the rivers only by narrow side channels (Plate 14). Baulks and strips of peat were found remaining in the beds of the Broads, notably along what are now parish boundaries, indicating removal of peat by man. At the same time evidence was found, from excavations for the construction of a power station at Great Yarmouth, that sea-level was relatively lower than at present from the eleventh to the thirteenth century, after which flooding began. Documentary evidence was found in support of these conclusions, that peat digging took place from about the eleventh to the thirteenth century, after which the areas stripped of peat were gradually flooded and formed the Broads as we know them today.

SILVA COMPASS

A compass is vital,
although not so easy
to use. This is the
make that seems to be
recommended most often.
Available all over the
place, from 88p to
£4.70.

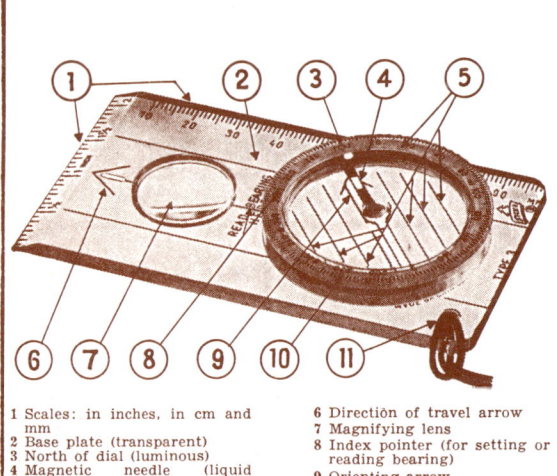

1 Scales: in inches, in cm and mm
2 Base plate (transparent)
3 North of dial (luminous)
4 Magnetic needle (liquid dampened with north end red and luminous)
  Compass housing with dial and orienting lines.
    On Silva Type 5 the ... lines are on the dial.
6 Direction of travel arrow
7 Magnifying lens
8 Index pointer (for setting or reading bearing)
9 Orienting arrow
10 Dial graduation (standard 360 degrees with 2 degree graduations).
11 Hole for safety cord and the cord

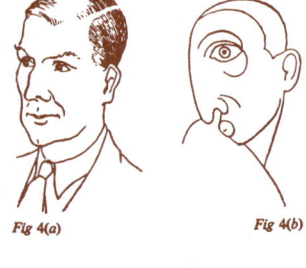

Fig 4(a)   Fig 4(b)

MAP READING VOL. 1
ARMY MANUAL.
pp132; 50p;
HMSO 1961.

Not full of pretty
colourful pics., but
plenty of useful info.,
especially if you're
planning a long
campaign.

2. This question of "likeness" is emphasized in Fig 4. The first head is like the original. It represents a particular person. It is like, because the sizes, positions and shapes of the various features correspond to those in the original. It is in fact drawn to scale, though we never think of it in that way, and because of that it could be recognized as a particular person. In just the same way a map, drawn to scale, enables particular pieces of ground to be recognized, or to be imagined, because the sizes, positions and shapes of the various features on the ground are reproduced correctly on the map.

The second head is recognizable as a head but it is not in the least "like" any head you have ever seen. You could not recognize a particular person from it. That is because, though the various features, eyes, nose, mouth, are recognizable and are roughly in the right places, their sizes, positions and shapes do not correspond to those in any original. It is not drawn to scale. It is a very bad map of a face.

(c) Escarpment   (d) Ravine

The Pennine Way

by Tom Stephenson

THE PENNINE WAY Tom Stephenson pp110; £1.50 HMSO 1969
PENNINE WAY COMPANION A. Wainwright pp 214 £1.10
Westmoreland Gazette 1968

Two books about the Great North Road of walkers. Tom
Stephenson was the main inspiration and realizer of the
route. His book is the official guide, and contains
1" and 2½" OS maps of the Way, but is rather general.
(Top, right)

Wainwright has been wondering in his lovingly
microscopic way across the North for years, recording
the uplands of the region. I think I'll keep his book
in my pocket when I go. (extracts below)

A "widdy", it is said locally, was a slate pencil. The English Dialect Dictionary gives no mention of this. but the Ordnance Survey 6 Inch map names a ruined building as "pencil mill", and a small inlier of Skiddaw Slates was formerly quarried there.

Hereabouts the mealy primrose *(Primula farinosa)* flourishes and despite the depredations of thoughtless visitors the blue gentian *(Gentiana verna)* still blooms on Widdybank Fell.

Upstream, round the thrusting shoulder of Cronkley Fell, is Holmwath, a Norse name meaning "island ford" Next the Way winds between boulders fallen from the crags of Falcon Clints and up to the foot of Caldron Snout where the Tees comes cascading some hundred and fifty feet down a natural and uneven stairway of dark rocks of the Whin Sill. From ledge to ledge the Way mounts besides the fuming, leaping water.

Above Caldron Snout the Tees formerly flowed lazily through a wide moorland waste. Now it is impounded in the Cow Green reservoir, the building of which was vigorously but vainly opposed by the naturalist and amenity societies. Above the fall, the Way enters Westmorland, and follows a rough and boggy track to the isolated farms at Birkdale. Beyond the upper house, after crossing Grain Beck, a track mounts to a cairn by some old mine buildings marked on the map as "Moss Shop". These "shops", of which there are many on the hills, were places where the lead miners lived during their working week, cooked their own food and slept on straw-filled bunks.

DURHAM AND WESTMORLAND

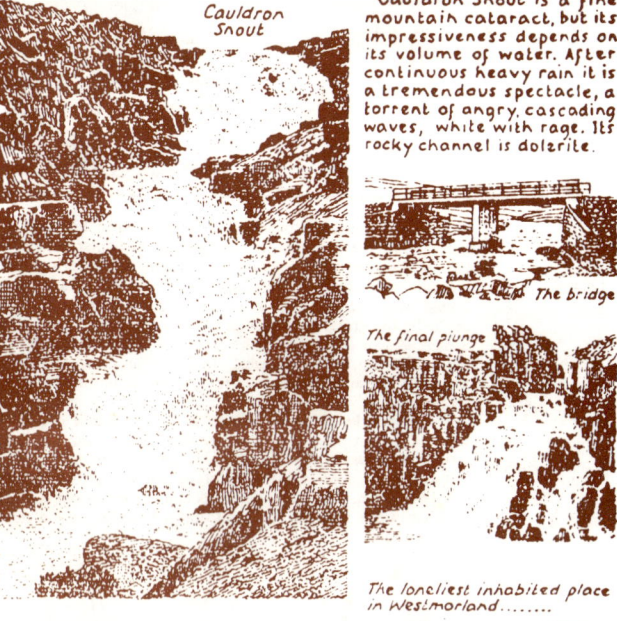

Cauldron Snout is a fine mountain cataract, but its impressiveness depends on its volume of water. After continuous heavy rain it is a tremendous spectacle, a torrent of angry, cascading waves, white with rage. Its rocky channel is dolerite.

The bridge

The final plunge

The loneliest inhabited place in Westmorland........

Birkdale, looking east

Falcon Clints, looking east

WIDDYBANK TO BIRKDALE

1" Ordnance Sheet 84

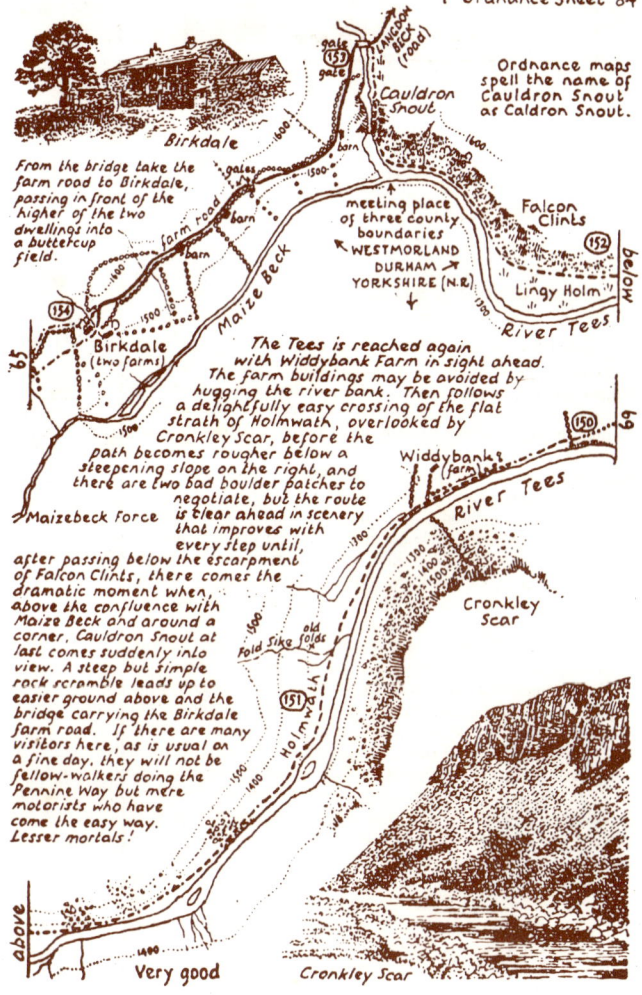

Ordnance maps spell the name of Cauldron Snout as Caldron Snout.

From the bridge take the farm road to Birkdale, passing in front of the higher of the two dwellings into a buttercup field.

meeting place of three county boundaries
WESTMORLAND
DURHAM
YORKSHIRE (N.R.)

The Tees is reached again with Widdybank Farm in sight ahead. The farm buildings may be avoided by hugging the river bank. Then follows a delightfully easy crossing of the flat strath of Holmwath, overlooked by Cronkley Scar, before the path becomes rougher below a steepening slope on the right, and there are two bad boulder patches to negotiate, but the route is clear ahead in scenery that improves with every step until, after passing below the escarpment of Falcon Clints, there comes the dramatic moment when, above the confluence with Maize Beck and around a corner, Cauldron Snout at last comes suddenly into view. A steep but simple rock scramble leads up to easier ground above and the bridge carrying the Birkdale farm road. If there are many visitors here, as is usual on a fine day, they will not be fellow-walkers doing the Pennine Way but mere motorists who have come the easy way. Lesser mortals!

Maizebeck Force

Widdybank (farm)

Cronkley Scar

River Tees

Very good   Cronkley Scar

Superb book - almost worth
getting a VW just to use it.
Every technical manual should be
written and illustrated like this.

HOW TO KEEP YOUR VW ALIVE - John Muir.
pp250; £2.50;
agents - Speed and Sport Publications,
Acorn House, Victoria Road, London W3.

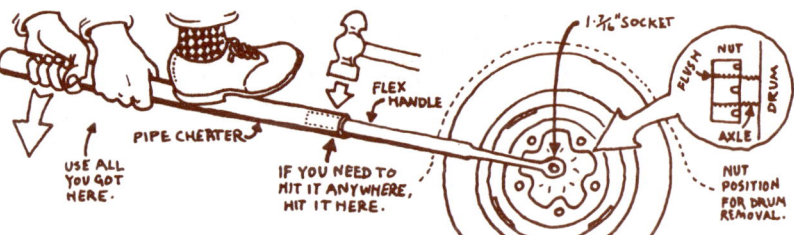

Automatic Choke Disarmament. Because of my reactionary position on auto-matic chokes, I refuse to tell you how to adjust it, but I will tell you how to make it _not_ work. Do you suppose this is being an act ivistic reactionary? Find the automatic choke. It's the round thing on the upper right hand of the carburetor. There is a wire coming to it, disconnect the wire and tape it so it won't ground on the engine. Look at the choke. It's a ceramic thing with a heat element in it held in position by a ring clamp and three screws (so it can be adjusted, which it has to be four times a year or it tends to over-rich your fuel and further ruin your engine's lubrication --- they didn't tell you that?) Loosen these three screws and you hold its life in your hands. Turn the cer-amic element so that it opens the butterfly valve in the top of the carburetor, turn it the other way and you'll see the valve start to close, just to get your direction right. Turn this ceramic so it opens the butterfly and then all the way in the same direction, as far as it will go --- now clamp it down with the three screws and you have disarmed the mother.

On the opposite side of the carburetor there is a swinging arm with teeth in it that presents various faces to the idle screw to make for a fast idle. In fact, it's called the fast idle cam. Now that you've disarmed the choke, you must tie this down so you can get a steady idle. A heavy rubber band around the fuel line slipped over the top of the fast idle cam will hold it back, or a piece of wire, whatever. You don't want it engaged at all. Disarming this choke is very much akin to putting your engine on a macrobiotic diet.

MOTOR CYCLE MECHANICS
Phil Irving.
Temple Press (out of
print at the moment)

Excellent guide to the
basics of bikes, from
frames through to
engines etc.

The main quality desired in a cylinder iron is freedom from wear; some grades of iron are better in this respect than others, mainly on account of their differing grain structure. It was once thought that rapid wear was due to insufficient hardness, and one or two makers adopted irons which could be hardened by heat treatment after all machining operations, except final grinding or honing, had been performed.

However, while a hardened barrel may have a lower rate of wear than a soft one under abrasive conditions—for example, when an engine is run in dusty surroundings minus an air cleaner—it is not necessarily any better, and may even be worse, than a softer iron of the correct analysis under the corrosive conditions which exist every time the engine is started up from cold.

At such times the upper end of the cylinder wall is almost free from oil, and the fact that it is cold causes the water vapour. formed as part of the products of combustion, to condense thereon. Partly because of the cold conditions and partly because of the usual enrichment by flooding of the carburetter or closing the air slide, combustion of the mixture is not complete and this results in the formation of acids which are dissolved in the condensed water vapour and attack the cylinder walls.

Part-sections comparing a flange-type barrel with one secured by through-bolts. The second form is superior structurally but more expensive.

DUETTO 2 LEADING SHOE FRONT BRAKE CONVERSION
Complete replacement back plate. Race proved design. No modifications neces-sary. Brake cable supplied. Exchange brake shoe service.
Illus. 23   _Cat. No. 41_

For 1965 Lightning models. Duetto 1.
For alternative 190mm, fitted to Light-ning and Spitfire. Duetto 3.
                                     Cat. No. 41

For 1967/8 Lightning, Thunderbolt and Royal Star. Fitted with 203mm single sided brake with 1½" width linings. Duetto 4.
                                     Cat. No. 41

EDDIE DOW.
15/16, Southam Road,
Banbury Road,
Oxford.
Catalogue 25p.

Eddie Dow specializes
in spares and mods for
BSA Gold Star bikes,
which were a classic
British type motor
bike.

INDEX

ABC of Preserving   B11
About Organic Gardening   B10
AD   B1
Agitprop   C2
Agricultural Testament   B6
Agriculture   B9
Air Structures   B2
Alternative London   C4
ALTERNATIVE MEDIA   C3-4
Architectural Design   B1
Ashley Iles   A6
Atelier Populaire   C6

Backyard Dairy Book   D11
Baskets and Basketry   A14
Bate, Harold   B5
Beekeeping   B11
Beverley, Poole & Co.   A7
Biology in Action   E4
Birth Control Handbook   E14
Bleibtreu, John   E4
Body Politic   E13
Books   C2
Bookshops   C2
Brewing Better Beers   B13
Buck & Hickman   A16
Buckminster Fuller   E2
Building Advisory Leaflets   B4
Building Research Station Digest   B4
Bulletin of Environmental Education   D2

Camping and Woodcraft   F2
Castenada, Carlos   E7
Chase Organic Seeds   B6
Circus Tents   B2
Clays and Glazes   A11
Communes, Directory of   C3
Communes Magazine   C3
Compendium   C2
Complete Guide to Gardening   B7
Composting   B5
Cooper, Charles   A15
CoSIRA   A1
Costs of Economic Growth   E9
Country Bizarre   C3
Craft of Film   C8
Culture Against Man   E12
Cymatics   E3

D'Arcy Thompson   E5
DESIGN   A2-3
Design for the Real World   A2
Design of Design   A3
Devcon   A10
Dialectic of Sex   E13
Dictionary of Symptoms   E14
Directory of Alternative Work   C3
Directory of Communes   C3
Domebook   B1
Dow, Eddie   D5
Dryad   A15
DYEING   A12-13
Dymaxion Maps   E2

EDUCATION   D1-4
Ehrlich   E8
ELECTRONICS   C11-12
Electrovalue   C11
Encyclopedia of Organic Gardening   B8
ENERGY   B5
English, H.W.   A17
ENVIRONMENT   E8-10
Environmental Handbook   E9
Environmental Revolution   E8
Evans, Sydney   A6
Eye and Brain   E7

Farallones Scrapbook   D2
Farmhouse Fare   B12
FARMING AND GARDENING   B6-10
Fertility Finder   B10
FIBREGLASS   A8
Fields, Factories, and Workshops   E10
First Steps in Winemaking   B13
Focal Press   C8
FOOD   B11-12
Foulkes, Thos.   A17
Foundations of Wireless & Electronics   C11
Foxwarren Machinery Services Ltd.   B9
Franks, H.   A18
Fulham Pottery   A11

GARDENING AND FARMING   B6-10
Gardening Without Poisons   B7
Gatto, A.   A7
Geology & Scenery in England & Wales   F3
Glasplies   A8

GKN Handybook   B4
Glasplies   A8
GLASSFIBRE   A8
Gordon, J.E.   A4
Graphics Handbook   C5
Grasses   B9
Gray, E.   A15
Green, D.   A17
Growth of Plants   B6
Grow Your own Fruit & Vegetables   B7
GRP   A8
Guerrilla TV   C4

Hampton, C.W.   A6
Handbook for Expeditions   F2
Handbook of Fixings & Fastenings   B4
Handbook of Seaman's Ropework   B3
Handbook of Woodcutting   A7
Harris, P. (radios)   A18
Harrison Meyer   A11
Hart Electronics   C11
Hayward, Charles   A6, A7
Hedgecoe, John   C8
Henry Doubleday Research Association   B8
Henry, Jules   E12
Home Preservation Of Fruit & Vegetables   B11
Howard, Sir Albert   B6
How Children Fail   D1
How Children Learn   D1

How Things Work   A2
How to Enjoy Your Weeds   B10
How to Keep Your VW Alive   D5
How to Work With Tools & Wood   A6
Hunt, D.   A7

ICI   A9
ICOM   A1
Intermediate Technology   A1
Into the Hidden Environment   E10
ITDG   A1

Jenkins, J.G.   A14

Kilns   A11
King, A.E.   A19
Kropotkin   E10

Landsmans Bookshop   C2
Lawrance Corner   A17
Lawrence, T.N.   A15
Leach, Bernard   A11
LIBRARIES   C1
Life Against Death   E12
Light Machines for Woodwork   A7
Light on Yoga   E15
Lives of Children   D3
Looking and Seeing   C7
LOOMS   A13
Lore & Language of Schoolchildren   D1
Lost for Words   D3
Loud Speakers   C12

Making Communes   C4
Making Wines Like Those You Buy   B13
Map Reading   F3
Massage Book   E15
MATERIALS   A4-5
Materials   A4
Mathematical Models   C10
Mathematician's Delight   C10
Mathematics   C10
METAL   A9-10
Metal Techniques for Craftsmen   A9
METHANE   B5
Min. of Agric. Publications   B9
Mitchell's Building Construction   B3
Mother Earth News   C3
Motor Cycle Mechanics   D5
Mountains & Moorland   F3
Mountaineering   F1
Mountain Rescue Handbook   F1

Natural Food Cookbook   B12
Nature and Art of Workmanship   A3
Nature of Design   A3
Neill and Summerhill   D3
New Essential First Aid   E14
New Glassfibre Book   A8
New Science of Strong Materials   A4

New Scientist   C9
NIMRA   A19
Noise   C12
Nuffield Science   D4

On Growth and Form   E5
Open Classroom   D1
Order in Space   C10
Organic Gardener   B10
Organic Gardening & Farming Magazine   B6
Otto, Frei   B2
OU Microscope   C8
Outdoor Equipment Suppliers   F2

Paper Making   A14
Parable of the Beast   E4
Pennine Way   F4
Pest Control Without Poisons   B7
Photography   C8
Pioneer Pottery   A11
Planecraft   A6
Pneumatic Structures   B2
Population, Resources, Environment   E8
Post Scarcity Anarchism   E9
Podmore   A11
Potter's Book   A11
POTTERY   A11
Power Research Guide   C1
POWER TOOLS   A7
Practical Screen Printing   C5
Print Reproduction Pocket Pal   C5
PRINTING   C5-6
PRINTERS   C6
Progressive Winemaking   B13

Readers Digest DIY Manual   B3
Reproduction of Sound   C12
Rewiring a House   B4
Ring Circuits   B4

School Nature Science Society   D4
Scientific American   C9
SECONDHAND SUPPLIERS   A17-19
Sense Relaxation   E15
Sign, Symbol, & Script   E6
Silva Compass   F3
Simble, J.   A7
Simple Weaving   A12
Sisterhood is Powerful   E13
Slide Rule   D2
Soil Association   B8
Specification   B3
Starrett Book for Student Machinists   A9
Starrett Co.   A9
Starting Right With Bees   B11
Stoneware & Porcelain   A11
Strand Glass   A8
Surplus Buying Agency   D4
Surplus Electronic Trading   A18
Synthetic Environment   E9

Tape Recorders   C12
Tarpaulin & Tent Co.   A19
Tassajara Bread Book   B12
Teachings of Don Juan   E7
Technics & Civilization   E11
Technological Society   E11
Tensile Structures   B2
Thurston, Violet   A13
Tie & Dye   A12
Tiranti   A15
Tools for Progress   A1
Tools for Woodwork   A6
TOOL SUPPLIERS   A15-16
Traditional Country Craftsmen   A14
Trylon Ltd.   A1, A8
TV   C4

Understanding the Earth   E10
Unicorn   C2
Use of Vegetable Dyes   A13
Utopia or Oblivion   E2

Valley Agricultural Co.   A17
Vision and Value   C7
Voices of Time   E6

Weavers Craft   A12
WEAVING   A12-13
Welding Craft Practice   A10
Wengers   A11
Wheelhouse, C.W.   A18
Which?   C1
Whiston, K.R.   A19
Whole Earth Catalog   E1
Wilderness Camping   F2
WINEMAKING   B13
Wireless World   C11
Women's Lib Bibliography   E13
WOOD   A6-7
Wool Suppliers   A13
Workshop Technology   A10
World of the Soil   B6

Yoga for Health   E15

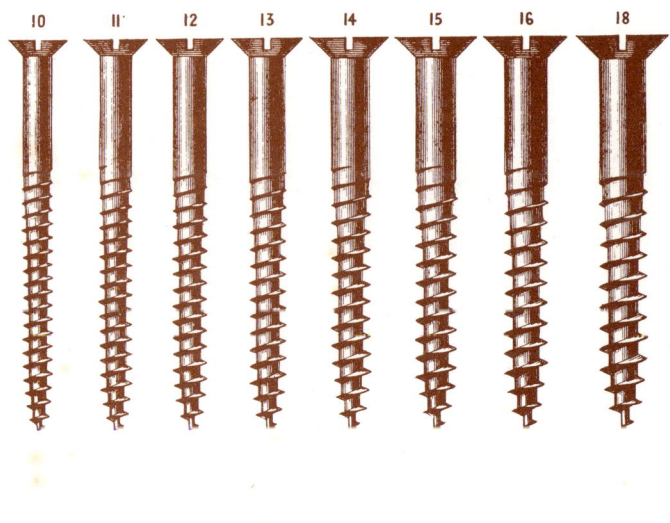

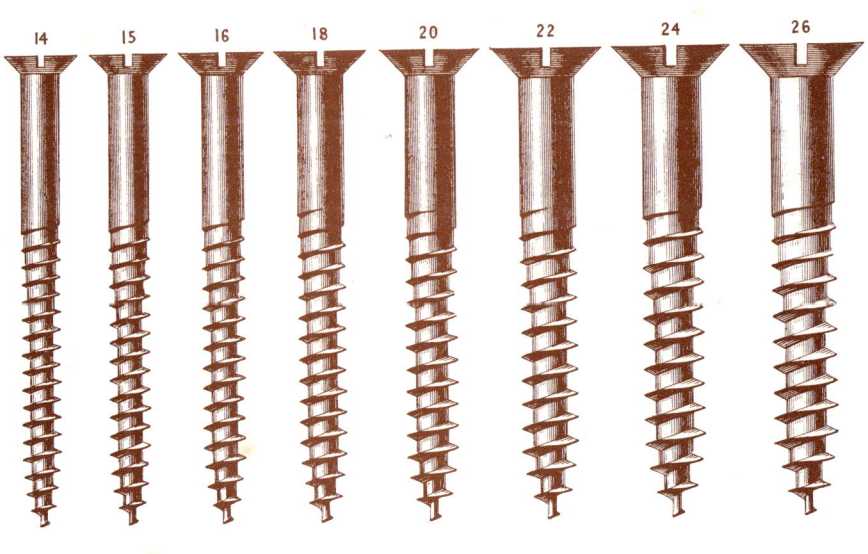